TROUBLING
EDUCATION

TROUBLING
EDUCATION

Queer Activism and Antioppressive Pedagogy

Kevin K. Kumashiro

ROUTLEDGEFALMER
New York and London

Published in 2002 by
RoutledgeFalmer
29 West 35th Street
New York, NY 10001

Published in Great Britain by
RoutledgeFalmer
11 New Fetter Lane
London EC4P 4EE

RoutledgeFalmer is an imprint of the Taylor & Francis Group

Library of Congress Cataloging-in-Publication Data
Kumashiro, Kevin K., 1970–
    Troubling Education : queer activism and antioppressive education / Kevin K. Kumashiro.
        p. cm.
    Includes bibliogaphical references and index.
    ISBN 0-415-93311-0 — ISBN 0-415-93312-9 (pbk.)
        1. Homosexuality and education—United States—Case studies. 2. Sex discrimination in education—United States—Case studies. 3. Gay activists—United States—Interviews. I. Title.

LC192.6 .K86 2002
306.43—dc21
                                                                        2001058885

Being an activist is a very strong part of my identity.
—*Pab, a student activist*

I look at high school students and I think, "Oh my God, how could I even spend one day being in the closet with these kids doing what they risk every day?"
—*Sam, a teacher activist*

I dedicate this book to those who insist on challenging oppression and who, day by day, are making our schools and society better places for all.

Contents

Acknowledgments

I am deeply grateful to many people for helping me with this project.

I thank my family—Sherrie Lou, Kenneth, Kristin, Kent, and Keane—who have shown only love and support for me and my work. They rock. I also thank my crazy Aunty Wilma for helping me stay sane via e-mail.

My many advisors and mentors in the University of Wisconsin-Madison School of Education gave invaluable advice and mentorship throughout the earlier version of this book, my Ph.D. dissertation. In particular, I thank my major advisor, Stacey Lee, for sticking by my side all these years, for giving me so much time and feedback, for guiding me through the many hoops of graduate school, for helping me strengthen my writing, and for everything else you have done to help me become the researcher and activist that I am today. Mike Olneck made me feel safe and supported enough to do research papers on all kinds of queer topics while keeping me grounded from the very beginning of my graduate student career, and Gloria Ladson-Billings inspired me to aim high in all that I do and encouraged and convinced me to follow my heart and pursue what I am most interested in for my dissertation. Amy Stambach helped me to strengthen my teaching skills and earn a living during graduate study, and was a constant source of encouragement; and Liz Ellsworth taught me to think in such different ways, helped me to think through and publish earlier components of this book, and just generally guided me in finding a space in the academy where I can do the work that I want to do and be happy while doing it.

I thank the many friends and activists who helped me find participants, and the many activists who volunteered to participate in my study but whom I did not ask to interview, as well as the activists who subsequently involved me in their own work, or who encouraged me to continue my work so that they might use it in the future.

My fabulous friends have supported me as I envisioned, embarked on, worked through, and now complete this project. I especially thank Lisa Loutzenheiser and Joy Lei for listening and advising and talking with me, and for never pointing out that I probably soak up more of their brilliance than I give back to them.

Swarthmore College provided me with a dissertation fellowship and resources that allowed me to finish writing the dissertation while teaching in the Program in Education with the most inspiring colleagues Lisa Smulyan, Eva Travers, Diane Anderson, and Kae Kalwaic. I also thank Bates College for providing me with resources, including a personal research fund, that helped me to complete this book as I gained new insight on what it means to implement these theories from my new colleagues Anne Wescott Dodd, Stacy Smith, Marcia Makris, and Clementine Brasier. At crunch time, my student assistant Carole Caldarone was a lifesaver.

Susan Talburt and James King were hugely generous with their suggestions, reflections, and encouragement. Eric Collum was invaluable in helping me to substantially revise and edit. And the editors and staff at RoutledgeFalmer helped me produce a book of which I can be proud.

I am sure there are others whom I have forgotten to mention, but I thank them as well, and apologize for letting their names slip by. They include the teachers who have taught me and the students who have moved me, the friends who have embraced me and the activists who have inspired me, the scholars who have mentored me and the strangers who have cheered me on.

Most importantly, I thank the participants of my study for taking the time to share their stories, for helping us think differently about activism and education, and for inspiring me to continue to do this kind of work. May the force be with you.

Permissions

CHAPTER 1

Introduction

Queer Desires in Education

In the spring of 1999 I had the opportunity to work with future teachers at a large university in the Midwest. I was teaching an introductory course on the relationship between school and society to thirty-three undergraduate students, most of whom were working toward certification in the teacher education program. We spent the first few weeks of the semester examining the paradoxical nature of schools that strive to give students equal educational opportunity but function to maintain various social hierarchies. As we discussed examples and theories of how and how often this happens, my students seemed to move, at least in their discussions, from feeling surprised to critically reflecting on their own schooling experiences to strategizing ways to address these problems. For this reason, I believe my students, just as I, honestly desired to teach in ways that were not oppressive.

Although I did not realize it at the time, our desires, while perhaps well-intentioned, revolved around affirming ourselves and remaining the same. For example, my students' desire to learn about issues related to social justice seems to have been limited to those issues that did not confront them with their own complicity with oppression. Some students (as written in their response papers on this topic) felt that schools are not responsible for social change and, instead, should follow the course set by others in society, as one student noted:

> I don't think that schools are responsible to initiate change. I think that artists, writers, lobbyists, activists, performers, the news media, thinkers of all types, spiritual leaders and political leaders are all responsible to initiate the social change attitude. Education can then take it from there.

Another felt that teaching in ways that address different forms of oppression will detract from that on which schools are supposed to focus—namely, academics:

> All the approaches deal so much with integrating racism, classism, sexism, and heterosexism into the curriculum, but will this take away from the true intention of schools to teach children academics?

In order not to detract from academics, some felt that teachers should be morally neutral. One student wrote,

> There are only eight hours in a standard school day. If cultures, races, sexual orientations, etc., are going to be added to the curriculum, what is going to be taken out of the present system? The school day is already jam-packed with the basic classes. How can a curriculum incorporate all ideas and still leave room for math and science? Will not it seem like teachers are teaching their values on different ideas to their students?

Some felt that teachers are not part of the problem, as exemplified by this student's comment:

> I don't think that I have ever experienced a situation when students were directly oppressed by teachers in any way. The teachers were there to teach, not to impregnate their own beliefs or biases upon the students.

Many of my students acknowledged and condemned the ways schools perpetuate various forms of oppression, but asserted that, as teachers, their jobs will be to teach academics, not disrupt oppression. By separating the school's function from the individual teacher's role, they were able to maintain their belief that they do not—and, as future teachers, *will* not—contribute to these problems.

Some of my students did agree that teachers need to address issues of inequity through their curriculum. However, they equated doing so with teaching about "minorities" and the disadvantaged in society, not about their own privileges and about themselves. They seemed to believe that their privileges did not make a difference in their education, and instead would shift the focus of our conversations to the people who were different from the norm at their school—they wanted to talk about *them*. As several students kept repeating in class discussions and in their final projects, if people can learn about different groups and develop empathy for them, then ignorance and the prejudice based on it will be effectively combated. For example, students who felt they were becoming more "open-minded about homosexuals" talked about realizing that there is "nothing wrong" with them, that they are just like normal folks, and that they hurt just like everyone else. As one student noted,

> This article made me sad. I had an uncle who was gay. I realize that he wasn't treated equal when he was in school. He was one of the greatest guys I ever knew. He died last year, so it really hurt me to know that other gay people are experiencing what he had to experience.

The expectation that information about the "Other" (i.e., groups who traditionally are marginalized in society) leads to empathy is often based on the assumption that learning about "them" helps students see that "they" are like "us" (Britzman, 1998a). In other words, learning about the Other helps students see the self in the Other and, thus, does not change how they see themselves.

This is especially the case when students learn about the Other in comforting ways. For example, one student stated,

> I started the semester much more close-minded about the issue of homosexuality. After hearing many stories and reading the class materials, I finally have come to realize that there is nothing wrong with homosexuality. I think it helped that I got to know Kevin before he told us his sexuality, by that time it did not matter if he was gay or not.

Significantly, this student, like most of the other students, referred to me as "gay," despite that I had discussed, in some depth, my bisexuality earlier in the semester (when I described my own experiences in school as a prelude to their autobiographical essay assignment). As I will soon argue, this tendency to think of sexuality as either/or often reflects a desire to stabilize and normalize a person's own sexual identity. To see me as gay is comforting because doing so put me on the "Other" side of the gay-straight binary (or on the same side for those who identify as gay/lesbian), while seeing me as bisexual or queer is to acknowledge that sexuality is more fluid. Students are not always willing or able to trouble their own identities, and in my class, perhaps some desired seeing me as "gay" because they could not bear the implications of seeing otherwise. This is not to say that such a change is insignificant; for many people, it is a big step. However, as my subsequent experiences illustrate, education cannot stop there. The desire to learn only what is comforting goes hand in hand with a resistance to learning what is discomforting, and this resistance often proves to be a formidable barrier to movements toward social justice.

As we moved to the next section of the course, we studied how teachers and schools might address the ways they function to maintain social hierarchies. At the end of this section, I asked students to read an earlier version of what is now this volume's chapter 2, and had planned an in-class activity to discuss and extend what I described in my essay as four approaches to challenging racism, classism, sexism, heterosexism, and other forms of oppression in schools (in other words, four approaches to "antioppressive" education). While planning my lesson, I had assumed that my students knew little about addressing oppression in schools but were committed to doing so, could implement the four approaches if they learned them, and therefore, should read about them and discuss their definitions and applications in depth. However, when the class session began, all did not go as planned. Almost immediately, we got stuck at my use of the term *queer*. One student wrote,

> You use the term "queer" throughout the article and it struck me as
> derogatory and actually really upset me until you clarified why you used it
> on page 11. As a suggestion, maybe you should explain how you use the
> term "queer" for a feeling of "self-empowerment" at the beginning. It

would make the reader feel more comfortable. The more I think about it, maybe you should not use the term at all. I don't really think it's appropriate for this type of paper. I know that I personally cringed every time I read it.

Another said,

Really don't like the word queer. I understand better why you chose the word queer but it's still a bit much [when said] over and over again—it just has a negative feel to it.

I had hoped to discuss the range of ways in which various forms of oppression play out and can be challenged in schools, but in a conversation where even some of the normally quiet students were speaking, many kept expressing feelings of discomfort and even anger at my use of a term that often meant something derogatory. Although I neglected before assigning the essay to discuss the history of the term, I did explain in the essay that *queer* has been claimed and appropriated by some people to emphasize a conscientious distancing from what is considered "normal" and a sense of self-empowerment (I will define the term in more depth later in this chapter). Nonetheless, many were offended that I used a term that they had been taught was "politically incorrect." For some, this may have meant reading the essay and disregarding the queer applications, while for others, this may have meant feeling no need even to read the entire essay. What they kept repeating in the class discussion was the notion that *queer* meant something negative, and that I should instead use *homosexual* or *gay* since those terms will not upset the (presumably) predominantly straight readership of my writing.

I believe there are two main reasons why we were stuck on *queer*. First, the notion that the term can be an affirming self-identification for some people reveals the socially constructed nature of identities. It can remind us that identities—including queer sexualities, but also including heterosexualities—can change in meaning and sociopolitical value in different historical and cultural contexts. To understand *queer* as an affirming and politically transgressive self-identification, my students would have needed to acknowledge the similarly socially constructed nature of heterosexuality, which for many of them was a self-identification considered normal and natural. Such a move is often difficult to make. Second, it is difficult to hear or see the word *queer* without feeling reminded of the culture and history of ignorance, bigotry, and hatred that often surround that term. In other words, *queer* often reminds us of the *existence* of heterosexism/homophobia, the *severity* of heterosexism/homophobia, and, if we have ever used the term in a harmful way (or failed to intervene in such a situation), our *participation* in heterosexism/homophobia. The preferred terms *homosexual* and *gay* do not stir up such connections, since the use of such terms does not carry as many harmful intentions and effects that *queer* does in everyday speech. By silencing the oppressiveness around the word *queer*, my students were able to more easily disregard heterosexism/homophobia as a significant form of oppression. Indeed, several students asserted that they did not believe that heterosexism/homophobia was as much of a problem as racism, classism, and sexism, which were the other forms of oppression addressed in my essay. As one student noted,

> I saw the title about Anti-Oppressive Education, but the majority of the examples used to explain the approaches dealt with homosexuality. I do not see homosexuality as the main problem. I would find it more helpful if more oppressive topics were discussed.

It is true that heterosexism was discussed in the essay more often than any other form of oppression, but only slightly. I could not help but wonder if the reason students felt that heterosexism was given "too much emphasis" was because it was not given the kind of emphasis that it is normally given, by which I mean only marginal attention. I do believe my students desired to learn. However, I also believe their desire for normalcy and for affirmation of their belief that they do not oppress others was stronger, preventing many of them from confronting and tolerating these new yet discomforting forms of knowledge. In desiring a sense of normalcy, they desired a repetition of silence surrounding heterosexism/homophobia, including their complicity with it, and thus, entered a crisis when they met *queer*.

Our getting stuck on the term was a crisis for me as well. I was completely surprised by their emotional reaction to my piece and unprepared for the resulting conversation. Ironically, this lack of preparation resulted from my desiring to be what many educators would call well-prepared. I had planned a lesson that proceeded rationally: first, summarize the essay; second, extend the theories in the essay to other forms of oppression. Furthermore, I had planned a lesson with a clear, desired end result: the selected reading and activity would help students think critically and teach subversively (the manner in which I try to think and teach). Finally, in trying to tailor my lessons to my students, I presumed to know my students: what they already knew, how they would respond to the lesson, where they needed to go, what would get them there. By leaving little room for what is uncontrollable and unknowable in education, and by expecting my knowledges to be affirmed and replicated by my students, my preparation also left little room for addressing ways that learning can be unexpectedly difficult, discomforting, and even emotional. While I did anticipate a crisis, I was expecting a different kind of crisis, one based on learning about the many ways oppression played out in their schooling years, not one based on resisting the very theories being presented.

There were a few students who expressed support for my use of the term *queer* and who thought positively of their experiences reading the essay. As one wrote,

> Upon reading the essay, I felt very happy. For once, I was reading an essay that dealt directly with the topic of discrimination in schools (especially with homosexuality).

Another even felt the essay and its queerness was educationally useful, and wrote,

> Personally, I had no problem with the use of the word "queer." I was not offended by the word. I was actually intrigued to read on and find out what the actual meaning of the word "queer" is.

Another wrote,

> This is a voice that I've never heard before. This brought a whole new dimension to my frame of thinking. I'm not sure what it is but information like this gets my mind going. It has been true for me that when I had

to work through a crisis, I grew and gained from the experience like no other time in my life. This is what life's all about for me: learning.

One student wrote of not initially understanding why I was using *queer*, but reasoned that feeling discomforted was perhaps part of the learning process of reading my essay. According to the student, wanting to learn meant wanting to learn something new, hear a different voice, imagine what has yet to be said, do the "unexpected." "Learning" meant learning things that are uncomfortable because they complicate a person's "frame of thinking."

As the class discussion ensued, I encouraged my students to enter into discomforting places and to think of learning as taking place only through crisis. Modeling my own advice, I forced myself to enter an uncomfortable place, departing from my lesson plan and teaching the unpredicted. Such a move, I should note, is very difficult for me, as it is for many teachers who desire control over the direction of the lesson and over what students learn. Patti Lather (1998) tells us that educators often try to avoid crises and close off stuck places in order to maintain a sense of control over what students learn (and, for that matter, over how they behave). Yet, we can never control what students learn. In fact, as my experiences show, attempts to control education can actually hinder antioppressive change.

Not until the end of the lesson did we discuss the four approaches. In retrospect, not expecting to address crisis not only led me to plan a lesson that could not be "achieved," but also, had I not departed from it, could have prevented me from working with my students where they were. This experience has led me to question what it means to teach in ways that challenge different forms of oppression. I am curious about what it means to address our resistances to discomforting knowledges, and about what it means to put uncertainties and crisis at the center of the learning process. I wish to explore new ways to think about antioppressive education. The goal of this book is to address such questions.

Troubling Educational Research

Educational research has contributed much to our understanding of the dynamics of oppression in school and the promises of some forms of antioppressive curriculum and pedagogy. As the above section suggests, more must be done to disseminate this research to classroom teachers and future teachers who traditionally respond to calls for antioppressive education with resistance, defensiveness, and fear. This is not to say, however, that existing educational research is itself unproblematic. Although some researchers speak with certainty and confidence, suggesting that they have found the answers to our problems, the "strategies that work," I will argue that every educational practice makes possible some antioppressive changes while closing off others. Furthermore, much in education remains unknown and underexplored, including perspectives that can significantly contribute to, critique, and offer alternatives to existing theories and practices in antioppressive education. Educators, therefore, have an ethical responsibility not only to learn and use the troubling or discomforting research already in existence, but also to engage in further troubling or complicating that research by looking beyond the theories and methods that we already know.

To this end, this book describes what I see as four primary approaches to antioppressive education suggested by the current field of research. Simultaneously, this book looks beyond these dominant frameworks for conceptualizing and addressing oppression, and explores insights and changes made possible by some of the theories and stories that are traditionally marginalized in educational research. One set of theoretical perspectives that I will explore is the recent feminist and queer readings of poststructuralism and psychoanalysis. As I will argue in chapter 2, I turn to these theories because they offer ways of thinking and talking about education, oppression, identity, and change that I find helpful for working against traditional ways of thinking and acting, teaching and learning. My exploration of these theories should not imply that these theories are the best theories for antioppressive education, since this body of writings is but one of many possible frameworks that can be helpful to such research. Poststructuralism and psychoanalysis will not give *the* answer, the panacea, the best practice; rather, they will help us imagine different possibilities for working against oppression.

Similarly, one set of stories or voices traditionally marginalized or silenced in educational research that can help us imagine new antioppressive possibilities is the stories of queer activists working against multiple forms of oppression. What do I mean by *queer*? In a narrow sense, I use the term *queer* to mean gay, lesbian, bisexual, two-spirited (this last term is specific to Native Americans; see Jacobs, Thomas, & Lang, 1997); transgendered, intersexed (neither male nor female; see Chase, 1998; Kessler, 1998); questioning, or in other ways different because of one's sexual identity or sexual orientation. (A catchall abbreviation for these identities that I will use here is GLBTsTgIQ.) Although *queer* often refers to sexual orientation, I do not limit its definition to that of gay, lesbian, or bisexual, partly because of the interconnectedness of sexuality and sex/gender (Butler, 1990), and partly because of the interconnectedness of heterosexism and gender oppression (Wilchins, 1997). The term *queer*, after all, like *fag* and *dyke*, derogates and polices not only people who feel attraction for members of their same gender, but also people who exhibit physical and behavioral traits that society deems appropriate only for those of the "opposite" gender (e.g., boys who "act like girls" and girls who "look like boys"). The range of reasons for identifying or being identified as queer suggests that being queer is as much a performance or identification (what we do) as an identity (who we are).

I should note that I sometimes use the term *queer* in the broader sense of nonnormative (i.e., not who we are supposed to be). While discomforting to many people because it reminds us of bigotry and hatred, it is exactly this oppressive history that gives the term its activist, in-your-face quality. For many queers, the term has come to mean a rejection of normative sexualities and genders, a reclaiming of the terms of their identities, and a feeling of self-empowerment (Butler, 1993; Capper, 1999; Pinar, 1998; Tierney & Dilley, 1998). For some, the term *queer* is expanding to include other marginalized groups in society (such as those with queer races or queer bodies), and the term *queer activist* is expanding to include those who do not identify as GLBTsTgIQ but nonetheless challenge heterosexism and gender oppression. Such expansions are important since the term has begun to normalize only certain ways of being queer, as when people equate "queer" with, say, "white, sexually active gay male." All of this is to say that this disruptive, discomforting term, with its multiple meanings and uses, seems appropriate for research on changing oppression.

Although I similarly use the term *activist* to identify people engaged in many different forms of activism, I limit my analysis to antioppressive activists—those who work against the forms of oppression that I describe in chapter 2. Right-wing or conservative activists (such as pro-life, anti–gay rights, and anti–affirmative action activists) are not antioppressive since they work to reinforce or conserve the norms of society and stabilize current social hierarchies. They work to repeat rather than to change social dynamics that privilege certain groups in society and marginalize others. They use power as it has traditionally been used to benefit some and limit the opportunities, threaten the safety, and subordinate the identities of others. While I believe that educators have much to learn from the experiences of activists who work to contribute to oppression, as well as from the experiences of nonactivists, I focus the analysis in this book on activists committed to challenging oppression. As I will argue in chapter 2, multiple forms of oppression are constantly played out in schools. The norm or status quo, which manifests in the traditional operation of schools, for instance, or in traditional pedagogies, is what is oppressive. Changing oppression, then, requires constantly working against this norm. This book looks beyond a repetition of the status quo, and even beyond good intentions and a critical awareness, in order to examine the particular kinds of *labor* involved in antioppressive activism and change.

Why focus on queer activists? As with poststructuralism and psychoanalysis, queer activists do not offer the "best" stories or voices for insight on oppression or education. They are but part of the many communities that have yet to significantly enter the conversation among researchers about antioppressive education. However, for several reasons, I feel a sense of urgency to focus on queer activists who work against multiple forms of oppression. I focus on queers and their oppression because queers remain "arguably the most hated group of people in the United States" (Unks, 1995a, p. 3); because queer sexualities continue to incite wide public panic, anger, and resistance, especially when discussed in the context of schools (Epstein & Johnson, 1998); because educators do not often feel the need to address homophobia and heterosexism in schools; and because my experiences as a queer researcher, teacher educator, and activist make me feel all the more capable of bringing about significant change in this area. I focus on activists because they are doing the kind of work that I would like to see educators and students doing (that is, not only voicing support, but also acting to bring about change); because they have never, to my knowledge, been invited into this conversation by researchers; and because they bring life experiences of becoming and being activists that can provide models for antioppressive education. I focus on activists who work against multiple forms of oppression because I hope to theorize approaches to antioppressive education that can address multiple and interested forms of oppression. And I focus on activists who are queer because they inspire me to continue to do the work that I do.

Calling Activists

I sought out a particular type of antioppressive activist. Since my focus was what it means to change *multiple* forms of oppression, I wanted activists who were engaged in projects or efforts that worked against more than one form of oppression, including heterosexism/homophobia (such as antiracist and antihomophobic activisms, or feminist and queer activisms, or queer Asian-American activisms). Since my focus was education, I wanted activists who were working with youth or were somehow in the field of education, be it formal education such as that gained in schools or informal education such as that experienced through community outreach. Since my focus was on queers and their oppression, I wanted activists who identified as GLBTsTgI, or queer, although I hoped to and did find at least one activist who identified as heterosexual but who engaged in antiheterosexist efforts. Since I wanted to interview them in person, I wanted activists living in close proximity to where I was living at the time, which was in the Midwest.

Of the adults, I wanted activists who were students of or had graduated from a college or university. There were three reasons for this. First, college students or graduates are more likely to have had the experiences of leaving their homes and maybe even their hometowns as they began their university-level education. Queer students living independently at college often feel a freedom to explore, research, and discuss their sexualities in ways they never felt they could while at home (Rhoads, 1994). Also, queers (as well as students of color) often have told me that they were not activists until they went to college. I wanted to see what it was about going to college that was helpful, if at all, in preparing activists to work against oppression.

Second, students and graduates who are activists are more likely than individuals who did not attend college to have taken courses in studies of oppression—such as ethnic studies, women's studies, and queer studies—and thus, are more likely to be conversant in theories about oppression. Having already acquired a familiarity with discourses, languages, and theories that are critical of various aspects of oppression, they will be better able to collaborate with the researcher in developing theory, a process known as "collaborative theorizing." Sue Middleton (1993) makes a similar argument about her choice of participants for a study on feminist pedagogy. She writes that

> the process of collaborative theorizing was helped by the women's theo-
> retical sophistication; all had done some higher education studies in the
> social sciences and had been involved in academic and/or grassroots
> feminist theorizing. This helped in avoiding what Liz Stanley and Sue
> Wise have termed "conceptual imperialism." (p. 69)

As I will explain in a moment, I wanted the participants to provide and analyze data with an awareness of my research questions and theoretical framework.

Third, students and graduates who are activists represent the type of students I believe schools need to help produce. Rather than produce "happy failures" because they have compromised academics in order to advance social justice (Metz, 1992), I argue that schools need to pursue excellence both in academics and in social justice. In part, this requires reconceptualizing excellence in academics and what is necessary to get there. But it also requires rethinking the purposes of schools. "Success" in school must involve, I argue, a balance of these two goals. Thus, I do not seek students achieving in higher education who are complacent about oppression, nor do I seek students active in antioppressive projects who did not succeed in and do not value academic education. Rather, I seek students who pursue and achieve both intellectual and political goals. They provide models for antioppressive education that cannot be criticized for not trying to "teach" students.

I began soliciting participants in April 1999, and did so in several ways. Primarily, I contacted, over the telephone or via e-mail, people I knew who fit these criteria and/or who I thought understood my definition of antiop-pressive activism and might be able to refer me to other possible partici-pants. My initial contacts included friends and acquaintances, teachers in local schools, and students, staff, and faculty of the local university, includ-ing staff of queer organizations, multicultural organizations, and health organizations. I also contacted leaders or members of queer organizations in the local area, such as youth groups, support groups, community organizations, churches, and education-related groups. To each of the potential participants, I sent out a letter or spoke over the telephone and described the goals and method of my research. As Kathleen Casey (1993) did in her research with feminist teachers, I wanted my participants to have a "brief description" of the context and purposes of my study before beginning the interviews.

Out of the twenty-plus individuals who volunteered to participate I chose seven activists who, when put together, constituted a diverse (though not necessarily "representative") group. They identified with six racial groups (African American, Asian American, Latino/a, Mixed Race, Native American, White American), six sexual orientations (bisexual, gay, lesbian, queer, straight, unsure), three gender identities (female, male, transgender), and ages from almost every ten-year bracket (teens, twenties, thirties, forties, fifties, and seventies). I felt that seven participants would offer a manageable number of stories to use in my study and at the same time provide a diverse range of experiences and perspectives. My attempt to assemble a wide range of stories was part of my attempt to always look beyond what I expected and look for perspectives that my own perspectives and assumptions may close off.

Feminist, Activist, and Collaborative Interviews

In designing the interviews, I used several research traditions: I drew on feminist researchers who work against detachment; activist researchers who explicitly work against oppression in the lives of the participants; and collaborative researchers who ask the participants to help them answer their research questions.

Feminists have long critiqued calls for objectivity and detachment (i.e., calls for the researcher to refrain from disclosing personal opinions and feelings to the participants), arguing that fears of biasing the interview are not only misguided, but also harmful (Fine, 1994; Gluck, 1991; Lather, 1991; Richardson, 1997). As Ann Oakley (1981) explains, "Personal involvement is more than dangerous bias—it is the condition under which people come to know each other and to admit others into their lives" (p. 58). In fact, the call for detachment actually dehumanizes the people being researched: it expects them to interact with an inhuman, "objective" questioner; it denies them humane responses to their emotions, their desires, their insecurities, and even their bodies (Honeychurch, 1998); and it denies them the opportunity to relate socially to the researcher as two people normally relate to and interact with one another. Many feminists have thus aimed to facilitate more personal connections and disclosure, and to minimize power differences between researcher and participant (Stacey, 1988). I should note that this movement toward a more egalitarian research process results not only from the affirmation of traditionally "feminine" capacities, such as compassion and caring (Gilligan, 1982; Noddings, 1984), but also from the recognition that the researcher can never be fully detached from or outside of the research process. As Michele Foster (1994) and James Scheurich (1995) have argued, the research interview is a dialogical, interactive event. What the interviewees say is often highly influenced by how they read, feel about, respond to, and relate to the interviewer at any given moment. Thus, the researcher should not pretend to be detached nor pretend to be interested, but engage in the process as honestly as possible. As I will explain momentarily, I tried in my interviews to make explicit the goals of my study, the assumptions and perspectives that I brought with me, and even my own experiences with education, oppression, and activism.

Activist researchers also critique calls for detachment and objectivity, but rather than focus on disclosure and the one-on-one interaction during the interview with the participant, they focus on action and intervention in the community, classroom, or situation of the participant (Gluck, 1991; Lather, 1991; Leck, 1994; Tierney, 1994). Concha Delgado-Gaitan (1993) argues that learning about oppression and about how to work against oppression go hand-in-hand with actively working to challenge oppression within the participant's community or classroom. What is important, here, is the recognition that, in the processes of researching and constructing knowledge, the researcher cannot help but impact the research context and the people in it. Faced with the impossibility of detachment, researchers should aim to ensure that what they do works against rather than contributes to oppression. As William Tierney (1994) argues, "if research is to be praxis oriented, if our purpose is somehow to change the world, then of necessity we must get involved with those whom we study" (p. 110). In Tierney's study of a colleague with AIDS, he "undertook the research not merely to collect empirical data but also to aid the individual under study" (p. 110). I should note that the term *activist* applies not only to the interactions researchers have with participants, but also to the knowledge produced through research. Because this knowledge is supposed to be accessible to both researchers and participants (through conversations, publications, and so forth), the value of the knowledge, and consequently the purpose of the research, must be determined at least in part by how the participants can put the knowledge to use and, in particular, how they can use it to work against oppression (Gluck, 1991; Lather, 1991). Researchers have an ethical responsibility to their participants to conduct research that will be useful to them; to do otherwise is to expect them to participate in and contribute their labors to a study that benefits only the researcher. In my own study, I tried to engage the participants in learning different perspectives on oppression and change that they can later use in their own activist efforts.

Collaborative researchers also believe in trying to have a positive impact on the lives of the participants and argue that doing so requires entering into a less hierarchical relationship (Bickel & Hattrup, 1995; Lather, 1991; LeCompte, 1995; Ulichny & Schoener, 1996). Traditionally, researchers assume control over the design and implementation of the research project, and their views of social change are often imposed onto the participants' stories and lives. Even feminist and activist researchers can act in ways that patronize or conflict with the desires of the participants. Collaborative researchers advocate a more cooperative or participatory approach in which the researcher does research *with* rather than *on* the participants. Collaboration can take place on many levels, including research design, data collection and analysis, and write-up (Ulichny & Schoener, 1996). Middleton (1993) argues that, especially when conducting analysis, collaborative theorizing helps to ensure that participants do not become merely the objects of study; such was the central goal of my interviews with the participants.

Unfortunately, I did not collaborate as much as I had originally hoped. A primary barrier was time. Although the participants expressed to me a shared commitment to activism and an interest in helping me with my project, most were unable to spend time outside of the interviews to do some of the background work needed for collaborative theorizing, which in this study meant reading my summary of the four approaches to antioppressive education and my preliminary data analysis (instead, I had to quickly summarize them verbally during the interview). Furthermore, the process of constructing their stories was not collaborative since most participants did not have a chance to look over, coconstruct, or even "approve" the ways I excerpted and presented their stories in the research write-up. So, my research was collaborative only to a point. This is not to say that more collaboration would necessarily make the project "better," since a collaborative construction of the stories would give not a "truer" reading but a different one, namely, a joint or shared one. Some of the stories that I represent in chapters 3 and 4 show participants grappling with theories of antioppressive education, while others do not, and yet I will argue that they can all help educators and researchers to trouble educational research and practice, though in different ways. In fact, while collaboration is desirable, it is not unproblematic; James Ladwig (1991) argues that it can be exploitative since the researcher is the one who often benefits significantly from the labors of the participant. Every methodology makes certain kinds of interactions, knowledges, and changes possible and others impossible. My methodology is not the "best" methodology, but simply a methodology that closely fits the goals of my project.

I interviewed each participant once or twice for a total of two to six hours in the summer of 1999. All interviews were tape-recorded and transcribed. I began the interviews by introducing myself and reiterating the basic premise of my study—namely, that researchers have conceptualized antioppressive education in certain ways, and that I will be asking them for help in rethinking these approaches. As they introduced themselves, I asked my participants how they wanted to be introduced in future write-ups. I wanted to resist introducing the participants with a list of identity categories that function to give the reader a presumably fixed lens through which to understand the stories of the participants (as if the stories make more sense *because* the reader knows this person is, say, gay). Some decided to list the ways they identify, while others had different choices, as will be seen in the following chapters. My first set of questions focused on what I called "moments of significance," or, moments of their lives, either in or out of school, that were significant in helping them either to address different forms of oppression or to become the activists that they are today. I also asked them to describe the forms of activism in which they are currently involved.

I did not conduct the interviews with the intent of learning about the participants, who they are, what they do, or why they do what they do.

Rather, I conducted the interviews to see what difference their stories can make *to my theoretical framework*, to see how they can help educators think differently about antioppressive education. I wanted to see how their stories confirmed the theories I describe in chapter 2, how they illustrated them, how they showed them in practice. And I wanted to see how they disconfirmed them, how they troubled them, how they stretched them or pointed to their gaps. I also wanted to see what the participants thought of the theories. The insights from their stories that troubled and exceeded my theoretical framework are the heart of chapters 3 and 4. The participants themselves were not the objects of inquiry; rather, they were resources who helped me trouble the theories. It was, then, the theories themselves that were the objects of inquiry.

The methodology I used as I collected and analyzed data and interrogated and reconstructed theory was a limited version of the extended case method, which, according to Michael Burawoy (1992) "derives generalizations by constituting the social situation as anomalous with regard to some preexisting theory (that is, an existing body of generalizations), which is then reconstructed" (p. 278). The "preexisting theory" is the theory that I describe in chapter 2: the four approaches to antioppressive education. The data that we put up against the theory were the stories that the activists told about activism and moments of significance. In the second interview (or for those interviewed only once, the second half of the interview), we talked explicitly about the theory, in light of my preliminary data analysis. Did they agree that certain of their experiences illustrated these approaches? Did they agree that certain experiences troubled, disrupted, or expanded these approaches? Did the way I defined the approaches fail to account for certain other experiences? To those participants who had a second interview (there were five of them), I offered to send each a copy of the transcript, my initial analysis, and my literature review to be looked over, appended, and commented on. Two of them agreed to look it over before the second interview, and although they offered no changes to the transcripts, they were able to begin the second interview by discussing the four approaches to antioppressive education without my having to explain them (as I did for the other participants). I believe the academic backgrounds of many of the participants enabled them to collaboratively theorize and analyze with me in much depth, as several of them had already read some of the writings I drew on and could refer in detail to theories and theorists.

The goal of presenting my theoretical framework to my participants was not merely to ask them for help in rethinking theory. I hoped that my framework could be helpful to them in rethinking their own practices and activism. In other words, I hoped that my relationship with the participants was not only one in which I benefited from their labors, but also one in which I gave something back. After all, collaboratively theorizing required that the participants learn the range of theories I am grappling with, read and interpret their experiences against this framework, and explore what new insights are made possible for education as well as for themselves. Therefore, I was excited when, after the interviews, several talked about having a clearer idea of how they came to do the activism that they do and felt encouraged to do more. Several also expressed interest in learning new ways to think about activism and change, especially when hearing about the strengths and weaknesses of the different approaches, and urged me to hurry and finish the write-up so that they and others could use it.

Re-presenting the Stories

Another way my research aims to be activist is in the changes it works to bring about in the readers of this book, and I hope this happens not just through what it says, but how it says it; not just through what is read, but how it is read. In other words, I hope that antioppressive change will result when readers read the voices and stories in this book in untraditional ways.

Traditionally, researchers have presented the voices of participants in the form of block quotations from the interview transcripts as if to convey to the reader what the participants were really saying, and allow the reader to verify the validity of the researcher's interpretations of and claims about what the participants were really saying. Poststructuralist researchers (e.g., Britzman, 1995; Fine, 1994; Kumashiro, 1999b; Richardson, 1997; Scheurich, 1995) have offered three main critiques of this practice. First, the interviewee's statements are always mediated and therefore influenced by the interviewer and context. Sometimes, what interviewees say can be less an answer to the interviewer's question than a speech act that solicits a particular type of response from the interviewer, as, for instance, when interviewees "test" interviewers to see whether or not they are "really" insiders (Foster, 1994). Second, interpretations by researchers within the write-up are always partial; they can never tell the whole story. Knowledge itself, after all, is always partial (Haraway, 1988). Third, the way readers read texts is always influenced by their own identities and life experiences (Richardson, 1997). Thus, presenting voices as if they are "literal representations" (Britzman, 1995) or transparent and stable "mirrors" of reality (Scheurich, 1995) obscures the history and context in which the text was and is produced, and the multiple labors involved in that production. Michelle Fine (1994) writes,

> As Joan Scott has written on the topic of "experience," the presumption that we can take at face value the voices of experience as if they were the events per se, rather than the stories about the events, is to dehistoricize and decontextualize the very experiences being reported. Scott argues that researchers who simply benignly transcribe social experiences fail to examine critically these constructions which seem so real to informants and are in such dire need of interpretation. (p. 21)

Researchers must reflect on ways in which the "voices" are both "an interpretation and in need of an interpretation" (p. 21). My goal, then, is to move away from a modernist representation of my participants' experiences, to a poststructuralist re-presentation of their experiences, one that makes explicit ways in which the participants' voices are contextualized, the researcher's interpretations are partial, and the reader's reading is situated.

I agree with William Tierney (1997) and Laurel Richardson (1997) that poetry can offer one such form of writing. Discussing a poem she constructed based on an interview, Richardson argues,

> When we listen to or read [it], rather than being swayed into thinking we have the one and only true story here, the facticity of its constructedness is ever present. By violating the conventions of how sociological interviews are written up, those conventions are uncovered as choices authors make, not rules for writing truths. The poetic form, moreover, because it plays with connotative structures and literary devices to convey meaning, commends itself to multiple and open readings in ways that straight sociological prose does not. The poetic form of representation, therefore, has a greater likelihood of engaging readers in reflexive analyses of

> their own interpretive labors of my interpretive labors of [the intervie-
> wee's] interpretive labors. (pp. 142–43)

In other words, while both forms of representation are constructions, poetry, more than prose, makes explicit, through its unconventionality, many ways in which the story is constructed. Poetry, in contrast with "straight" prose, can offer queer representations of my participants' experiences.

Some forms of poetry can also more closely resemble speech patterns of everyday conversation than does formal prose (Richardson, 1997; Tedlock, 1983). As Dennis Tedlock (1983) argues, both "good syntax" and "good scansion" are "more likely to be obtained in dictation than in continuous discourse" (p. 7). Everyday speech involves nonstandard sentences, broken phrases, frequent and meaningful pauses, changes in volume and rhythm, and stresses on particular words, and these communicative devices are intrinsic to a form that makes substantial and unconventional use of breaks, stanzas, spacing, punctuation, capitalization, repetition, and so on. Drawing on Tedlock, I argue that, although the written word can never be an exact substitute for oral speech and thus can never move an individual in exactly the same way that the spoken word can, the closer resemblance to speech of some forms of poetry makes those forms a more useful vehicle for capturing qualities of speech and reproducing the power of speech to move the listener. My choice of poetry, then, is an attempt to have my participants and me speak to the reader. Readers cannot read stories as mere recordings of the participant speaking to the researcher, but they can read stories as events where the participant and the researcher are speaking to the reader. The mode of address changes, the audience changes, and as a result, the reader's response can also change. I do not want the readers to read the stories in ways that they have always read stories; I want the readers to read these stories in ways that disrupt traditional reading practices and that call on them to respond in different ways.

To this end, in chapters 3 and 4, I re-present the words and experiences of my participants in the form of poetry. There are, of course, many forms of poetry, and I have chosen what might be called *narrative poetry*, by which I mean poetry in which the speaker narrates a story using everyday speech. The lines in every poem are quotations from the interview transcripts. The stanzas are abridged versions of the interview (what would otherwise be a block quotation, but without ellipses). The selection, construction, and ordering of the stanzas reflect my interpretation of my participants' stories. In other words, for each participant I combed through the transcript to find instances of their discussing a particular topic, then pieced together these instances to reflect my understanding of their story. I have also put to use my admittedly limited understanding of such literary devices as pauses, cadence, repetition, connotation, and mode of address as I try simultaneously to guide the readers in their interpretation while reminding them of the constructedness of this process.

I do not purport to say, "this is *the* story," or even, "this is my participant's story." Rather, I claim only a partial interpretation. Furthermore, I purport neither to give the reader an unbiased window through which to understand my participants' experiences, nor to provide the reader with presumably objective data against which my claims can be "tested." Rather, I present a literary lens that I hope will force readers to acknowledge their own lenses and interpretive labors in understanding my participants' experiences. My goal is to work against ways in which imposed interpretation and purported objectivity often do violence to the words and lives of the people being researched. This is not to say that poetry is the way that all researchers should represent and use data. As I try to argue throughout this book, there is no one best way. Rather, different approaches with their different strengths and weaknesses can each accomplish different things. For my project, I believe it is important to resist feeling knowledgeable about who the participants are or what they are "really" saying.

Of course, this is not to say that learning about others by hearing the voices and stories of people traditionally silenced in schools and educational research is unimportant. On the contrary, I believe hearing such stories is very important. "Critical ethnographers" (e.g., Anderson, 1989; Fine, 1991; LeCompte, 1995; Simon & Dippo, 1986; Weis, 1990; Willis, 1977) have critiqued the tendency of researchers to speak *for* the Other, and have advocated "giving them voice" or "liberating their voices" through multiple, long, block quotations that reflect not only diversity but also contradiction, opposition, and complexities. Such research helps to disrupt simplistic understandings of the Other.

However, in this book, my goal is not for the reader to know the Other. In fact, using voices to speak as the Other in an effort to learn about the Other can be problematic (Talburt, 2000). My goal is also not to amplify the stories of the Other; that is a different project. My goal is not even to have the reader listen to the language and words that the participants use to tell their stories, since the process of constructing the poems required me to completely rework (and, perhaps some might say, violate) their language. Poetry is not useful for all projects and goals, and it is not useful for "hearing stories" or "giving voice." But my goal here is quite different. In this book, my goal is to *use* their stories. My goal is to treat my poetic constructions as *cultural texts* that I read in multiple ways and then ask, How do the different ways that I read the text help me to think differently about antioppressive education? What is important in this book is not as much the "meanings" of the texts as the process of "reading" the texts, and the poetic form of representation seems to fit this goal nicely.

Queer Activist Reading Practices

In this book, I will juxtapose insights from educational research on antioppressive education with stories of queer activists as I explore different ways to challenge multiple forms of oppression in schools. As I look beyond existing theories and practices, I will work toward developing new conceptual and cultural resources for educators and researchers committed to social justice.

In chapter 2, "Theories and Practices of Antioppressive Education," I review the developing literature on antioppressive education by summarizing and critiquing what I see as the four primary approaches that educational researchers have taken in conceptualizing (1) the nature of oppression and (2) the curricula, pedagogies, and policies needed to bring about change. These approaches are: education for the Other, education about the Other, education that is critical of privileging and Othering, and education that changes students and society. I will argue that engaging in antioppressive education requires more than just using an amalgam of different approaches. In order to address the multiplicity and situatedness of oppression, and the complexities of teaching and learning, educators also need to make more use of insights from poststructuralism, feminist and queer readings of psychoanalysis, and other theories that remain marginalized or unexplored in the field of educational research. Both students and educators need to "look beyond" existing theories and practices. I conclude

chapter 2 with a preliminary examination of the implications of poststructuralist and psychoanalytic notions for classroom instruction in the "core"
disciplines (social studies, English, mathematics, and science) in K–12
schools. These notions of unknowability, multiplicity, resistance, and crisis
suggest approaches to antioppressive education that are paradoxical in
nature in that they constantly work to queer their very center.

In chapter 3, "Readings and Rereadings of Identity, Culture, and
Oppression," I discuss different ways to think about oppression and the
identities and cultures that situate it. I pay particular attention to the complex and contradictory ways that multiple forms of oppression intersect and
play out in everyday life. I begin by drawing on my own life experiences and
on the four approaches in chapter 2 as I describe three dominant frameworks for understanding multiple oppressions, or three "reading practices": a focus on difference, a focus on normalcy, and a focus on
intersections. I then turn to the stories of four queer activists—Pab,
Christopher, Matthew, and Beth—who live and work at some of these intersections (of heterosexism, racism, gender oppression, religious oppression, and so forth) as I complicate these reading practices. With the first
three participants' stories, I incorporate poststructuralist insights into my
earlier "reading practices" as I explore how different routes make possible
different insights into the complexities and contradictions of oppression.
With the fourth participant's stories, I take poststructuralist insights one
step further by exploring yet another route of reading, one I call "looking
beyond," as I explore how some routes can help not only complicate our
understandings of oppression but also change our very senses of self. I suggest implications for education throughout the chapter.

In chapter 4, "Addressing Resistance through Queer Activism," I draw
on the previous chapters as I turn more explicitly to the implications of
queer activism for addressing resistance in education. I turn to four queer
activists—Sue, Debbie, Matthew, and Pab—to see how their stories of
activism help me address students' desire for repetition and resistance to
crisis and change. As I read their stories, I search for elements in each story
that suggest a different way to "read" that story, and explore what insights
are made possible when I read these stories through these suggested routes
of reading. I will argue that my readings of the stories suggest to me four
useful antioppressive practices: doing "homework"; inverting and exceeding binaries; juxtaposing one text with another; and catalyzing for action

and change. Throughout the chapter, I will try to model each of these four practices. In other words, what will be important in this chapter is not only *what* I read, but also *how* I read it. Each of my four readings will both describe a practice (insofar as I discuss and interpret the story) and model it (insofar as I discuss and interpret the story in a particular way). Following each story, I will suggest practical implications for classroom teachers.

In chapter 5, "Conclusions," I briefly reflect on how different ways of concluding this book can invite as well as disinvite readers to look beyond my own arguments and analyses. I draw on the stories of Christopher (an activist from chapter 3) about how schools seem to want to "dispose" of some students, including his own adopted child, as a way to remind myself of my goals as well as my limitations. I then call on readers to continue this paradoxical work involved in antioppressive educational research and practice.

As I suggested earlier, I do not aim to offer strategies that work. Rather, I hope to offer conceptual and cultural resources for educators and researchers to use as we rethink our practices, constantly look for new insights, and engage differently in antioppressive education. I encourage readers to read this book in a way that resists looking for answers and that instead invites them to reflect constantly on their own assumptions, identities, theoretical frameworks, and educational practices and puts to use whatever insights are gained. Looking beyond themselves and their own practices, and even looking beyond my theories and arguments, readers need to engage in a reading practice that always asks, What difference is made possible in my own practices by this book?

To this end, I intersperse short vignettes throughout this book. These vignettes are selections from my interviews with an antioppressive educator, Sam. My hope, in juxtaposing her stories with the chapters of the book, is that the reader will feel invited to look beyond what I say in the book and to see how the ideas and practices of an antioppressive educator trouble my own analyses. Of course, the vignettes are no more the "real" story than are my poems. They appear with no context, no discussion, and no interaction between the speakers and the listener/reader. They are partial stories. And my hope is that reading my partial readings alongside these partial tellings will incite theorizings by the reader that not even I could have imagined. Including the vignettes—with contents and a form (block quotations) that overlap, extend, and contradict my own arguments—is my attempt to refuse to present this book as final, complete, and *the* answer.

I encourage readers to think of reading this book as an event that constitutes the kind of antioppressive educational practices that I articulate throughout its discussion. It is queer in its unconventionality and it is activist in the changes it aims to bring about. In this way, my book is not a mere exercise, and not a final product, but a resource that I hope can be in some way helpful to the reader, as it was for the researcher, and as I hope it was for the participants.

VIGNETTE 1

KEVIN: You get to pick your own pseudonym.

SAM: I always wanted to be called Sam. Short for Samantha. Instead of my name. So, Sam.

KEVIN: How would you like me to introduce or initially describe you in the book?

SAM: Well, let's see, an aging lizard [*laughter*]. No. You know, that's the name of older lesbians? Lizards.

KEVIN: I knew there was a group.

SAM: Yeah, the Lizards. 'Cause we all are, you know, our skins are all weathered. I guess I would describe myself as over fifty. And, a parent, you know, a mom. An educator. A lesbian, of course. And an activist. Yeah. I'm pretty middle class, that's important. And a feminist, definitely, feminist.

KEVIN: Can you describe a significant moment, such as a success story, related to your queer activism? Something that you did, who or what did you do this with, how do you think they or it changed, why do you think this is significant or successful?

SAM: Well, as far as dealing with youth, I feel the most significant event that happened was three years ago, when a student came to me, a gay student, and introduced himself and said that being in the support group was not enough for him. He wanted a way to be social with other kids. And I was like, "Okay, well, we need to start an alliance or a club"—of course that's a scary word, *club*—"in our school." And he's just such a terrific kid. So a bunch of us got together, some teachers, and we invited some key people that we knew would help us in any adversarial task. We ended up forming a gay-straight alliance at our high school. And this has snowballed and now there are ten gay-straight alliances in [the county], and I feel that the one that this young man helped us start at this school was really the foundation of that. And it's incredible to me that by being kind of a risk taker, and our high school is seen as suburban, conventional, conservative, so when other schools looked at us, and thought, Oh my God, look what they did! then they took the risk and they did it. And this was done with another friend of mine, who's also a teacher at the same school, and we're really close. And I think having somebody to do it with was instrumental. I know I could never have done it alone. I see that as so incredible. We had a conference for the kids last fall, and there were 150 kids, or 120 kids, I guess, that attended from all these schools. And I thought, This is incredible. This started from one kid talking to me. And I get calls all the time, "I want to start one, what did you do, how did you do it?" So I think that's probably it.

KEVIN: How do you think this student was changing as a result of helping to form and then being a part of this gay-straight alliance?

SAM: I think it gave him connections, especially, well, with other gay, lesbian, questioning, or bisexual kids. Not just [in] his school, because that was pretty few. So he was able to broaden his social experiences, which is so lacking for gay kids. And I think it made him a lot stronger, I mean, he was a really strong kid anyway and happened to be also an excellent student. And I've seen him since, he's transferred here [to the nearby university]. And when I see him come back and visit, just the confidence he has. I think that's probably a lot of what it did. And having that interaction between student and teacher in creating something and knowing that students have power.

KEVIN: What was it about the student-teacher interaction that was significant or helpful? What do you want other teachers to know about that relationship that would help them help students in similar ways?

SAM: That you have to maintain your, let's see, how should I put it? Your professionalism. Yet you have to let that student in to your human side. And with me, because I am a lesbian, and I have my own children, I think it was easier, because I could connect to him, on that basis, too, not just what I'm teaching in the classroom. I mean he didn't happen to be a student of mine, but yet, I think teachers are, especially gay and lesbian teachers, are so freaked out about getting close to students that they just close them out, they just shut them out. And I think there are ways to do it. And I know it's an advantage because I'm older, because they see me more like the mom. I know it's been harder for my colleague who's very young, and it's been harder for her to make that separation for the kids? And so I think, you know, letting them into your life a little bit, letting them know your history, your struggles, what you've done, as far as changing society. And another thing is, kids like to see that we're a family. You know, that's really important. They like to look at the pictures on my desk. They see, Oh my gosh. I'm gay, but maybe I could have a family. You know, [my teacher] does it. And being able to share that, too, instead of, "Where do teachers live? In a broom closet? You know, Do they just, like, float suspended? Or do they really feel, and . . ." you know?

Theories and Practices of Antioppressive Education

In an attempt to address the myriad ways in which racism, classism, sexism, heterosexism, and other forms of oppression play out in schools, educators and educational researchers have engaged in two types of projects: understanding the dynamics of oppression and suggesting ways to work against it. Whether working from feminist, critical, multicultural, queer, or other perspectives, they seem to agree that oppression is a dynamic in which certain ways of being (or, having certain identifications) are privileged in society while others are marginalized. They disagree, however, on the specific cause or nature of oppression, and on the curricula, pedagogies, and educational policies needed to bring about change. Collectively, they point to what I see as four ways to conceptualize and work against oppression: education for the Other, education about the Other, education that is critical of privileging and Othering, and education that changes students and society. Of course, many educators and researchers blend and modify these four approaches, including the thinkers I cite in each category, but I use this categorization to help me highlight the primary strands of thought in this field of study.

In this chapter, I examine each approach in terms of its conceptualization of oppression, its implications for bringing about change, and its strengths and weaknesses. I argue that although educators have come a long way in detailing approaches that address different forms and different aspects of oppression, they need to make more use of feminist and queer readings of poststructuralism and psychoanalysis in order to address ways that oppression plays out differently in different situations. In addition to bringing poststructuralist and psychoanalytic perspectives into the first three approaches, I devote significant attention to them in the fourth approach, where I also explore their implications for instruction in the "core" disciplines of K–12 schools (social studies, English, mathematics, and science). Broadening the ways we conceptualize the dynamics of oppression, the processes of teaching and learning, and even the purposes of schooling is necessary when working against the many forms of oppression that play out in the lives of students. Doing so requires not only using an amalgam of these approaches (which many educators already do), but also "looking beyond" the field to explore the possibilities of theories that remain marginalized in educational research.

Before turning to my analysis, I should explain some of my terminology. I use the term Other to refer to those groups that are traditionally marginalized, denigrated, or violated (i.e., Othered) in society, including students of color, students from under- or unemployed families, students who are female, or male but not stereotypically "masculine," and students who are or are perceived to be queer. They are often defined in opposition to groups traditionally favored, normalized, or privileged in society, and as such, are defined as *other than* the idealized norm. Although my analysis focuses on only four forms of oppression, I believe it extends to other forms of oppression and to other traditionally marginalized groups, such as students with disabilities, students with limited or no English-language proficiency, and students from non-Christian religious backgrounds. Future research should further explore these connections.

Education for the Other

What is Oppression?

The first approach to addressing oppression focuses on improving the experiences of students who are Othered or in some way oppressed in and by mainstream society. Researchers taking this approach have conceptualized oppression in schools in two ways. First, schools are spaces where the Other is treated in harmful ways. Sometimes the harm results from actions by peers or even by teachers and staff. For example, numerous researchers have documented the discrimination, harassment, physical and verbal violence, exclusion, and isolation experienced by female students (Kenway & Willis, 1998), by queer students or students perceived to be queer (P. Gibson, 1989), and by students of color, such as Asian American students (U.S. Commission on Civil Rights, 1992). Sometimes, however, the harm results from inaction by educators, administrators, and politicians. For example, a number of researchers have documented the shocking, shameful, and substandard conditions, such as insufficient instructional resources and unsafe buildings and classrooms, of many urban schools serving economically poorer students and students of color (Kozol, 1991), while others have pointed to the lack of attention female students receive by teachers who simultaneously give too much of their attention to disruptive male students (Orenstein, 1994). The first way, then, that researchers have illustrated oppression is by pointing to the recognizably harmful ways in which only certain students are treated in and by schools—in other words, to the external ways in which Otherness is marginalized.

Oppression, however, is not always easy to recognize. The second way that researchers have conceptualized oppression is by looking at assumptions about and expectations for the Other—especially those held by educators—that influence how the Other is treated. In particular, they look at the internal ways of thinking, feeling, and valuing that justify, prompt, and get played out (and even reinforced) in the harmful treatment of the Other. Sometimes these dispositions, both conscious and unconscious, are about who the Other is, as is the case with racial and ethnic prejudices and stereotypes that influence how teachers treat their students of color (L. S. Miller, 1995), or sexist ideologies and stereotypes that influence how teachers differently treat their female and male students and how students treat one another (Kenway & Willis, 1998; Mac an Ghaill, 1994). Sometimes these dispositions are about who the Other should be, as is the case with assimilationist beliefs that students of color should conform to the mainstream culture and become more like middle-class White Americans (L. S. Miller, 1995). And sometimes these dispositions are about who the privileged must be in order *not* to be the Other, as is the case with sexist and heterosexist assertions that all boys should exhibit hegemonic masculinity in order to be "real" men (Askew & Ross, 1988).

Students have responded in a variety of ways to these oppressive treatments and dispositions. Some have "overcompensated" by hyperperforming in academic, extracurricular, and social activities (Friend, 1993); some have accommodated enough to succeed academically but have maintained a sense of connection to their ethnic culture and community (M. Gibson, 1988); some have resisted the dominant values and norms of school and society (Fordham, 1996; Willis, 1977); some have experienced an array of "hidden injuries," such as the psychological harm of internalizing or even resisting stereotypes (Osajima, 1993); and some have endured depression and turned violence onto themselves by abusing drugs, starving and scarring their bodies, and even attempting or committing suicide (Orenstein, 1994; Uribe & Harbeck, 1992). Thus, to the onlooker, some of these students "succeed" in school, whereas others are marginalized, fail, and drop out, while still others exhibit no signs that distinguish them from the majority of the student body. But despite the apparent differences between those students who "succeed" and those who "fail" or simply fail to distinguish themselves, all experience oppression.

Bringing About Change

Researchers applying this first approach to antioppressive education have suggested two ways in which to address oppression. Responding to the notion that schools are "harmful spaces," many researchers have argued that schools need to be and to provide helpful spaces for all students, especially for those students targeted by the forms of oppression described above. These "spaces" have been conceptualized on two levels. On one level, the entire school needs to be a space that is *for* students, and in particular, that welcomes, educates, and addresses the needs of the Other. For example, the school needs to be a safe space where the Other will not be harmed verbally, physically, institutionally, or culturally (Governor's Commission on Gay and Lesbian Youth, 1993; U.S. Commission on Civil Rights, 1992). The school needs to be an affirming space where Otherness is embraced, where normalcy (cultural or sexual) is not presumed, where students will have an audience for their Othered voices, and where the Other will have role models (Asante, 1991; Malinowitz, 1995). The school also needs to be a financially and materially sound space where buildings are safe, instructional materials are available, and programs and personnel are sufficiently funded.

On another level, the school needs to provide separate spaces where students who face different forms of oppression can go for help, support, advocacy, resources, and so forth. For example, the school needs to provide therapeutic spaces where harmed students can go in order to work through their trauma, such as that resulting from harassment or assault; to receive the affirmation provided by support groups; and to come to know and accept who they are by learning about their differences (Crystal, 1989; Reynolds & Koski, 1995). The school also needs to provide supportive spaces where the Other can receive advocacy, such as that provided by teachers willing to serve on committees that address sexual discrimination and harassment and to signify their advocacy by, for instance, putting pink triangles on their classroom doors (Kenway & Willis, 1998). Student alliances that engage in political action, such as gay-straight alliances (Woog, 1995) and Asian American student organizations (S. J. Lee, 1996), should also occupy such spaces. Finally, the school needs empowering spaces where the Other can find resources and tools to challenge oppression themselves, such as informational pamphlets by various organizations, and a wide variety of literature in libraries and resource rooms (see, for example, the lists of queer resources in Besner & Spungin, 1995; Committee on Gay, Lesbian, and Bisexual Issues, 1997; Unks, 1995b). Many have even argued that schools should be, or at least provide, learning spaces exclusively for the Other, such as single-sex schools or classrooms (Salomone, 1997).

In response to the harmful dispositions of teachers, researchers have argued that educators need to acknowledge the diversity among their students, as well as embrace these differences and treat their students as raced, gendered, sexual, and classed individuals. For example, researchers suggest that rather than assume that students of color are intellectually inferior to White American students or culturally deficient, educators could incorporate the students' home cultures into their classrooms and pedagogies, teaching in a "culturally sensitive" or "culturally relevant" way (Ladson-Billings, 1994; Philips, 1983; Sheets, 1995; Vogt, Jordan, & Tharp, 1993), or even teaching students about the "culture of power" so that they will know what it takes to succeed in mainstream schools and society (Delpit, 1988). Rather than employ traditional and, as many have argued, masculinist pedagogies that tend to benefit boys and marginalize girls (as in teacher-centered lectures or competitive debates where teaching/learning is rational, abstract, and detached from personal experience), educators could teach in ways that are equitable (American Association of University Women, 1992; Sadker & Sadker, 1994), are traditionally "feminine"—such as by personally "connecting" and constructing knowledge *with* their students (Belenky, Clinchy, Goldberger, & Tarule, 1986)—or are sensitive to the differences between how boys and girls think and evaluate (Gilligan, 1982). Furthermore, educators could teach in a way that challenges the sexism—and concomitant heterosexism (Epstein, 1997)—prevalent among boys (Connell, 1997) and young men (Sanday, 1990).

Concerning queer students, rather than assume that all students are heterosexual or sexually "innocent"—which is not to say that they are asexual, but rather, that their heterosexuality is unstable (Watney, 1991)—and for that matter, that students can, should, or do leave their sexuality outside of school, educators could acknowledge and address the fact that students do bring sexuality into schools for a variety of reasons, such as to resist norms (Walkerdine, 1990) and to denigrate Others (Epstein & Johnson, 1998), and that students are not all heterosexual (some are queer, some are questioning). Finally, rather than assume that a student's class background or community has no bearing on how he engages with schooling, educators could acknowledge the realities of day-to-day life that can hinder one's ability to learn—as J. Alleyne Johnson (1997) did when she addressed the death of a classmate in an inner-city school—and could draw from the student's own knowledge, experiences, and outlooks; as Paul Sylvester (1997) did when he transformed his classroom of predominantly working-class students of color into a "minisociety" in which students ran their own businesses.

In short, these studies urge educators not to ignore the differences in their students' identities, and not to assume that their students are "normal" (and expect them to have normative, privileged identities) or neutral, in other words, without race, sex, and so forth (which is often read as "normal" anyway). Rather, educators could work to learn about, acknowledge, and affirm differences and tailor their teaching to the specifics of their student population.

Strengths and Weaknesses

The strength of this approach is that it calls on educators to recognize that there is great diversity among the student population, and, more importantly, that the majority of students—namely, all those who are not White American, male, hegemonically masculine, heterosexual, and middle-class or wealthy—are marginalized and harmed by various forms of oppression in schools. Educators have a responsibility to make schools into places that are for, and that attempt to teach, all their students. To fail to work against the various forms of oppression is to be complicit with them.

However, educators cannot use only this approach, as it has at least three limitations. First, by focusing on individual prejudice, cultural difference, and the interpersonal discriminatory treatment of the Other, educators fail to attend to other causes of oppression as well as other signs of oppression (McCarthy, 1993). Oppression consists not only of the marginalizing of the Other; it also consists of the privileging of the "normal." By focusing on the negative experiences of the Other this approach implies that the Other is the problem: without the Other, schools would not be oppressing anyone. Furthermore, this approach has little to say to schools without populations of traditionally marginalized groups of students (such as schools with White American, middle-class enrollments with no gender disparities in grades and no "out" queer students). Yet, as the remaining approaches will soon reveal, since the dynamics of oppression are not confined to the ways in which certain students are treated by educators and other students, disrupting oppression requires more than preventing harmful interpersonal interactions.

Second, in order to teach for the Other, educators need to define the Other, but the process of doing so is both difficult and problematic. After all, identities and characteristics of groups are difficult to define, since the boundaries of groups are constantly shifting and contested, which means that any attempt to describe a group can simultaneously function to prescribe what it means to belong to that group. For example, safe spaces, supportive programs, and other resources often seem to target only a portion of a particular group, raising the question, Who is the Other that these resources are for? If these resources target homophobia, are they only for students who identify as gay, lesbian, and bisexual, and perhaps those who are questioning their identities as well? What about students harassed because they are *perceived* to be gay/lesbian/bisexual based on their gender expression, or children of gay/lesbian/bisexual parents? They are all harmed by homophobia, and they all deserve support, but one could argue that they need different kinds of support. Similarly, pedagogies seem to target only subpopulations of a particular group, raising the question, what does it mean to tailor a pedagogy to a particular group? Does teaching in traditionally "feminine" ways reinforce the binaries of masculine/male and feminine/female? Does empowering girls to enter nontraditional fields challenge gender inequities even while reinforcing gender binaries? What about people who do not fit the normative categories of "boy" and "girl" (Bornstein, 1994; Chase, 1998)? A pedagogy tailored to address, in this case, gender inequities is not necessarily able simultaneously to address ways that the gender categories themselves are oppressive. In fact, pedagogies and resources that target a particular group or identity often fail to address students who are marginalized on the basis of more than one identity, such as multicultural curricula and resource centers that challenge racism but silence queer sexualities.

The situated nature of oppression (whereby oppression plays out differently for different people in different contexts) and the multiple and intersecting identities of students make difficult any antioppressive effort that revolves around only one identity and only one form of oppression. Perhaps what is needed, then, are efforts that explicitly attempt to address multiple oppressions and multiple identities, and that keep goals and boundaries fluid and situated. In other words, what is produced or practiced as a safe space, a supportive program, a feminist pedagogy, or a culturally relevant pedagogy cannot be a strategy that claims to be the solution for all people at all times, but is rather a product or practice that is constantly being contested and redefined. Rather than search for a *strategy that works*, I urge educators to address the articulated and known needs and individuality of the students, while constantly *looking to the margins* to find students who are being missed and needs that have yet to be articulated. Educators could create safe spaces based on what they see is needed right now, but constantly re-create the spaces by asking, Whom does this space harm or exclude? They could create supportive programs, but constantly re-create the programs by asking, What practices does this program foreclose and make unthinkable? They could engage in equitable and relevant pedagogies, but constantly rethink their pedagogies by asking, Whom does this pedagogy miss or silence? Without constantly complicating the very definition of the Other, an education for the Other will not be able to address the ways it always and already misses some Others.

A third weakness of this approach is its assumption that educators can accurately assess the needs of their students, especially their Othered students. As I will later argue, teaching involves a great degree of unknowability. Elizabeth Ellsworth (1997), for example, points out that there is always a "space between" the teacher/teaching and learner/learning, between, for instance, who the teacher thinks the students are and who they actually are, or between what the teacher teaches and what the students learn. What does it mean, then, to give students what they need if we acknowledge that we cannot know what they need and whether our efforts are received by students in the ways that we want them to be received? This is not to say that educators should not try to teach, but that the very notion of what it means to teach needs to change. I will discuss this factor of unknowability when I turn to the fourth approach to working against oppression. For now, my point is that the first approach is necessary to work against the harmful effects of oppression, but in helping only the Other (and in presuming to know the Other), it alone is not enough.

Education about the Other

What is Oppression?

Turning from interpersonal interactions to the school curriculum, some researchers have attempted to work against oppression by focusing on what all students—privileged and marginalized—know and should know about the Other. Given that knowledge can lead to oppressive as well as antioppressive actions (as described above), and given that a primary goal of schooling is to teach and learn more knowledge, these researchers suggest that antioppressive knowledge is central to challenging oppressions in school.

Researchers have pointed to two kinds of oppressive knowledges. The first kind of knowledge is the knowledge about (only) what society defines as "normal" (the way that things generally are) as well as what is normative (the way that things ought to be). In this case, Otherness is known only by inference, often in contrast to the norm. Such partial (i.e., incomplete) knowledge often leads to misconceptions. For example, learning that White New England settlers and their descendants are the "authentic" Americans implies that people of color are not real Americans (see Giroux, 1997, for a discussion of Whiteness and racial "coding"). Learning that normal and moral human beings fall in love with, marry, and procreate with members of the "opposite" sex implies that same-sex attraction is an illness, a sin, and/or a crime (Sears, 1987). Learning that there are exactly two genders and that members of each gender exhibit only certain behaviors, appearances, feelings, and occupations implies that anyone who deviates has an unnatural or inappropriate gender (Chase, 1998; Connell, 1987). Schools often contribute to this partial knowledge through the selection of topics for the curriculum: U.S. history textbooks, for instance, routinely celebrate industrial inventors but include little if any discussion of labor exploitation (Anyon, 1979).

The second kind of knowledge encourages a distorted and misleading understanding of the Other that is based on stereotypes and myths. Students learn or acquire this form of partial (i.e., biased) knowledge both outside and inside of school. Outside of school, for example, students learn about queers from sensationalist and stereotypical accounts in the media and popular culture (Lipkin, 1995); they learn about Asian American men and women from exoticized portrayals in films and television (Okihiro, 1994); and they learn about the "proper" roles for girls or women and boys or men from their families, their communities, the popular press, and so forth (Holland & Eisenhart, 1990; McRobbie, 1978; Willis, 1977). But even inside school, students learn little that challenges these stereotypes and misrepresentations. For example, students learn little if anything about the gay liberation movement in history textbooks (Lipkin, 1995); they see few portrayals of queers in health textbooks, and many of these only in the context of sexually transmitted disease (Whatley, 1992); they hear and/or engage in few discussions about queers, except when making jokes or disparaging comments, and since these often go unchallenged by the teacher, they consequently learn that it is acceptable to denigrate queers (Unks, 1995a); boys in particular learn that normalcy does not include queer sexualities (Epstein, 1997; Mac an Ghaill, 1994).

In short, researchers have suggested that the "knowledge" many students have about the Other is either incomplete because of exclusion, invisibility, and silence, or distorted because of disparagement, denigration, and marginalization. What makes these partial knowledges so problematic is that they are often taught through the informal or "hidden" curriculum (Jackson, 1968), which means that, because they are taught indirectly, pervasively, and often unintentionally, they can carry more educational significance than the official curriculum (Jackson, Boostrom, & Hanson, 1993).

Bringing About Change

Researchers have offered two complementary ways to combat these two harmful forms of knowledge. They have suggested that curriculum be expanded to include specific units on the Other, such as curricular units on labor history and resistance (Apple, 1995); feminist scholarship, or any of a number of fields in women's studies (Schmitz, Rosenfelt, Butler, & Guy-Sheftall, 1995); literature by and/or about queers (Sumara, 1993) or the representation of queers in films (Russo, 1989); and various topics in Asian American studies (Hune, 1995) and ethnic studies (S. Chan, 1995). Furthermore, rather than limit their lessons about the Other to once or twice a year when this topic is exclusively addressed, they have suggested that educators integrate lessons and topics about the Other throughout the curriculum. For example, educators might teach about queer resistance movements in class discussions of the civil rights movements of the 1960s, or of the impact of changing the boundaries of voting districts in local elections (which helped activist Harvey Milk get elected to the San Francisco Board of Supervisors in the 1980s), or of the grassroots mobilization around the AIDS epidemic and the AIDS Memorial Quilt. More routine opportunities to integrate diversity include the wording of math problems; lists that suggest possible topics to cover for science research projects; discussions of the personal lives of historical figures, authors, political leaders, and celebrities; and the use of guest speakers (Loutzenheiser, 1997).

Such integration can work against the notion that teaching and learning about the Other can be achieved with a day's lesson, say, on Native Americans, and then another on the physically disabled. In addition, the movement away from discrete lessons about the other can work against the tendency to treat different groups as mutually exclusive. Such an approach enables educators to address the intersections of these different identities and their attendant forms of oppression, by, for instance, examining queer themes in ethnic literature (Athanases, 1996); queer sexualities in communities of color (Sears, 1995; Wilson, 1996); and issues of class, race, and sexuality in feminist movements and feminist spaces (Anzaldúa, 1987; Maher & Tetreault, 1997; Schmitz et al., 1995).

Strengths and Weaknesses

The strength of this approach is that it teaches all students, not just the Othered students, as it calls on educators to enrich all students' understanding of different ways of being. By increasing students' knowledge of the Other, and perhaps helping students see similarities between groups, this approach challenges oppression by aiming to develop in students an empathy for the Other (Britzman, 1998a). This approach also attempts to normalize differences and Otherness by encouraging students to think of and treat other ways of being as just as "normal" and acceptable as normative ways of being.

Like the first approach, however, this second approach does not always bring about change unproblematically. There are at least three reasons for this. First, teaching about the Other could present a dominant narrative of the Other's experience that might be read by students as, for instance, *the* queer experience, or *the* Latino/a experience. Otherness might become essentialized and remain different from the norm. Second, teaching about the Other often positions the Other as the expert, as is the case when students of color are asked to explain the African American or some other "minority" perspective (Fuss, 1989; hooks, 1994). Such a situation reinforces the social, cultural, and even intellectual space or division between the norm and the Other. Third, the goals of teaching about the Other and working against partial knowledge are based on the modernist goal of having full knowledge, of seeing truth, of finding utopia. However, many researchers have argued that the modernist desire for full knowledge is misguided since partial (or, "situated") knowledge is the only form of knowledge that is possible (Haraway, 1988). Furthermore, practically speaking, there is only so much time in the school year, and it is literally impossible to teach adequately about every culture and every identity, especially given the multiplicity of experiences within any cultural community (for example, a straight Jewish woman's experiences often differ significantly from a straight Jewish man's experiences).

All of this is not to say that educators should avoid teaching about the Other and amplifying voices of the Other. Rather, we could reconsider the *uses* of such lessons. Learning about and hearing the Other could be undertaken not to fill a gap in knowledge (as if ignorance about the Other were the only problem), but to disrupt the knowledge that is already there (since the harmful/partial knowledges that an individual already has are what need to change) (Luhmann, 1998). As I will argue further on, changing oppression requires *disruptive* knowledge, not simply more knowledge. Students can learn that what is already known or is becoming known can never tell the whole story, especially since there is always diversity in a group, and one story, lesson, or voice can never represent all. In fact, students can learn that the desire for final knowledge is itself problematic. Learning is about disruption and opening up to further learning, not closure and satisfaction.

To put it another way, lessons about the Other should not aim to tell students the "accurate" portrayal of the Other. Rather, such lessons could be treated as both catalysts and resources for students to use as they learn more. Disruptive knowledge, in other words, is not an end in itself, but a means toward the always shifting goal of learning more. For example, novels from writers of color have traditionally been used to teach students about different cultures, or to give students entry into different cultural experiences (O'Neill, 1993). The problem with such a use of novels comes when students believe that, after "understanding" the novel, they will "understand" the represented culture or group. Yet every novel has silences and every novel privileges certain ideologies over others; every novel, in other words, provides only a partial perspective. Therefore, using novels to learn the truth about others is problematic. Rather than ask, What does this novel tell us about, say, Native Hawaiians? teachers might ask, What questions does this novel raise about Native Hawaiians? Which stereotypes of Native Hawaiians does this novel reinforce, and which ones does it challenge? What is not said in this book about being Native Hawaiian, and how do those silences make possible and impossible different ways of thinking about Native Hawaiian peoples and experiences? The value of lessons about the Other comes not in the truth it gives us about the Other, but in the pedagogical and political uses to which the resulting (disruptive) knowledge can be put.

I should note, however, that even when such questions are asked there are significant limitations inherent in the second approach to antioppressive education. The assumption that information and knowledge lead to empathy does not account for times when feelings do not reflect intention, and for that matter, when neither feelings nor intention gets played out in behavior. And even if empathy were to be achieved, it could be argued that it might simply reinforce the binary of "us" and "them"; for, as argued in chapter 1, the expectation that information about the Other leads to empathy is often based on the assumption that learning about "them" helps students see that "they" are like "us," and therefore does not disrupt ways that students see themselves (Britzman, 1998a). Especially for traditionally privileged students, teaching about the Other does not necessarily force a separation of their sense of self from a sense of normalcy; and it does not necessarily illuminate, critique, or transform the processes by which the other is differentiated from and subordinated to the norm. This is not to say that empathy has no social value. On the contrary, I believe that students need to have empathy for others, and especially for Others, and that pedagogies that aim to cultivate such a sensitivity are important components of antioppressive education. However, since the roots of oppression do not reside solely in the thoughts, feelings, and behaviors of individuals, challenges to oppression need to encompass more than empathy.

Like the first approach, this second approach to challenging oppression works against the marginalization, denigration, and harm of the Other. However, while such efforts do help the Other, they do not necessarily bring about structural and systemic change, redefine normalcy, and disrupt processes that differentiate the Other from the privileged. In addition to addressing Otherness, we need to make visible and work against the privilege and normalization of certain groups and identities. The next two approaches help us do just that.

Education that is Critical of Privileging and Othering

What is Oppression?

Many researchers have argued that understanding oppression requires examining more than one's dispositions toward, treatment of, and knowledge about the Other. They assert that educators and students need to examine not only how some groups and identities are Othered in society, but also how some groups are privileged, as well as how this dual process is legitimized and maintained by social structures and competing ideologies. Schools, after all, are part of society, and understanding oppression in schools requires examining the relationship between schools and other social institutions and cultural ideas (Stambach, 1999). For example, understanding the marginalization of female students (and faculty) requires looking not only at sexist interactions and cultures, but also at employment structures and curricular ideologies that favor males (Luke & Gore, 1992). Similarly, understanding social and economic reproduction and oppression on the basis of class requires looking at structural factors—in particular, at the imperatives and contradictions of capitalism—to see how such things as the commodification of culture, the paradoxical nature of working-class resistance, and the technical control of teachers all contribute to the legitimization and maintenance of the existing socioeconomic order (Apple, 1995). Understanding the underachievement of Hmong American women in higher education requires looking not only at cultural differences, but also at "economic, racial, and other structural barriers to educational persistence and success" (S. J. Lee, 1997). Similarly, understanding the oppression of queer students requires moving beyond an emphasis on homophobia and individual fear, to consider heterosexism ("heteronormativity") and how the social demands of being "normal" are what help to produce queer-based oppression (Britzman, 1998a).

Researchers have also noted that schools do not stand outside of these structures and ideologies, innocent of the dynamics of oppression, but are institutions or "apparatuses" that transmit "ruling ideologies" (Althusser, 1971), maintain "hegemony" (Gramsci, 1971), and reproduce existing social order. Researchers have argued that schools and other social institutions serve two functions: they privilege certain groups and identities in society while marginalizing others, and they legitimize this social order by couching it in the language of "normalcy" and "common sense." Thus, the role of the school in working against oppression must involve not only a critique of structural and ideological forces, but also a movement against its own contributions to oppression.

Bringing About Change

Researchers applying the third approach to working against oppression advocate a *critique and transformation* of oppression. In particular, they suggest that we teach a critical awareness of oppressive structures and ideologies, and strategies to change them.

This process begins with more knowledge, and not knowledge about the Other, but knowledge about oppression. As Gloria Ladson-Billings (1995b) argues, students need to be able to "recognize, understand, and critique current social inequities" (p. 476). Developing this critical awareness requires learning that that which society defines as "normal" is a social and contested construct (Apple, 1995) that both regulates who we are supposed to be and denigrates whoever fails to conform to "proper" or "normal" roles (Greene, 1996). Simultaneously, developing this critical consciousness requires *un*learning or critiquing what was previously learned to be "normal" and normative (Britzman, 1998a), especially when what we previously learned helps to mask the privileging and Othering of different identities: examples include notions that being White makes a person "authentically American," or being heterosexual makes a person moral. In other words, teaching such critical thinking involves making visible the privilege of certain identities over others, and the process by which this privilege is masked. This process of learning about the dynamics of oppression also involves learning about oneself. Students can learn how their identities correspond to both the privileged and Othered identities about which they are learning, and they can learn how they often unknowingly can be complicit with and even contribute to these forms of oppression when they participate in commonsense practices that privilege certain identities. Developing this critical perspective can happen when teachers practice what Maher and Tetreault (1994) call a "pedagogy of positionality" that engages both students and teacher in recognizing and critiquing how we are positioned and how we position others in social structures.

But this approach does not stop there. As I argued above, "critical" education involves both the critique *and transformation* of structural oppression (Giroux & McLaren, 1989). Knowledge about oppression is but the first step of a larger process. Also necessary are thinking skills that students can use to formulate effective plans of action. Ellsworth (1992) describes the assumptions underlying critical pedagogy as "the teaching of analytic and critical skills for judging the truth and merit of propositions, and the interrogation and selective appropriation of potentially transformative moments in the dominant culture" (p. 96). When students have knowledge about oppression as well as critical thinking skills, they will be "empowered" to challenge oppression. As Paulo Freire (1995)—whose work on "liberatory education" has become the foundation of "critical pedagogy"—and feminist researchers influenced by him (hooks, 1994; Weiler, 1991) have argued, critical education or "consciousness raising" (what Freire calls *conscientização*) entails learning "to perceive social, political, and economic contradictions, *and to take action against the oppressive elements of reality*" (Freire, 1995, p. 17; my emphasis). Similarly, Maher and Tetreault (1994) have argued that "if the classroom setting can help students to understand the workings of positional dynamics in their lives, . . . then they can begin to challenge them and to create change" (p. 203). Critical education, in other words, teaches about oppression, but also teaches what it means to act against oppression and work toward change. In fact, teaching and learning about oppression take place only through social action; learning happens when acting in the world, and critical learning happens when acting critically in the world (Freire, 1995). This emphasis on both knowledge and action is characteristic not only of many critical and feminist pedagogies (such as those listed above), but also of queer (Malinowitz, 1995) and multicultural pedagogies (such as that suggested by McLaren, 1994, who advocates a "critical and resistance multiculturalism," and by Sleeter & Grant, 1987, who advocate a "social reconstructionist" multiculturalism).

Strengths and Weaknesses

The strength of this particular approach is that it calls on educators not only to teach about oppression but also to try to change society. It is important for students to develop the knowledge and thinking skills necessary to understand the processes of Othering and normalizing, as well as their own complicity in these processes. These understandings can lead not only to empathy for the Other, but also to the ability and the will to resist oppressive ideologies and change social structures.

There are, however, several difficulties with this approach. First, the notion that oppression is structural in nature implies that oppression has the same general effect on people. My critique does not deny that members of any particular group share common experiences with oppression, or that certain groups historically have been subject to the same general form of oppression. However, because all individuals have multiple identities, members of the same group will have different experiences with oppression. Structural explanations cannot account for this diversity and particularity. Experiences with oppression involve many contradictions (Apple, 1995). For example, in her research on nursery classrooms, Valerie Walkerdine (1990) has argued that females who at one moment were able to exert power over males, at another were rendered powerless by them, because in each situation a different discourse was being cited. In other words, in each situation, a different discourse or way of thinking was being implicitly referred to, called up, and worked within, and this "citation" of different discourses gave actions and words different meanings in the different contexts. So, in one context, several female students were able to control the toys and limit the activity of the boys while playing "house" by citing the discourse of domestic labor (woman as housekeeper). In another context, several male students engaged in a particularly sexist and demeaning conversation with the female teacher, and the teacher excused their behavior by citing the discourse of normal childhood sexuality (boys will be boys) even though the boys were citing the discourse of woman as sexual object (Middleton, 1997). Such fluidity of identity and power relations cannot be explained by patriarchal structures that position males over females (and teachers over students). A framework that allows for a more situated understanding of oppression is needed.

Second, the goals of consciousness-raising and empowerment assume that knowledge, understanding, and critique lead to personal action and social transformation. However, awareness does not necessarily lead to action and transformation. A student may learn all the knowledge and skills theoretically needed to engage in subversive political action, but may not choose to act any differently than before. Consider Deborah Britzman's (1998a) argument that all learning involves an unlearning. If the unlearning involved in learning the necessary knowledge and skills leads the student into a state of "crisis" or paralysis (such as feeling emotionally upset), the student will first need to work through the crisis before being able to act (Kumashiro, 1999a). I will explain the notion of crisis in more detail in the next section, but my point here is that rather than leading to a desire for change, crisis can sometimes lead to more entrenched resistance. In addition, as I argued earlier, teachers can never really know whether students learned what they were trying to teach, or how students will be moved by whatever they do learn. The goal that students will first learn and then act "critically" is difficult to achieve when there is much that the teacher cannot and does not know and control.

The recognition that they can neither know what students learn nor control how students act based on what they learn leads many teachers to feel paralyzed. After all, educators are often trained to delineate what we want students to understand, plan a lesson to get them there, and then assess whether they indeed came to this understanding. The recognition that teaching involves much that cannot be known or controlled may seem disconcerting, but according to Ellsworth (1997), it has significant promise for antioppressive education and for radically different models of what it means to teach. Rather than try to get students to think and act in a particular way, to repeat what is being taught or already known, Ellsworth urges educators to teach students always to reflect critically on what is being taught and learned, to think critically even about critical theories and critical pedagogies, and to go where not even critical educators could have predicted. Such an unpredictable and uncontrollable goal is not unlike what I described in the previous approach as a way to work against the essentialization that so frequently occurs when teaching and learning about the Other—both involve *looking beyond*. Critical pedagogy needs to move away from saying that students need *this* or *my* critical perspective since such an approach merely replaces one (socially hegemonic) framework for seeing the world with another (academically hegemonic) one. Rather than aim for *understanding* of some critical perspective, antioppressive pedagogy should aim for *effect* by having students engage with relevant aspects of critical theory and extend its terms of analysis to their own lives, but then critique it for what it overlooks or forecloses. As with any pedagogy, critical pedagogy can be understood as making some insights and changes possible and making others impossible.

One of the unspoken assumptions of critical pedagogy raises the third difficulty in this third approach to antioppressive education: its goal of consciousness-raising puts into play a modernist and rationalist approach to challenging oppression that is actually harmful to students who are traditionally marginalized in society. As Ellsworth (1992) argues, the "key assumptions, goals and pedagogical practices fundamental to the literature on critical pedagogy . . . are repressive myths that perpetuate relations of domination" (p. 91). In particular, the rationalist approach to consciousness-raising assumes that reason and reason alone is what leads to understanding. However, rational detachment is impossible: our identities, experiences, privileges, investments, and so forth always influence how we think and perceive, what we know and do not know. To accept the possibility of such detachment is really to perpetuate a mythical norm that assumes a White, heterosexual, male perspective. Those who are traditionally marginalized remain outsiders, called upon as "experts" to speak with their own voices and educate the norm, only to be deemed not rational because they speak from a visible (or nondominant) standpoint. Furthermore, the life experiences of traditionally marginalized students can bring a historical and personal connection to lessons on oppression that those who fit the mythical norm typically do not have. Personal experiences as people not privileged on the basis of, say, race can exceed the expectations of a pedagogy that relies on rationality and that represses other ways of knowing and relating. Such lessons serve to "Otherize" students who cannot be engaged by a pedagogy that presumes to address the mythical norm. What this means is that critical pedagogy is helpful for challenging oppression but itself needs to be treated critically.

Education that Changes Students and Society

What is Oppression?

In response to these limitations, some researchers have turned to poststructuralist theories of discourse to help formulate different conceptualizations of oppression (Britzman, Santiago-Valles, Jimenez-Muñoz, & Lamash, 1993; Butler, 1997; Davies, 1989; Kumashiro, 1999a, 1999b; McKay & Wong, 1996; Talburt, 2000). As I discussed in the previous section, Walkerdine's (1990) study on nursery classrooms suggests that oppression and harm are produced not merely by the actions and intentions of individuals or by the imperatives of social structures. Rather, oppression is produced by discourse, and in particular, is produced when certain discourses (especially ways of thinking that privilege certain identities and marginalize others) are cited over and over. Such citational processes serve to reproduce these hierarchies and their harmful effects in society.

To illustrate this notion of citation, we can look at the "model minority" stereotype of Asian American students, which says that they are all smart and hardworking "academic superstars" (S. J. Lee, 1996). As I have discussed above, researchers have explained the harmfulness of stereotypes as being a result of individual prejudice and discrimination (L. S. Miller, 1995) or of a White-dominated racial order that claims to be meritocratic and nonracist by pointing to the "success" of "model" minorities (Osajima, 1988). They have argued that the power of a stereotype to harm either exists inherently in the stereotype (so that an individual using a stereotype is like an individual wielding a weapon) or derives from social structures and ideologies (so that using a stereotype is like assisting in the maintenance of systemic racism). They have also argued that this stereotype has tangible consequences in that it may cause differential treatment of students by teachers and even psychological harm (Crystal, 1989; S. J. Lee, 1996;

Osajima, 1993). These theories imply that challenging oppression involves either prohibiting individual acts of oppression—from stereotypes to hate speech (Butler, 1997)—or dismantling structural forms of oppression (through critical pedagogy).

Poststructuralism offers a different view. As I have argued elsewhere (Kumashiro, 1999b), the reason that voicing a stereotype or assuming it to be true can cause harm is because every such use cites past oppressive uses of that stereotype, especially the history of how that stereotype has been used within a particular community of people (Butler, 1997). For example, if someone were to tell me that I should be a better student because I am an Asian American, it is possible for me to conclude that the speaker is making racist assumptions about me because I have heard other people talk about and generalize about Asian Americans in similar ways before. The speaker's words could have racist meaning to me because I am able to read them as constituting part of the history of how the model-minority stereotype has been and is being used in the mainstream United States. If I believed that the speaker was judging me based on this stereotype and I valued the speaker's judgment, the speaker's words could then produce in me feelings of failure or abnormality. And the effect of this stereotype could extend beyond emotions and self-identity if the stereotype were believed by people in affirmative-action offices and advisory commissions on race, which have often failed and continue to fail to address racial inequities experienced by Asian Americans. What is significant, here, is that in each of these situations, the discourse of model-minority Asian Americans keeps getting cited, keeps getting repeated, not only reinsisting that Asian Americans are "like this," but also reproducing the power to marginalize and harm Asian Americans.

Indeed, oppression itself can be seen as the repetition, throughout many levels of society, of harmful citational practices. In the above examples, the association between "Asianness" and "success" (i.e., the process in which Asianness cites successfulness) gets repeated over and over. In U.S. society, there are many other associations that characterize oppression: Whiteness and authenticity, femaleness and weakness, heterosexuality and normalcy, queer sexualities and sinfulness, limited English-language proficiency and lack of intelligence, to name just a few. What is harmful is when we have to live through the repetition of these histories, which we do constantly through interpersonal conversations and interactions; institutional, economic, and legal imperatives; and moral and religious doctrines.

Of course, the meaning and effects of stereotypes do change in different contexts and over time. This is perhaps most easily illustrated when examining the relationship between two different forms of oppression, and we can do that by turning to research on queer Asian American males. What is helpful in this discussion is another poststructural concept: *supplementation*, which means to cite, but also to add something new in the process (Crowley, 1989). Research on queer Asian American males reveals that the forms of oppression they experience in traditionally marginalized communities are both similar to and different from those in mainstream society (Kumashiro, 1999b). In Asian American communities, queer Asian American males often experience a form of heterosexism that cites the heterosexism in mainstream society. However, in addition to defining queer sexuality as abnormal and sinful, Asian America often assigns it a racial marker: heterosexuality is marked as an Asian virtue, queerness as a "white disease." In queer communities, queer Asian American males often experience a form of racism that cites the racism (i.e., "orientalism") of mainstream society that ascribes a deviant femininity to Asian American men. However, rather than define the feminized Asian American male as sexually undesirable, many queers consider him "exotic" and, thus, sexually hyperdesirable. The racialized heterosexism in Asian American communities and the queered racism in queer communities exemplify how oppression can acquire different meanings and effects in different contexts even while continuing to cite and repeat aspects of its own history.

The notions of citation and supplementation help us understand ways in which oppression is multiple, interconnected, and ever-changing. Not surprisingly, they also help us think differently about what it means to change oppression. As already noted, some researchers argue that people often associate certain identities with certain attributes because over time those associations have been repeated and thus naturalized. Therefore, in contrast to prohibiting harmful words and actions, or to developing a critical awareness of harmful structures and ideologies, they have argued that change requires becoming involved in altering the citational practices that constitute these associations (Butler, 1997; Kumashiro, 1999a; Talburt, 2000). They suggest that the prohibition and/or the critical awareness of the repetition of harmful associations/histories do not necessarily change them. What does is a particular kind of labor. When activists labor to supplement harmful associations they are participating in altering them and are constituting a reworked history. When enough members of a community participate in this kind of labor, the meanings and effects of different identities and identifications change. One example of this kind of change is the ongoing work among queers to disrupt the harmfulness of the term *queer*. Mainstream society often defines heterosexuality as "normal" while treating queer sexualities as illnesses, but more and more queers are working to supplement the term *queer* by continuing to cite its deviation from the norm while adding an insistence that normalcy itself is problematic, or at least, that not being heteronormal does not make queerness akin to a crime or an illness. More than merely psychological, this change has contributed to changes in how more and more legal entities, medical establishments, religious organizations, and academic institutions treat queers.

Bringing About Change

Thus far in this chapter, I have suggested ways in which poststructuralist concepts can help address some of the weaknesses of the first three approaches to antioppressive education. These concepts included ways in which identities are shifting, ways in which knowledge is partial, and ways in which oppression is citationally produced. As I have introduced such concepts, I have also drawn on closely related concepts from another theoretical framework—namely, psychoanalysis—to develop such notions as the space between teacher and learner, the connection between knowledge and ignorance, and the crisis involved in learning and unlearning. In what follows, I will expand on these concepts as I more fully develop this fourth approach to antioppressive education. Like other researchers (e.g., Britzman, 1998a, 1998b; Ellsworth, 1997; Felman, 1995; Luhmann, 1998; Pitt, 1998; Talburt, 2000) I draw on the combined body of research that I call recent feminist and queer readings of poststructuralism and psychoanalysis. These theories tend to be quite abstract, and therefore, I will discuss them as they apply to the "core" disciplines (social studies, English, mathematics, and science) of K–12 schools, focusing on three themes: a problem of resistance, a curriculum of partiality, and a pedagogy of crisis. I should note that I make substantial reference to my preceding discussion of the first three approaches as a way to show how poststructuralism and psychoanalysis take antioppressive educational theory in new directions. I should also note the reason that I devote substantial time to this fourth approach and to concrete classroom examples is because these theories will be central to my analyses in the following chapters.

A Problem of Resistance. Curriculums in the core disciplines often perpetuate oppressive knowledges. For example, when U.S. history curriculums focus on political leaders, military conflicts, and industrial inventors, they are including the voices, experiences, and perspectives of only some in society, especially those with racial, economic, and/or gender privilege. Left silenced or pushed to the margins are such topics as immigration, the gendered division of labor, and civil rights movements, all of which have the potential to reveal the roles that the Othered in society have played in U.S. history (Anyon, 1979; Asante, 1991; Lipkin, 1995; Minnich, 1990). Compounding matters is the recognition that the structure of history curriculums, not just their content, is problematic. More and more historians are arguing that signs that the author wrote the text and constructed a particular version of history belong in written accounts of history (Cronon, 1992). However, many history textbooks continue to silence the narrative or authorial voice (Paxton, 1999), implying that the account being told is objective and impartial (Richardson, 1997) and that "history" consists of facts, not readings or interpretations of events, despite that any telling of history involves selectively including and excluding materials (Paxton, 1999).

Similarly, many science classrooms purport to be teaching a "neutral" subject despite its oppressive history. For example, what many have come to call "real" science is only the science that originated in the Western (or White) world (Harding, 1994). Until fairly recently, only men were considered capable of thinking scientifically (Battersby, 1989). Depending on what it asks (or chooses not to ask), publicizes (or chooses not to publicize), and finds (or lacks the resources and authority to find), science can politically and materially benefit some populations more than others (Harding, 1994). This happened with the AIDS epidemic when the science community refused to devote significant time and resources until the "problem" changed from an African/Haitian/gay disease to a virus that could spread to mainstream America (Treichler, 1988). Science can normalize only certain ways of being, as when it talks about sex/gender in dichotomous terms, thus reinforcing the notion that there are only males and females and nothing else, despite that significant numbers of human beings and other living beings in the natural world are intersexed (Kessler, 1998; Letts, 1999). Even progressive educators help maintain the privileging of certain groups in society when they require that students think "scientifically," objectively, and rationally (Ellsworth, 1992).

Mathematics is no different. Historically, mathematics has served as a tool of colonialism and imperialism (Bishop, 1990), which should not be surprising given that mathematics has an underlying "logic of control": mathematizing and quantifying nature and time and space are ways for humans to control not only nature, but also society, since defining "reason" as, in part, the ability to think "mathematically" allows certain people (i.e., the "mathematical" ones) to extend their control over others (Fleener, 1999). Furthermore, mathematics often purports to be a transparent language—one free of the ambiguity of spoken language and that therefore gives unmediated access to the world—even though no language is transparent (Shulman, 1996). Not only is any language encoded with culturally specific and gendered meanings (Shulman, 1994), but so too do people understand and use the languages of mathematics differently depending on the cultural context or situation (Bishop, 1994; Powell & Frankenstein, 1997). Therefore, indirectly, teaching only certain forms or languages of mathematics is a way of teaching only certain cultural norms and values (Shulman, 1994) and only certain ways of making sense of the world (Macedo, 1991).

Perhaps most commonly critiqued for teaching partial materials are English classrooms that insist on teaching the "canon." Biases based on class, race, gender, sexuality, and other social markers often play out in the curriculum when the authors and characters of the literature being read consist primarily of middle-class or wealthy White, male, heterosexuals (Palumbo-Liu, 1995; Schmitz et al., 1995; Sumara, 1993). By learning about only certain groups and perspectives in society, students are not learning about alternative perspectives and the contributions, experiences, and identities of those Othered, and by not learning such knowledge, students are not troubling the (mis)knowledge they already have.

In response, many educators have called for diversity and an inclusive, multicultural curriculum as a way to learn about the Other, and to affirm differences. (Educators have also called for critical awareness of these problems within the disciplines, and I will discuss this later in the chapter.) Unfortunately, educators often stop after "adding on" differences as if adding, say, *women* here and *Jews* there solves the problem. As I discussed earlier in this chapter, there are a number of problems with adding differences to the curriculum, not the least of which is the recognition that the very act of naming and including difference could operate in contradictory ways. What does it mean to add Latinos/as, queers, or the working poor? In fact, what does it mean to "be" any of the things being added? Who counts as the "different"?

By adding, say, Black Americans, do we expect their voices to "speak" to racial differences (hooks, 1994)? If so, are we adding only those people whose difference is specifically and only their race (and not also, say, their gender, sexuality, or disability) and, in the process, ignoring what it means for Black American women or Black American queers or disabled Black Americans also to be Black (but to be Black in perhaps a different way)? Does Blackness, in other words, take on normative (or, regulatory) qualities within the inclusive curriculum just as it has within Black liberation movements (Cohen, 1996)? Activists at the intersections of oppressions have long argued that, ironically, identity-based activist movements function just as mainstream society does in excluding its own margins (Powell, 1999), such as feminist movements and women who are of color (McKay, 1993), antiracist movements and people of color who are queer (Conerly, 1996), or queer rights movements and queers who are female (Blackwood & Wieringa, 1999). Adding difference is problematic when the difference is itself normative.

Yet, *difference* always exceeds singular categories since identities are already multiple and intersected. For example, what it means to be a woman is already racially normative (Higginbotham, 1992), just as what it means to be masculine is already heterosexually normative (Kimmel, 1994). Similarly, racial identities such as those of Asian Americans are already gendered, as with orientalist stereotypes of Asian Americans in the mainstream U.S. imagination (Okihiro, 1994), and are already heterosexualized, as when Asian American communities reify "traditional Asian values" that are centered on heterosexist familial roles (Kumashiro, 1999b). It is a problem, then, to speak of identities always and only in their separate(d) incarnations, which not only denies ways in which identities are already intersected, but more importantly, masks ways in which certain identities are already privileged. Treating identity as singular allows only certain identities to count as authentic or to matter when learning about what it means to be of that group. This should not be surprising given that identities have meaning only because they are defined in opposition to an Other (Butler,

1993). Authenticity requires the existence of the nonauthentic: to say *who we are* and *what we are focusing on* is simultaneously to say *who we are not* and *what we are not focusing on*. The naming of difference, then, whether in activist communities or inclusive curricula, can serve less to describe who a group is, and more to prescribe who a group ought to be.

Furthermore, the focus on difference fails to change that which is not different—namely, the norm. As argued earlier, although a curriculum that aims for inclusion may succeed in teaching that the Other is as normal or important as the norm, it does not necessarily change the very definition of "normal" and ways in which we traditionally see ourselves as such. In other words, adding difference does not really change teaching and learning practices that affirm our sense of normalcy. And perhaps this is exactly why schools continue to teach in oppressive ways; perhaps we desire teaching and learning through normalized lenses (Doll, 1998; Morris, 1998). Perhaps we desire teaching and learning in ways that affirm and confirm our sense that *what we have come to believe is normal or commonsensical in society* is really the way things are and are supposed to be. After all, imagine the alternative: imagine constantly learning that "what is normal" and "who we are" are really social constructs maintained only through the Othering, marginalization, or silencing of other possible worlds and selves. Imagine constantly learning, in other words, of our own complicity with oppression.

My point here is that perhaps we resist antioppressive practices because they trouble how we think and feel about not only the Other but also ourselves. A good example is the refusal of many academics to engage with queer theory. As Diana Fuss (1991) tells us, since the definition of *straight* requires the existence of *queer*, and since the privileging of heterosexuality requires the Othering of other sexualities, any effort to change what it means to be queer requires simultaneously changing the meanings and values we place on being straight. So, too, with all other binaried identities. Our desire to teach and learn about the Other in traditional ways is a desire to maintain some sense of identity and normalcy, and to affirm the belief that we are not contributing to oppression. Therefore, difference is not merely something we have yet to learn, but something that we desire not to learn, something we at least subconsciously resist (Britzman, 1998a; Luhmann, 1998). We resist learning what will disrupt the frameworks we traditionally use to make sense of the world and ourselves.

The problem with schools, then, is not merely that only certain voices are included. Since we can never hear all voices, such a view of the "problem" of curriculum leads either to a false sense of hope that the inclusion of a representative selection of voices will solve it, or to a sense of despair of ever rectifying it. We need to acknowledge that there is a reason certain voices are silenced in the first place (Scott, 1993). We need to acknowledge that the desire to continue teaching the disciplines as they have traditionally been taught is a desire to maintain the privilege of certain identities, worldviews, and social relations. And we need to acknowledge that trying to "solve" the problem by adding differences can comply with oppression if we define differences in problematic ways and then add them to a framework where the same identities remain privileged.

A Curriculum of Partiality. Given the problems with traditional practices of inclusion, and given the impossibility of fully including all differences and voices, some researchers have suggested a different way to think about inclusion and curricular change. The emphasis, here, is less on what each voice teaches directly, and more on what the collection of voices teaches indirectly.

Any assembly of voices indirectly tells an underlying story, one that will always exceed what the individual voices say explicitly. And the story then frames how we make sense of what it is we are learning, and of how it is our learnings relate to what we already know and to who we think we are. Some stories reinforce dominant frameworks for thinking about and acting in the world, others challenge them, and still others do both. Thus, stories always have political effects (Richardson, 1997). The inclusion of more and different voices will tell not a "truer" story, but a different one, one with different political implications (Scott, 1993). When we desire to include the same voices, or to include different voices in ways that differences have traditionally been added on, we are desiring (subconsciously or not) to continue using the same stories to make sense of the world. Ironically, because these stories are the ones that define normalcy, we often desire exactly what is harmful to ourselves.

It is easy to add difference to the curriculum in a way that complies with oppression. For example, in English classrooms, Gayatri Spivak (1990) tells us that the inclusion of "ethnic literature" into the curricula can reflect an objectification of difference, where writers and literary critics of color, by making people of color into objects of (new) investigations, ironically contribute to a "new orientalism" or new form of colonialism. In fact, historically, the formation of "ethnic canons" arguably reflects a commodification of difference, a creation of a type of currency in political correctness, since calls for inclusion grew as much out of the desire for change as the desire to appease the discontented (Palumbo-Liu, 1995). Capitalist structures and colonialist ideologies do permeate English curricula and can constitute its underlying "story."

Similarly, oppressive stories often permeate social studies curriculums. For example, often absent from lessons on what many call the Second World War are any discussion of the role women played in transforming the workforce in the United States; of the persecution of queers in Nazi Germany alongside Jews and other targeted groups; and of the forced relocation of Japanese Americans, many of them U.S. citizens, to internment camps primarily in the western United States. Such a unit indirectly tells a certain story about the war: The Nazis were evil for persecuting the innocent Jews, the United States was the force of good in the face of this evil, the men in the United States helped save the world, and women/queers/Japanese Americans were not heroes, victims, or otherwise part of this event. Were a teacher to try to cover more perspectives, the unit could expand to include women's, queers', and Japanese Americans' voices. But if the expansion rests at saying "these other groups were also there, and now we have the full story," such a move does not really change "the story"—at least not the story of the United States.

However, it is possible to include differences in ways that change the underlying story and the implications of the story for thinking, identifying, and acting in oppressive and/or anti-oppressive ways. Rather than perpetuate a story of the United States as a force of good (along with the implication that the nation is a big brother to the world, a place of freedom and righteousness, a meritocracy), the unit can include voices in ways that teach about the U.S. perpetuation of racism and homophobia (as when the nation freed Jews, but put queers right back into prisons), and perhaps tell a story of how the United States acted in contradictory ways. Rather than a story that privileges men, the unit can include voices in ways that tell a story of how patriarchal divisions of labor both influenced and were influenced by the war. The inclusive curriculum, in other words, can not only tell more about women, queers, and Japanese Americans; it can also change narratives of the United States' role in simultaneously challenging and contributing to various oppressions. Were the curriculum also to include the contradictory voices within these different groups, the underlying stories could change in yet other ways. Such an insight can lead students to ask such questions as, What story about the United States does the presence of these voices and the absence of others tell us? When we add different voices, how does the story change? What knowledges and identities and practices do different configurations of voices make possible? Which stories justify the status quo? Which stories challenge the marginalization of certain groups and identities in society? As students learn about differences, they can also constantly reflect on ways in which *what they learn* makes different knowledges, identities, and practices possible.

The same applies to math and science curriculums. Just as there are social and political reasons why history consists of only what we have come to call history, so too is there a reason why mathematics and science consist of only what we have come to call mathematics and science (Harding, 1994). This is not to say that what we now know in mathematics and science has not been immensely helpful in improving our lives, but just as there is much more to learn within what we call (Western) mathematics and science, so too are there alternative ways to know and act in the world through other mathematics and sciences. If science and mathematics classrooms have traditionally taught in only certain contexts and attempted to answer only certain questions, then students can be invited to learn sciences and maths in different contexts (Frankenstein & Powell, 1994), and use sciences and maths to answer different kinds of questions and solve different kinds of problems, especially problems relevant to their own lives and communities (Ladson-Billings, 1995a). They can even use sciences and maths to (con)test prior scientific/mathematical findings that have been used to privilege and marginalize different groups, such as findings that perpetuate stereotypes. Also, if science and mathematics classrooms are centered on approaches that claim universality despite their necessary partiality, then students might critically respond by exploring alternative approaches, such as approaches that explore chaos and contradiction and the impossibility of totality (Fleener, 1999). Students can seek not an understanding of *what science and math are*, but an exploration of *what different approaches to math and science make possible and impossible in terms of understanding the world and addressing different problems.*

To put it another way, mathematics and sciences can be taught in ways that constantly look beyond what is being learned and already known. As with teaching social studies, educators can approach the teaching of math and science in paradoxical ways: simultaneously learning and using knowledge to complicate current worldviews, identities, and practices while critiquing and troubling that knowledge by questioning the ways we teach and learn it, the perspectives and practices made possible and impossible, and the ways it contributes to or challenges oppression. Educators can teach students to be not only mathematicians and scientists, but also math critics and science critics (Harding, 1994), just as we teach students to be social critics (not only sociologists and historians) and literary critics (not only readers and writers).

In English classrooms, since curriculums often face problems with the politics of representation (and the difficulties of inclusion), students can learn to read texts in critical ways. As I discussed earlier in the chapter, including different literatures can be problematic if students read texts as merely a means of getting to know differences. Any given text will reflect the realities of some people but miss those of others; will represent the voices of some groups but silence those of others; and as a result will challenge some stereotypes while reinforcing others. Even texts used to tell "representative" stories are problematic when we expect that they actually "tell" us about difference. As I argued in chapter 1, texts are never transparent media that give us access or entry to a different reality, and are only partial representations of what it is they tell us about. There is always a difference between the text or telling and the object of the telling. In fact, using texts as ways to know difference is problematic when we acknowledge not merely that texts have silences, but that they have *necessary* silences. Just as I earlier argued that identities have meaning because of what they are *not* (i.e., whom they exclude), so too do texts have meaning because of what they leave unsaid (Marshall, 1992). The unsaid is what gives the said its meaning. U.S. literature, for example, never has to explicitly privilege Whiteness since what is unspoken (though still present), namely, the "Black shadow," does much to accomplish this task (Morrison, 1992). Yet, conventional readings of texts, such as readings that look at universal meanings (such as their themes, the intentions of the writer, and the development of the characters) or that look at personal connections to the texts (such as similarities between the reader and the character, and the reader's opinions about how the story could have ended differently) treat what is said in the text as its reality, as the embedded "meaning" of the text (O'Neill, 1993). Such readings fail to treat as central to their analysis what is unsaid (as well as what we *do not want* to have said), how both the said and the unsaid constitute the underlying story, and how the effects of that story are often hegemonic.

Just as social studies, science, and mathematics curricula need to look beyond what is being represented, so too do English curricula. In particular, since different ways of reading texts have different effects, students can learn to read texts in multiple and antioppressive ways. This can be done on two levels. First, students can learn to read for silences and the effects of those silences on the "meaning" of a text (Ellsworth, 1997). For example, they can ask, "what is not said in this novel about, say, queer youth, and how do those silences make possible and impossible different ways of thinking about queer youth, about homophobia, about the reader's own sexual identities, and about change?" Educators can teach that the partiality of texts is exactly what makes texts useful for antioppressive education. Second, students can learn to examine their desire to read in particular ways and their resistance to reading in other ways, and can do so with the understanding that some reading practices are desired because they are more comforting (though more oppressive) than others (Morris, 1998). For example, they can ask, What are different ways to read this text, what different knowledges about the Other does each reading give, and—perhaps most importantly— why do we traditionally learn to read about the Other in only certain ways?

Antioppressive education is not something that happens when the curriculum is no longer partial. Rather, it happens when critical questions, such as those described above, are being asked about the partial curriculum. It is not a curriculum that is fully inclusive or that centers on critical texts. Rather, it is a process of looking beyond the curriculum. It is a process of troubling the official knowledge in the disciplines (Apple, 1993). It is a process of explicitly trying to read against common sense. And perhaps that is why this process is so difficult. Official or commonsense ways of thinking about the disciplines and the world have traditionally influenced our identities and life experiences (Sumara & Davis, 1998), and we are often invested in maintaining these practices. We often resist antioppressive change.

A Pedagogy of Crisis. Antioppressive education that aims to change students and society cannot do so without addressing the ways students and society resist change. As I discussed in the previous section, we do not often desire learning about our own complicity with oppression, and when we do learn such things, the process is rarely easy and cannot always be done rationally (Ellsworth, 1997; Felman, 1995; Luhmann, 1998; Pitt, 1998). Learning that *the very ways in which we think and do things is not only partial but oppressive* involves troubling or "unlearning" (Britzman, 1998a) what we have already learned, and this can be quite an emotionally discomforting process, a form of "crisis" (Felman, 1995). In particular, it can lead students into what I call a *paradoxical condition of learning and unlearning* (Kumashiro, 1999a) in which students are both unstuck (i.e., distanced from the ways they have always thought, no longer so complicit with oppression) and stuck (i.e., intellectually paralyzed and needing to work through their emotions and thoughts before moving on with the more academic part of the lesson). Such a paradoxical, discomforting condition can lead students to resist further learning and unlearning and therefore may be seen by educators as something to avoid. Yet education is not something that involves comfortably repeating what we already learned or affirming what we already know. Rather, education involves learning something that disrupts our commonsense view of the world. The crisis that results from unlearning, then, is a necessary and desirable part of antioppressive education. Desiring to learn involves desiring difference and overcoming our resistance to discomfort.

Consequently, educators need to create a space in their curriculums in which students can work through crisis. Shoshana Felman (1995) discusses how her students worked through a crisis they experienced by giving testimonies (self-reflections and analyses) of their experiences of the crisis. She argues that teaching and learning really take place only through entering and working through crisis, since it is this process that moves a student from being stuck and into a different intellectual, emotional, and political space. In noting that both teaching and psychoanalysis involve "liv[ing] through a crisis," Felman explains that both "are called upon to be *performative*, and not just *cognitive*, insofar as they both strive to produce and to enable, *change*. Both . . . are interested not merely in new information, but, primarily, in the capacity of their recipients to *transform themselves* in function of the newness of that information" (p. 56; emphasis in the original). How so? In revisiting the crisis through testimony, students are not merely repeating the crisis but are supplementing it, giving it new readings, new meanings, and associations with different emotions. They are, in the words of the poststructuralist concepts I described earlier, *laboring to alter citational histories* as a way to work through crisis and bring about change.

Ideally, what results from working through crisis is a change in the relationship students see between themselves and the binary of normalcy/Otherness. As Britzman (1998a) argues, efforts to challenge oppression need to involve changing ourselves, rethinking who we are by seeing the Other as an "equal" but on different terms. It should not be the case that "one looks for one's own image in the other, and hence invests in knowledge as self-reflection and affirmation" but that "in the process of coming to know, one invests in the rethinking of the self as an effect of, and condition for, encountering the other as an equal" (p. 81). Thus, in addition to self-reflection (in which they ask how they are implicated in the dynamics of oppression), students can engage in self-reflexivity (in which they bring this knowledge to bear on their own senses of self). To put it another way, schools can encourage students to "queer" their understandings of themselves. By this, I do not mean that we should define everyone as the Other, or think that the norm is no different than the Other, but deconstruct the norm/Other binary. We might look, for example, at how our sense of normalcy needs, even as it negates, the Other, as heterosexuality does the homosexual Other (Fuss, 1991) or literary Whiteness, the Black shadow (Morrison, 1992). Or, we might look at how the normal is dangerously close to the perverse, as homosociality (same-gender socializing) is to homosexuality, a closeness that causes "homosexual panic" (Sedgwick, 1991). And then we might ask, How does this knowledge come to bear on my sense of self? By changing how we read normalcy and Otherness, we can change how we read Others and ourselves.

Examples of learning through crisis are perhaps most easily foreseeable in social studies classrooms that focus specifically on issues of social difference and oppression. Lessons that critique, for example, the harmfulness of stereotypes and the invisible histories of institutionalized oppression can involve revealing our own privileges, confronting our own prejudices, and acknowledging the harmfulness of practices that unintentionally perpetuate stereotypes or are complicit with institutionalized oppression. Unfortunately, what happens in classrooms often is not crisis and change, but rather repetition and comfort for both student and teacher, as when students understand difference in commonsense ways or when teachers strive to develop in students knowledges and practices that mirror their own.

This is the case not only in social studies classrooms. In English class-rooms, for instance, essays are often assigned to allow students to show who they are or what they know. The problem is that, as with research and liter-ary texts, the writings of students are never transparent re-presentations of, in this case, their minds and souls. All texts, and words themselves, are par-tial. And even if they are not partial, the use of writings as demonstrative or representative of who the students are or what they know limits the poten-tial of the writing process to bring about antioppressive change in the writer (and, arguably, in the reader as well). As Laurel Richardson (1997) suggests, writing can be not only representative, but also performative, whereby the process of writing brings about difference in the writer. In many English classes, instructors assign essays in which students are to explain the theo-ries covered in class, synthesize the readings, critique the readings, or con-nect the readings to the students' lives or observations. For such assignments, the standards for evaluation are often signs of repetition: stu-dents are expected to repeat the main points of the readings, critique them with support from other writings, or make connections to their personal lives that draw on frameworks they have earlier used to make sense of their lives or observations. In addition to the *content* of the essay, repetition is often required in the *structure* of the essay: essays are considered "aca-demic" when they reference other writings and invoke the authority of someone who spoke earlier (Zenger, 1999), and are considered "well writ-ten" when they adhere to already existing models of what is "good academic writing." By learning to be "good writers," students are necessarily being constructed into subjects that were predetermined by "standards" in acade-mia. In saying this, I do not advocate abandoning all academic essay writing, since different types of writing assignments accomplish different things. However, I do suggest interrupting the privilege of certain ways of writing by troubling what we say it means to write well. Writing will not be antioppres-sive if it is always forced to repeat and adhere to partial stories or frame-works of what it means to learn or to write well.

This applies even to assignments that ask students to reflect solely on their own lives. Janet Miller (1998) critiques the ways many educators assign autobiographies in their classrooms, noting that "telling one's story" not only presumes a rational development of a singular subject from igno-rance to enlightenment, but also privileges the developmental model as *the* story, making other stories unthinkable and untellable. Such a modernist use of autobiography merely repeats stories already told, "reinscribes already normalized identity categories," and forecloses the possibility of seeing oneself in ways neither the student nor the teacher could have predicted. Miller argues that autobiography should engage not in repetition, but in resignification and making one's story unfamiliar and unnatural to both the student and the teacher. Can we imagine an assignment in which teachers ask students to write in ways that trouble familiar stories? Can we imagine an assignment in which the product is less important than the process? Can we imagine an assignment in which students are helped to resist repeating their own as well as their teachers' knowledges, identities, and practices, and to engage in the discomforting process of resignifying knowledges, identities, and practices (which might be possible when rereading one's life through different "lenses")? Writing, like reading, can be about changing "who we are" and "how things are" but such a move cannot come about if we insist on repeating the same stories of what it means to *do* a writing assignment or to *be* an English student.

So, too, with mathematics and sciences. One commonsense view of when a student has "learned" math and science is when "the foundations have become 'obvious' and disappeared from view; one is able to take the basic axioms for granted and use them correctly and unselfconsciously" (Shulman, 1996, p. 449). In other words, students have learned math and science when they have begun to think in ways consistent with the tradition of mathematics and science. Not surprisingly, given the colonialist, patriarchal, Eurocentric, and heterosexist nature of (Western) mathematics and science, commonsense definitions of good teaching and effective math and science education that center on such views of learning math and science actually hinder efforts toward equity in education (Secada, 1995). Teaching in commonsense ways cannot help but maintain social inequities. This is not to say that we should abandon all instruction in how we currently "do" math and science, but I do suggest interrupting the privilege of current ways of doing. At the very least, educators can recognize that different communities and cultural groups develop different practices for working with numbers and thinking numerically—not only cultural groups around the world, but also within the United States, including ethnic communities, children in different age groups, and professional groups (D'Ambrosio, 1985; Nelson-Barber & Estrin, 1995). The "numeracy" (Street, 2000) being taught in mathematics and science classrooms, then, is only one of many approaches to calculating, solving, predicting, modeling, and so forth. Antioppressive mathematics and science classrooms can teach in ways that draw on Lisa Delpit's (1986, 1988) theory of the culture of power: teachers need to learn about and build from their students' own cultural proficiencies in order to make connections between ways the students are already numerate and ways they need to be numerate to succeed in mainstream schools and society.

If educators are to contest the proper domains of math and science and to critique the ways their classrooms are already complicit with oppression, then it seems contradictory to require that all students acquire certain standards of knowledge about and skills within these fields, especially given that our knowledge is always partial. Meeting standards is, like some forms of essay writing, a practice of repetition, one that closes off the possibilities of learning what has yet to be known by both student and teacher. Furthermore, the use of standards assumes that teachers can know and control the processes of teaching and learning. Yet, as Ellsworth (1997) tells us, teaching involves a great deal of unknowability. We cannot fully know who our students are, we cannot control what they learn, we cannot know with certainty what it is they actually learn, and we cannot even be certain that what we want them to learn is what is in their best interest to learn. To acknowledge the unknowability of teaching is to acknowledge that teachers cannot say ahead of time what we want students to learn, what we will do to get them there, and how we will then determine if they got there—which is a popular format for lesson planning. Education cannot only be about requiring that students learn what we traditionally or currently consider to be the important knowledges and skills in the disciplines.

In fact, not even antioppressive approaches to education should predetermine what students need to know or be able to do, since theories and practices of antioppressive education are as partial and uncontrollable as any other theory and practice. Ellsworth (1997) has argued that teachers addressing their students are not unlike a film addressing its audience, for

> no matter how much the film's mode of address tries to construct a fixed
> and coherent position within knowledge, gender, race, sexuality, from
> which the film "should" be read; actual viewers have always read films
> against their modes of address, and "answered" films from places different from the ones that the films speaks to. (p. 31)

Working against oppression, therefore, cannot be about advocating strategies that are always supposed to bring about the desired effect. Consider, for example, Didi Khayatt's (1997) discussion of the role queer teachers play in challenging heterosexism and homophobia. Critiquing the notion that queer teachers "should" come out, she points to the different, contradictory ways that students—queer and straight—can read that supposedly empowering act. She does not tell educators *not* to come out, but argues against making the common assumption that that act has the same meaning to all students. Strategies to bring about change must be situated, and must recognize that teaching involves unknowability and that learning involves multiple ways of reading.

This does not mean that educators are powerless to name goals or to engage in practices that work toward those goals. I am committed to challenging oppression in schools, and am focusing this entire book on exploring different approaches to doing so. However, I do believe that we need to resist believing that we know what it means to do antioppressive education effectively or unproblematically. The unknowability involved in teaching requires that even antioppressive educators must constantly trouble our own practices and look beyond what we already know.

Strengths and Weaknesses

I have argued throughout this chapter that the context-specific and complex natures of oppression make problematic any attempt to articulate a single strategy that works for all teachers, with all students, in all situations. Although poststructuralism does not offer *the* one answer, it is helpful in complicating the first three approaches to antioppressive education and in developing a complementary fourth approach. In particular, poststructuralism suggests curricular and pedagogical reforms that help to address the complexities of antioppressive education by developing such notions as partiality, resistance, crisis, and unknowability as they apply to teaching and learning. Perhaps the most significant contribution poststructuralism makes is its insistence that the very ways in which we think are framed not only by what is said, but also by what is not said (Marshall, 1992). Critical theorists made this explicit in their analysis of school curriculum and the "hidden" curriculum. But the same applies to the field of educational theory itself, raising the question, Are notions of "oppression," "education," "teaching," and "learning" framed by theories, disciplines, and perspectives that make only certain ways of thinking possible, only certain kinds of questions askable? Ellsworth (1997) argues that the field of educational research has tried to address oppression by conducting research primarily within the social science disciplines and by theorizing primarily within "critical" frameworks. Drawing on the humanities (film studies, in particular), she argues for radically different ways of thinking about antioppressive education.

Ironically, this insight from poststructuralism reveals a limitation of this fourth approach to antioppressive education, namely, that many more perspectives remain underexplored and that this fourth approach alone is not enough. Poststructuralism and psychoanalysis themselves grew out of the histories of thought in Western Europe that continue to dominate educational theorizing in the United States. Very little research and theorizing has drawn on the histories of thought in, say, Asia, Africa, or the indigenous Americas, and future research needs to examine the different insights and possibilities for antioppressive education that they make possible.

The conceptualization of antioppressive education embodied by this fourth approach also raises at least four ethical questions that warrant more discussion among educators committed to social justice. First, is it ethical to intentionally and constantly lead a student into crisis? The fourth approach suggests that allowing students to continue living through the repetition of comforting norms, identities, knowledges, and practices is tantamount to perpetuating the oppressive status quo, which means that *not* teaching and learning through crisis is what is unethical. However, what results is a vision of social justice premised on constantly working through crisis. Could such a situation lead to a life with little feelings of hope or even peacefulness?

Second, are all experiences with crisis antioppressive? While asserting that learning takes place "only through crisis," the fourth approach also suggests that the form, context, and degree of crisis, along with how students work through it, can all determine whether or not a particular experience actually brings about antioppressive change. Students are all in different places, living through different forms of repetition, and open to different kinds of change. What will disrupt repetition with one student may not work with another, and what may invite one student to explore alternative ways of identifying, thinking, and acting may incite another to express greater resistance. Not even the notion of learning through crisis, then, can be standardized and applied to all students without itself becoming an

approach to teaching that presumes to know more than it knows and pre-
scribes what it can never prescribe. Students learn through crisis differently, and benefit from different experiences with crisis. More research on
different types of experiences with crisis is needed.

Third, does working through crisis involve invading a student's privacy? It is certainly possible for teachers to ask students to critically reflect
on their own lives, explore alternative ways to think about and act in the
world, and work through "stuck" places in ways that do not require public
disclosure and/or exhibition. And perhaps teachers need to do so, since
requiring that students bear all presumes that any disclosure or exhibition
can actually re-present the students' thoughts, feelings, complicities, histories, and movements in ways that unproblematically communicate them
to an audience, which, as I argued in chapter 1, is impossible. However, not
much has been written about how to have students work through crisis without forcing them to disclose and perform themselves in ways that invade
privacy and belie the partiality of any representation of that process.

Fourth, do all forms of repetition constitute oppression, and do all
resignifications constitute antioppressive change? The notion that oppression consists (at least in part) of repetition does not mean that all repetition
is harmful. Repetition can lead to feelings of comfort and security, an affirmation of identity and knowledge, and a stabilization of traditions, meanings, and institutional practices; while such processes can help to
perpetuate an oppressive status quo, they can also create viable alternatives
to the norm. What is harmful, then, is not repetition per se; what is harmful
is when repetition contributes to the production and reproduction of
oppressive dynamics in schools and society. Similarly, not all changes are
antioppressive. Disrupting repetition can lead to other forms of oppression. Further research is needed to clarify these distinctions as they pertain
to classroom experiences.

Looking to Activism

As I call on educators to make use of an amalgam of the four approaches
outlined in this chapter, and as I call on researchers to explore more implications of traditionally marginalized or yet-unexplored perspectives on
antioppressive education, I acknowledge that engaging in such efforts pre-

supposes a commitment on the part of educators and researchers to subversive views of the purposes of education, of the roles and responsibilities of teachers, and of how we want students and society to change. I also acknowledge that, even with this commitment, the difficulties in implementing changes in our present educational system and in today's political climate are substantial. Yet, I believe this chapter shows that more and more educators are educating themselves of the dire need to engage in antioppressive education, and that more and more educators are making a positive difference in the lives of their students. I expect this trend to continue, and hope that this chapter helps in this effort.

In the remaining chapters, I aim to bring into the field of antioppressive educational research another body of underexplored perspectives—namely, those of queer activists working against multiple forms of oppression. I am interested in seeing how their stories and insights come to bear on these four approaches to antioppressive education. Do they complicate these approaches? Do they suggest different ways to conceptualize and work against oppression? Do they trouble the very meaning of antioppressive education that I have thus far developed?

SAM: We don't teach our students to think. Our public schools don't do that. We don't give our students a chance to problem-solve and think for themselves.

KEVIN: What do you think we're doing in public schools instead?

SAM: We're asking everybody to color within the lines. We want them to reach standards. That's the whole thing right now is, "How can we get everyone up to a certain standard?" Well, the only way to do that is to have everything extremely curriculum based, where it's exposure-memorization-recall type of model. And then only the very high functioning will be allowed to go on and problem solve. Because if you look at our AP classes in high school, actually some of them are not as hard as your regular classes because the student is allowed to do more independent thinking instead of, "you must learn exactly what I'm teaching you, and give it back to me."

KEVIN: Can you talk more about how learning involves crisis and emotion, based on your experiences?

SAM: [pause] I think that—boy—a lot of things. When you suddenly opened up this whole new way of thinking to a student, they don't have any place to go with it.

KEVIN: What do you mean by that?

SAM: Well, if you brought up a lot of emotional feelings by talking about stereotypes and some of the things we were talking about—mistreatment—how would that student in the grade school, secondary type of school—how would they deal with that? We divide school up into these fifty-minute slots, each one is for a different subject, and you're faced with twenty-some students, and who do they continue that crying or confusion with? When can they connect? I mean it goes back to connecting with somebody. Because how would you then come back? You know, it takes a while. This stuff has to sink in. When we present workshops, the participants usually leave kind of like this [Sam's face expresses a sense of being overwhelmed]. And they need to go home and think and be able to reconnect. You know, we often say we have to do some kind of follow-up because otherwise people will just be blown away, and we have to bring them back, and let them go through it. So I'm thinking that that's something that's definitely lacking in education. It's like we don't have time for the process, the natural process to occur. And the questioning. We also don't—I'm probably going off in the wrong way—but I'm thinking we don't allow students to question, to ask questions. We don't even teach students how to ask questions, or to question. Because that's not part of our public schools, it's not what we've done. So when you do this, they can't have time to question. And that's also coming back to, "Am I free to ask this, teaching some of these deeper questions, to understand?" And I think that can become a crisis. And I think sometimes, you know, just from talking to other teachers who bring up really different—quote—"subjects"? I often hear that kids just shut down, they would not discuss this. And that was it. They would then avoid that teacher. Other students would be, you know, miraculously changed and want more. And be really probing. I mean how many students can go home and talk to their families about it? I mean that's a whole other thing that we're not talking about. And I think that's really missing.

KEVIN: What do you think the solution could be?

SAM: Well, a lot of schools are talking about the block system, which would allow more time for discourse. Because it would be fewer classes and longer times to be together. And I think teachers are like, "Oh my God, what would I think of to do all that time?" But maybe there would be more discussion. I mean we still use the lecture format in schools. And, I think also having a chance to share with your peers, you know, more small group opportunities, or to do projects together. I was just thinking of this thing that just happened. There's a student in my school who's your typical upper-middle-class, flawless young woman, you know, just pretty and sweet and popular and big house and the perfect family type of thing. And she came to me because another teacher said, "Go to [Sam]," because she needed her community service project and I can usually think of stuff for kids, even though I don't know the kids. So I got her involved in this, I had been wanting to do this project, maybe I told you about it, for the Jamaican school that I had visited in Spring Break, I went to a school.

KEVIN: Oh, right.

SAM: And I decided that, since they have absolutely nothing, that would be a project that I could do with my friends, and just collect school supplies and books and help them start a school library. So I was like, okay, I'll just throw this out to this, you know—[*makes a high-pitched squeal*]—type of kid. And, she really took to it. And I think part of it, now that I'm seeing the whole picture, because I met her mom and I've talked to her dad and I've gone to her house, I realized that Mom kind of jumped on to the bandwagon and channeled her and got ideas about how to make this project really big. Dad got involved, he's an exec at [a clothing company], he asked [the company] to pay for all the shipping for all the stuff and they said yes. Dad's been pulled in. Mom turns out to be a freelance journalist. She wants to do a story about it. She's encouraging her daughter, you know, "This is an opportunity." The daughter, when we were together, sorting through stuff, I showed her all the pictures of the kids and you know, it started. "Oh my God! Jamaica's more than these all-inclusive resorts! These are kids." She'd ask me these questions, she'd pick up something that we'd collected, "Do you think that they could use this? Would they be interested in this?" And she was starting to move to a poor, you know, very poor, poor community. The kids have nothing, it's so far removed from her life. How would she ever have a chance to know what that was like? But she was starting to figure it out. And it's really helped me make a connection because I have a tendency, as you noted in there before that, okay, the White kids, the middle-class kids, you know, you kind of do them a disservice by using them as like, "Well, I don't have to reach out to them, they got it." Which is so wrong.

KEVIN: Before, you said some students resist learning about these kinds of things. How do you think we can overcome that? What has been helpful for you?

SAM: I think it's trust. I think it's trusting that teacher. Students get angry when you tell them something about their culture, about their family, or about how people relate to others. It's so threatening if you point out that that's very racist or that's hurtful. And then they're just like, Oh my God, that's so scary, you know, and so I'm just going to be angry, I'm just going to be mad. But if you've got that trust and that basic relationship, they're going to come back. And you know, it may not happen right away. They may be really angry. And I guess I have this ideal situation because I'm with my kids for four years, and I see them grow. And, with the boys, it's usually junior year that they really start to change. And they'll come back and they'll bring up something that we talked about maybe freshman year, something I brought up. But then they're able to see it. Or then they've separated it. Another thing I see—oh my God, more with boys than with girls—they start to separate and they start to get their own values away from Mom and Dad. And they'll come back to me and say, "my dad is such a racist, I could never feel the way he does, and now I'm finally able to talk about it and realize I'm going this way." And you know, and it's so wonderful, and I'm like, "well, that's what school's supposed to be about. School's supposed to help you become a person, not just echo what your parents want us to teach." And you know, that's what I always say to my students: You're going to be exposed to all this stuff and a lot of it is going to be scary because it's going to be different than what you hear at home at the dinner table. Then you've got to take it on, and decide what you want to keep and what you want to throw away. I'm not telling you you have to believe in the theory of evolution, but you've got to at least know about, know it's there, then you've got to sit down and decide. And that is so scary for kids. Especially for low-functioning or middle-functioning, you know? But I do think trust, trust in that teacher, that, Well, they're a good person or they care about me, so she can't be, you know, misleading me. I may not accept everything or I may not do everything she wants, but I know she's a good person, and I trust her. Kids don't trust adults. You know, basically they hate a lot of teachers because they screw them over all the time with the grading system and different ways that they expect them to live up to norms.

KEVIN: When you said someone came back to you as a junior, it made me think, Sometimes we have to wait three years. That's a long time!

SAM: I know. Isn't it amazing? But I've noticed that with my own children. If they have an incredible experience, they may not talk about it, and then all of a sudden one day they're like, "You know, when I did this, or climbed this mountain, or this happened?" and I'm like, "I can't believe, that was six months ago and you're just telling me?" But it's the process time.

KEVIN: Maybe it's how they revisit it in their own minds.

SAM: Yeah. And so how do we allow for that in schools? We really don't.

CHAPTER 3

Readings and Rereadings
of Identity, Culture,
and Oppression

As I turn to stories of queer activists, I feel it is important first to develop a more complex understanding of what it is that I am hoping to change, which is not only oppression, but also the identities and cultures that situate oppression. Drawing primarily on the poststructuralist perspectives developed in chapter 2, this chapter examines different ways of making sense of or "reading" the multiple oppressions that play out in everyday life. I focus on stories of four queer activists—Pab, Christopher, Matthew, and Beth—who live and work at some of these intersections. As I explained earlier, my goal is not to explain the experiences of the activists. Rather, my goal is to examine how different modes of interpretation—what Elizabeth Ellsworth (1997) calls "routes of reading"—can lead to different conceptualizations of identity, culture, and oppression, which in turn can lead to different conceptualizations of antioppressive activism.

The four approaches developed in chapter 2 suggest at least three different ways to "read" identity, culture, and oppression: the first and second approaches suggest a reading that focuses on Otherness and difference; the third approach, on privilege and normalcy; and the fourth approach, on the intersected and situated nature of Otherness and privilege. I begin this chapter by describing these three routes of reading, illustrating each with examples from my own life, and reiterating their strengths and weaknesses. Turning to the stories of the four participants, I then explore the readings made possible when these three routes incorporate poststructuralist critiques and insights. In other words, I then explore the insights on identity, culture, and oppression made possible with poststructuralist rereadings of difference (in Pab's stories), normalcy (in Christopher's stories), and intersections (in Matthew's stories). I will argue that the poststructuralist variations of these routes of reading illuminate many complexities and contradictions in our experiences with oppression, and disrupt any one way to "understand" oppression.

One of the poststructuralist notions developed in chapter 2 (namely, the notion of "looking beyond") suggests yet another approach to reading, one that defies notions of common sense because it does not aim even to understand that which is being read. I develop this route of reading as I turn to the stories of the fourth participant, Beth, and explore how reading can lead as much to different understandings of identity, culture, and oppression as it can to changes in our own identities, cultures, and social relations. Throughout this chapter, but especially in the section on Beth, I will argue that antioppressive routes of reading and rereading can lead as much to noncommonsense knowledges of and practices in our world, as it can to nonnormal or queer identifications of and feelings about ourselves. Antioppressive routes of reading can involve queering our very selves.

Before turning to my own experiences, I should note that this chapter focuses on complicating our understandings of oppression, and on laying the groundwork for the discussion of educational implications that takes place in chapter 4. I do conclude each of the four sections on the activists with a brief discussion of educational implications, but refrain from explaining these implications in depth. Instead, I ask the reader to reflect on how these implications are being modeled by my readings, and on whether new insights on oppression and on education are made possible when I refuse to claim that a particular reading means that educators "should" do something.

Reading My Experiences in Antioppressive Ways

In elementary school, I internalized many stereotypes and messages about who I was supposed to be and consequently read my identities and experiences through these normative lenses. For example, I read myself through a racist lens that viewed White Americans as the norm in U.S. society and stereotyped Asian Americans as the smart, hardworking minority. I read myself through a sexist lens that valued a particular form of masculinity and denigrated other expressions of masculinity and all expressions of femininity among boys. And I read myself through a heterosexist lens that defined heterosexuality as "normal" and normative and characterized queer sexuality as something to fear and hate. As a boy who was Asian American, nerdy, and queer (though I had not yet self-identified as queer), I wrestled subconsciously with these harmful readings. My responses were paradoxical. I tried to conform to the stereotype of Asian Americans as good students, to compensate for feeling inferior to other boys, and to repress and negotiate my queer sexual desires. But I also tried to avoid admitting to myself, and showing others, that I was being harmed, and I ended up throwing myself into arenas, such as those of academics and music, in which I could and did excel. On the surface, then, I was a school success, but my success was, in large part, a mask—a mask that concealed my feelings of difference and my fear of isolation while in school. My experiences have led me to ask, Are there ways of reading queer Asian American masculinities and sexualities that explicitly disrupt racism, heterosexism, and other forms of oppression?

Readings that Focus on Otherness and Difference

Many researchers have talked about the genders and sexualities of Asian American boys by focusing on cultural differences. They argue that notions of what are normal and queer vary from culture to culture. For example, mainstream U.S. society often defines "masculine" or "real" boys as those who constantly demonstrate aggression, competitiveness, and excellence in a number of areas, including athletics and physical fitness (Kimmel, 1994). However, some believe that "traditional Asian cultures" condemn physical displays of aggression, and privilege the mind over the body (Sung, 1985). The "typical" Asian American boy, then, might seem queer or effeminate by U.S. standards since he lacks the dominant or hegemonic form of masculinity, but that is because he exhibits a different form of masculinity, one that is valued in his own culture.

The focus on cultural difference has also been used to differentiate Asian American heterosexuality from normative heterosexuality. For example, mainstream U.S. society often encourages sexualized interactions between boys and girls, such as dating, and even condones interactions that are overtly sexual and sexist, such as boys' sexual harassment of girls and women, defining such interactions as mere expressions of "natural childhood sexuality" (Walkerdine, 1990). In contrast, "traditional Asian cultures" expect that sexual attractiveness, expressions, and interactions will be underplayed, subtle, and private, and that boys in particular will control their sexual desire so as not to distract from making learning their top priority (Sung, 1985). The "typical" Asian American boy, then, may appear queer (or asexual) by U.S. standards, but by underplaying his sexuality while hyperachieving in academics he also exemplifies traditional Asian values.

The cultural focus has even been used to differentiate Asian American queers from other queers. Connie Chan (1995), for example, argues that psychological models used to describe the "stages" of queer sexual identity development are based on Western conceptualizations of sexuality and on the experiences of White American queers. "Traditional Asian cultures," however, value different expressions of sexuality, and do not consider public expressions of queer sexuality and participation in queer communities to be the highest stages in, or the "achievement" of, an individual's sexual identity development. Some queer Asian boys privately express same-sex attraction, but publicly appear heterosexual and refrain from "coming out" and identifying as queer. The "typical" Asian American queer boy, then, may appear abnormal, with an "unachieved" queer identity, but he is normal within some Asian queer subcultures.

Educators who focus on cultural difference can expect that many Asian American boys—straight and queer—will, in general, value and exhibit different masculinities and sexualities (compared to White American boys) since they come from different cultures. They can engage in an education *for* the other by acknowledging the differences among their students and tailoring their interactions with their students to those differences, such as by encouraging them to be themselves, explore their own interests, and take pride in their cultural traditions and heritage. Furthermore, educators with a knowledge about cultural differences can pass on this knowledge to their students, teaching an understanding of and an empathy for differences. Knowledge about and appreciation for differences, in other words, can also help educators engage in an education *about* the other as both they and their students learn ways in which some groups are culturally different from the mainstream, and ways to act accordingly. As I reflect on my own schooling experiences, I can recall no route of reading offered to me that disrupted commonsense ways of reading difference as something inferior, something problematic, or simply something to hide. I needed a reading practice that could help others see me, and help me see myself, in affirming ways.

While this route of reading is able to help educators acknowledge and affirm differences among students, it does have several weaknesses. By relying on notions of a "traditional Asian culture" to describe Asian Americans, educators can end up overlooking ways in which Asian and Asian American cultures are tremendously diverse and ever-changing. And even if Asian American cultures were not diverse, by defining Asianness as culturally different, educators do not necessarily contest the White American heterosexual norms from which Asianness differs. In fact, focusing on cultural difference can absolve educators of addressing oppression if they believe that Asian cultures traditionally confine all sexual expression to the private realm, and therefore, that challenging sexism and heterosexism by discussing issues of sex and sexuality in the classroom is culturally inappropriate.

Readings that Focus on Privilege and Normalcy

Offering a different reading of oppression, some researchers have focused on that which the Other is *different from* as they advocate engaging in "critical" education. They examine U.S. society not only for ways in which Asian American masculinities and sexualities are Othered, but also for ways in which Whiteness and heterosexuality are privileged. They suggest that the harm experienced by queer Asian American boys results not only from cultural insensitivity and individual prejudice, but also from the social structures and competing ideologies that help to define normalcy in society. As I argued in chapter 2, queer Asian American boys confront at least two forms of structural/ideological oppression: a racism that privileges Whiteness and "Otherizes" Asianness, and a heterosexism/homophobia that privileges heterosexuality and "Otherizes" queerness. Therefore, some researchers argue that addressing the experiences of queer Asian American boys requires addressing the simultaneous nature of these oppressions— that is, the ways in which queer Asian American boys are doubly oppressed or "doubly marginalized" (Hom & Ma, 1993).

Educators who focus on multiple privileges and norms can unravel with their students the shared ways that oppressions operate—especially ways that the dual processes of privileging and Othering are often invisible because they are masked by common sense. As I argued in chapter 2, mainstream U.S. society often privileges Whiteness by defining White Americans as the "real" or "authentic" Americans and stereotyping Asian Americans as perennial foreigners (whose home can only be in Asia) or the model minority (whose extraordinary success proves that the "American dream" is not hindered by racism). Similarly, mainstream U.S. society often privileges heterosexuality by defining it as the way people naturally are or the moral way to be, while defining other sexualities as queer, as illnesses, and, in many places, as crimes. These processes of privileging and Othering can be the focus of an education that aims to critique and transform multiple oppressions. Educators, in other words, can teach students to think critically about the notion that it is "only natural" that people think about differences in only certain ways, and to ask, Why and how has society come to think about racial norms and sexual differences in these ways? Furthermore, as educators teach students to ask about the political, material, and even psychological effects of these oppressive ideas, they can also engage students in resisting and challenging these oppressive structures and ideologies, and imagining and creating less oppressive situations for queer Asian Americans and others in schools and society.

Compared to the first route of reading, this second route sheds light on more of the complexities of oppression experienced by queer Asian American boys—namely, the dual processes of privileging and Othering and the simultaneity of multiple oppressions. It reminds us that a queer Asian American boy may have experiences in school radically different from those of a straight Asian American boy or those of a queer White American boy. And by reminding us that multiple oppressions can be experienced simultaneously, it suggests that education similarly needs to address multiple oppressions simultaneously, which means ensuring that antiracist pedagogies are not heterosexist, antiheterosexist pedagogies are not White centered, and so forth. However, this route of reading does have a major weakness: it relies on an additive model of oppression. As the next route will reveal, the experiences of queer Asian American boys are more complex than the sum of experiences of Asian Americans and queers; they confront additional forms of oppression.

Readings that Focus on the Intersected and Situated Nature of Oppression

Some researchers have suggested that queer Asian American boys do experience the forms of racism and heterosexism described above, but they also experience different forms of racism and heterosexism from within their queer and Asian American communities, respectively. As I discussed in chapter 2, the forms of oppression in traditionally marginalized communities often supplement forms of oppression in mainstream society, by which I mean they cite them and then add something new (Butler, 1997; Kumashiro, 1999b).

Queer Asian American boys often experience a form of heterosexism in Asian American communities that supplements the heterosexism in mainstream society. As with mainstream society, Asian American communities often normalize heterosexuality and denigrate queer sexualities and queer individuals, but they also assign racial markers to different sexual orientations. Heterosexuality is often racialized *as Asian*, as a requirement of Asianness, such as when the "traditional Asian values" of getting married, having children, and passing down the family name imply that being a virtuous or "real" Asian American, at least among adults, requires practicing heterosexuality. Similarly, queer sexuality is often racialized *as White*, as characteristic of White Americans, such as with the notion that Asian Americans who are queer are not "really" Asian, are more White than Asian, have the "White disease" (Wat, 1996). As I reflect on my own childhood, I realize that my sexual repression and confusion resulted from my internalizing both the heterosexism of mainstream society and the racialized heterosexism of Asian America. I had feelings for boys, but told myself I was merely "curious" about them, not attracted to them, and paid heed only to my attraction for girls. I did not want to be queer, but also I did not consider being queer a possibility, perhaps because I saw no queers who were Asian American. Not until going to college did I meet other queer Asian Americans, learn about queers in Asian history, and start to critique both the heterosexist "traditional Asian values" and the racist-heterosexist notion that only White Americans are queer. Not until unlearning the racialized heterosexism of Asian America did I start coming out to myself.

Queer communities, too, can be oppressive spaces when they exhibit a form of racism that supplements racism in mainstream society. Like mainstream society, queer communities often privilege Whiteness and Otherize

Asianness, and like mainstream society, they often assign gendered markers to each racial identity, stereotyping White American men as masculine and Asian American men as feminine (Okihiro, 1994). However, queer communities also often give this gendered form of racism a hyper-sexualized dimension. While being an Asian male is often read in mainstream society as unmasculine (wimpy, nerdy) and, therefore, sexually undesirable, it is often read by other queers as "exotic" and, therefore, hyperdesirable. In fact, some queer men actually fetishize queers who fit the stereotype of the feminine Asian American youthful boy (Kumashiro, 1999b).

Recognizing that unique forms of oppression play out in marginalized communities forces educators to rethink what it means to challenge oppression. Traditionally, educators expect that Asian American boys can turn to their families and communities to find relief from racial oppression, and similarly, that queer boys can turn to their queer "families" and communities to find relief from heterosexism and homophobia. But boys who are both queer *and* Asian American face the paradoxical situation of identifying with both communities while finding solace in neither. With racialized heterosexism in Asian American communities, and queered racism in queer communities, they often feel excluded from, and unsafe and unsupported in, both. Even their identities can leave them with a sense of exclusion and paradox: they cannot be both queer and Asian American if queers are "supposed" to be White and Asians are "supposed" to be straight. Educators committed to addressing the complex experiences of queer Asian American boys will have difficulty doing so without engaging in this third route of reading, or at least in a route that explores these poststructuralist insights on the intersected and situated nature of oppression.

In what follows, I argue that the poststructuralist insights I discussed in chapter 2 can help to address weaknesses of or simply to expand on each of the routes of reading I used to examine my own experiences with oppression. As I turn to the stories of three of the participants, I will develop poststructuralist versions of the routes of reading (i.e., poststructuralist rereadings) and explore how they each make possible different insights on identity, culture, and oppression. As with the original routes of reading, the focuses of the altered routes continue to be (1) difference, (2) normalcy, and (3) intersections. However, my goal is to look beyond the repetition of what are now becoming familiar insights on oppression; my goal is to read for difference.

First Route: Rereading Difference in Pab's Stories

Pab's stories remind me of the first time I held hands with another man. He was not a man I was dating or in any way involved with sexually. Rather, he was a new friend, and in that context, holding hands was commonplace. This was 1992, my first month in Nepal as a Peace Corps volunteer, and my hand-holding friend was one of the Nepali language trainers who was himself Nepali. Before heading to Nepal, I had read through a number of orientation materials that alerted us soon-to-be volunteers of this shift in norms regarding culturally appropriate expressions of affection. In Nepal, we were told, same-gender friendships (such as between two males) were commonly expressed in very physical ways, such as by holding hands, walking arm in arm or arm over shoulder, sitting in one another's lap, hugging. In contrast, opposite-gender friendships, along with opposite-gender sexual relationships, involved very little physical contact in public.

Ironically, despite the ease with which same-gender pairs could express their affection for one another physically, same-gender *sexual* relationships (or, queer relationships, such as two men "in love") were taboo. While queer relationships did not carry the stigma of immorality that they did in Western societies (perhaps because Christianity was not a central religion in South Asia), they nonetheless were not socially acceptable, at least among adults, who were expected to "outgrow" such inclinations. This irony should not be surprising, given Eve Sedgwick's (1991) notion that homosociality (same-gender socializing) and homosexuality are very close in social expression but rigidly differentiated in symbolic meaning and cultural acceptability. This makes me wonder, If same-gender sexual relations were to become more recognized in Nepal, would public displays of affection between members of the same gender become less acceptable? And, would public displays of affection between members of different genders become more acceptable? In other words, would the mere acknowledgment of queer sexualities serve to trouble cultural norms that presently permitted public displays of affection only between two people who could not possibly attribute sexual desire to their touching?

My guess is that the answer would be yes. After all, cultural norms (of men as masculine) that privilege homosociality among men go hand in hand with cultural norms (of men as not-feminine) that prohibit homosexuality among men (Sedgwick, 1991).

I bring this all up because my hand-holding incident troubled the boundary between homosociality and homosexuality. Why? Because I was somewhat sexually attracted to my friend. So, while my friend (who I believed felt no sexual attraction to me) probably read our hand-holding in one way, I read it in quite another. In particular, although he probably meant it to express friendship, I nonetheless felt excited by this shared act. Later, another Peace Corps volunteer came up to me and asked how it felt to be holding hands with him. Nervous at being outted, I gave a flippant answer about just going with the flow, since it was my new friend who grabbed my hand, not the other way around. But I wondered, why did the volunteer ask me that question? Since I was holding hands with my friend while standing among a group of other volunteers, I was acutely aware of the possibility that our hand-holding could have taken on multiple readings. Some may have read it as an expression of friendship commonplace among Nepalis (as in, "Oh, they're just doing the Nepali thing"). Some may have read it as an awkward expression of friendship, appropriate in Nepal, but inappropriate when involving a non-Nepali (as in, "Kevin's not Nepali—why is he holding hands with him?"). Some may have read it the same way I did (as in, "Ooh, I wonder if Kevin's queer, and is excited by the chance to hold hands with this cute guy"). And some may have read it in yet other ways. Complicating matters was that I had not yet explicitly disproved the expectation that I was heteronormal; in other words, I had not yet come out as queer. Further complicating matters was the fact that my Asian facial features and small body build made me passable as a Nepali. I looked like one of the Nepali ethnic groups, but I was a U.S. volunteer with primarily White colleagues.

Nonetheless, I would be surprised if anyone read the hand-holding as queer (as in, "They're both queer, they're attracted to one another, and that's why they're holding hands"). My friend, after all, was gradually getting the reputation among the volunteers as a (hetero)sexual predator who made constant sexual advances toward the women volunteers (which meant he would not be my friend for very long). More importantly, that act (of men holding hands) in that culture left little, if any, space for queer readings, in part because holding hands was "supposed" to mean friendship, and in part because adult Nepalis were not "supposed" to be queer.

Years later, and back in the United States, I again confront Nepali culture and its heterosexism. But not in the form of same-gender hand-holding, which often disappears when "Nepali culture" is transported to the United States. This is not surprising: cultures change over time and place, and elements of a culture that could make a diasporic group (i.e., a group that has emigrated from their "home" country) stand out in a negative way (such as same-gender hand-holding in a homophobic society), as with elements that could otherwise help a group "fit in" and accommodate (M. A. Gibson, 1988), will understandably be changed. And they can be changed without the threat of disrupting what it means to be Nepali.

In contrast are elements that members of a group often want to maintain because they are seen as central or core parts of their cultural heritage and identity. In their quest to defy assimilation, diasporic groups often search for and embrace a sense of tradition, privileging certain cultural elements as their essential culture, the culture that has historically been "of" their group (Hall, 1990). In this case, Nepali Americans, like other Asian Americans, often embrace a "traditional Asian culture" (Yanagisako, 1985) or "traditional Nepali culture" that privileges the heterocentric family unit. What is problematic with defining an "essential" culture is that all cultures, even in the "homelands," change over time, and cultural traditions, norms, and identities shift in meaning and practice from one era to another and from one place to another (Yanagisako, 1985). Defining a tradition requires choosing and privileging only certain histories and cultural practices, as when notions of a "traditional" South Asian culture ignore times in history when South Asian cultures and religions embraced queer sexualities (Shah, 1993). Defining a tradition can even involve reworking contemporary practices in the "homeland," as in Southeast Asian American communities where parents continue to arrange marriages for their daughters, but marry them off at ages younger than is common in Southeast Asia (Smith-Hefner, 1993). Defining a tradition is less a process of discovery than it is of imagination and differentiating oneself from others.

My point here is that the ways in which cultural elements are reworked, redefined, and revalued may help a group to develop an identity that affirms a part of themselves, but may also help to maintain forms of oppression already in play, and perhaps create new ones as well. It is important to "read" culture in antioppressive ways. What I have tried to show in this section is a reading of hand-holding that reveals the contradictory ways in which cultural practices can change even while beliefs in the existence of traditional or essential cultures persist. I have tried to show a reading that reveals the oppositional ways in which the definition of a "traditional" culture tells us who we are (from Asia) by telling us who we are not (namely, the White American norm and everything racialized as White, including the queer). And I have tried to show a reading that suggests who a group *has been and is* as much as who a group *should and should not be*.

This brings us to Pab. Pab was born in Nepal and is currently attending high school in a large, predominantly White American community in the Midwest. I found Pab to be insightful and inspiring. She reminds me that teenagers have countless insights to offer educational research. Yet, I do not wish to imply that Pab is a typical teenager. She has been involved in literally dozens of student and community organizations and projects, has held leadership positions in many of them, and has spoken about sexuality and race on a number of panels to young students and adults alike. Not surprisingly, she was recommended to me by many different people as the perfect person to interview for my research. I was very glad and grateful that she agreed to participate:

> A lot of people see me as a person that's gay
> even though I do tend to like guys
> I've just had a girlfriend for all my relationships in the past few years.
> And that's a strong part of my identity.
> I always knew I looked at women.
> I never told anybody about these things
> I mean I went about my normal life
> I was a great person
> had tons of friends
> you know?
> Everything like that.
> I talked about guys a lot
> but I did like guys
> you know?
> But I never talked about the female part that I liked
> I just made really good friends with the females I liked.

I always thought that if I was a guy
everything would be so much better because
I loved playing sports.
I didn't hang out with guys
all of my close friends had been girls.
There's just this little part where if I was a guy
I thought the world would be so much better.
I still have desires to be male
but not desires enough where I'm gonna,
'cause I love being a female
I love the friends I've made
I love the life that I've lived and the emotions I have
and I don't think I'd have the same kinds
if I was a guy
or do the same things I'd be doing.
There's times I'm with my girlfriend
where I would like to have the choice of
spending my life with her and marrying her and having kids with her
and having my own kids
'cause that is important to me,
'cause I want to adopt but
having kids from my own body is important.
And there's just times where it seems that would be still be a lot easier.
And even like the sex part of it is just like, like, 'cause,
I'm not afraid to go very personal, I hope you don't mind.
Like even the sex part
it gets a little bit questionable because I've always had this thing where
the penis is very important in the relationship.
And there's no penis involved and I'm very happy about that.
But there's points where I'm just like,
I wish there was.
If we had some ways that two women could have babies
and if society was more accepting
and if I hadn't been taught all my life that
for sex to be great
there had to be two different parts of a body

two different kinds, two different sexes involved
then I think it'd be better also.

Oh
there's still a time when I don't accept myself.
I think the largest reason is 'cause my mother.
Communication is just really hard
and to keep it a secret from my mom has made it the
most difficult part of my life
just 'cause I'm so open to everybody else
and yet with my mom
I can't tell her anything.
And it makes it really hard.
I don't know if you've ever read the book
A Lotus of Another Color [a book on queer South Asians],
but I read that
and I read through other books
and I did a whole entire research paper on it
and I tried to understand why it's just so oppressive in South Asia
but I didn't understand because like
in our history there are like,
back in the Mahabharata days in India
everybody was so open
and all of a sudden
because sexuality is never talked
sex is never talked about
sexuality therefore is not even a question
and my mom grew up with that.
I think she'd find it weird if she met a
South Asian gay person.
She'd probably think, How?
[*laughter*]
She wouldn't understand like, because
the family raises you to be straight.
I think that would be most upsetting to her.
She like has that Nepali thing where
she wants grandchildren and

she wants a son-in-law and

she wants a normal life.
If I told her I was gay it would be
a threat to a dream that she's always had.
And she could respond and she could say,
"Great, I knew, I'm glad you told me,
you can still have kids and you can adapt."
But I think the real thing that would happen is she'd
freak out
and she would never kick me out
she'd never disown me
but we'd have a lot of tension for a while
and soon she'd come about
but it's just not something that I'm ready to deal with.

Did you say you've read *A Lotus of Another Color*?
There's an interview with a woman where she's talking about
being lesbian and being Asian and being a minority within a minority
and, within a minority,
and how that's an oppressive state of mind because you
oppress yourself and how society sees it as being oppressive,
and we need to be accepted by our Asian society
but we also need to be accepted as ourselves.
And I think helping that acceptance
so we can accept ourselves
I think that would be the largest thing
is if we said, "It's okay."
I think to have more people say it's okay.
Just to kind of accept it?
That I'm Asian, I'm a woman, I'm queer.
I think that's the largest thing, is just to accept it.

I'm not saying I'm always oppressed
and I'm not going to sit here and say,
"Well, I've been oppressed my whole life."
But, I don't know.
It's horrible because uh,
I'm trying to find money for school again and I can't

because I'm a minority
so therefore in society I get all the treatments that a minority gets
you know
but when it comes down to affirmative action
I can't be helped because I'm South Asian
and South Asians have a high rate of success in their ACT and SAT
scores.
"They're smart."
And the money.
"They're very high class"
you know?
And therefore I don't fit into the affirmative action stereotype
but I fit into all the other stereotypes of being oppressed.

I know throughout life like
I've always dealt with, um,
memories are really hard for me.
I've moved around   .
I've lived in—how many cities have I lived in?
I've lived in four different states
two different countries
one two three four five six seven different cities, eight different cities,
so I've had different types of friends.
Like when I was little I always had friends that were of different nation-
alities.
And, like just growing up and then coming to [this state]
and then coming to a place,
I lived in [two different cities] for a while
and everybody was just White,
and just trying to find myself amongst everybody who's White
and I'm like one of the only students of color
and one that is able to acknowledge, you know?
It's really hard, in that like,
I think the worst memory is people being like,
"Well, you're not actually Asian
'cause you don't dress Asian or

you don't hang out with the Hmong people or the gangbangers
or you're not really smart
you don't get perfect on your ACT scores
or you're not great in math."
And I've just kind of been this person who's known as an
activist in school
and so they see me as being White because I'm with friends
White friends all the time.
And it's really disturbing because
even with all the Asians I've known like,
I'm really into my culture
but in a different way
where I don't speak Nepali everyday
where they may speak Hmong with their friends everyday
but, and my family doesn't live a total Nepali lifestyle
we live a very mixed lifestyle,
but I'm willing to go back to my culture
and learn my heritage
and I want to live both lifestyles.
And it's also very difficult because within that
there's the fact that I live a very gay lifestyle
just because I've been with a female for so long.
It's hard too because I can't show them gay around the Asians.
Like, if you tell people dealing with racism,
"Be that strong individual
be part of your culture
or remember that culture,"
and part of that culture is to be homophobic,
and identify with your own kind,
that takes away from identifying with different types of people
that happen to be people who are homosexuals or whatever
you know?
I think that's a large conflict.
I don't know.

I can be Asian and gay.

I can be both, and I can be cool with everybody, you know?

I wish I could live in a world where I could just be all of it at once.

Trying to find a group that accepted me,

I hang out with more of the gay people than minorities.

I keep reminding my friends,

"You know what,

I'm Asian,

we gotta deal with that."

When I read Pab's stories, I cannot help but be reminded of the stories of Michael, a queer Asian American man I interviewed several years ago (Kumashiro, 1999b). Both Pab's and Michael's stories point to a racialized heterosexism in Asian American communities. For Michael, being Asian required getting married and having children, and thus, required the performance of heterosexuality. So, too, with Pab; her mother, who in some ways symbolizes for Pab "traditional" Nepali culture, wants grandchildren and a son-in-law. Her mother would find it "weird" if she met a South Asian who was gay, since they are all "raised to be straight." In fact, Pab also told me that, for her mother, seeing Pab as queer is not even in the realm of possibility. According to Pab, "traditional" Nepali culture is heterosexist.

It is also sexist. Michael told me that "traditional Asian cultures" place significant pressure on males, especially firstborn sons, to get married, have children, and carry on the family name. Daughters also face significant pressure to conform to normative Asian traditions. In fact, daughters are the ones who often are expected by parents and community members to keep alive the "traditions" of the culture. Research on Southeast Asian girls in the United States, for example, suggests that parents hold gendered expectations of them. Parents want their sons to learn how to integrate into and succeed economically in mainstream U.S. society, but want their daughters to remain at home, learn the traditions of their home country, and personify what it means to be Hmong or Khmer (B. L. Goldstein, 1988; Smith-Hefner, 1993). Similarly, Gayatri Gopinath (1997) argues that Asian Indian communities in the United States often treat Asian Indian women as the "guardians of tradition" who uphold what is "essentially Indian." While men are often expected to become "American" and enter the public realm, women are expected to remain "ethnic" and maintain the private realm.

What results from this oppressive view of "Asian culture" for queer Asian American women is a paradox, an impossibility of identity. If an Asian woman is straight, she is "essentially Asian," but if she is queer, she has the "White disease" and is "more White than Asian." If she is straight, she assumes the role in the private realm of wife/daughter-in-law/mother, but if she is queer, she has no prescribed role in the traditional (heterosexual) family household. Even stereotypes in mainstream society make the identity of queer Asian American woman impossible, since Asian women are supposed to be ultrafeminine while (White) lesbians are supposed to be butch (J. Lee, 1996). One is essentially Asian, one is essentially not Asian; one is an insider, one is an outsider. Not surprisingly, Asian American women who are queer are often invisible both in Asian American communities and mainstream U.S. society.

It was not always the case that South Asian cultures silenced queer identities and relationships and cited homophobic discourses. As Pab learned when conducting research on the Mahabharata era in Indian history, there have been times when dominant cultures in South Asia were much more queer-friendly. There are, arguably, many elements of South Asian cultures that can be labeled "traditional." Who decides? Defining "traditional" South Asian culture is an act that is already influenced by particular perspectives and values, and that always carries political and material consequences. In her Nepali and Nepali American communities, Pab found it difficult to embrace her ethnic identity and "go back to my culture and learn my heritage" without embracing a homophobic culture and heterosexist identity. But her research revealed multiple traditions regarding queer sexuality, and troubled the notion that "traditional Nepali culture" required her to be heterosexual. Changing the ways she read culture and tradition led to changes in her own identities.

Not many people desire learning that what are often considered "traditional" or "essential" are socially constructed and that any definition of who we are is partial. In fact, as I argued earlier, some desire to look back in time to find some core of their culture or identity—namely, some singular, unchanging notion of who they are—as a way to affirm their differences from the mainstream and develop a sense of community, especially in a racially oppressive context. For example, in Pab's experiences, identifying as Nepali when faced with a White-dominated community (where "everybody was just White") and a racist society (where she gets "all the treatments that a minority gets") can be seen as a political act that enables an individual to find a sense of belonging and support, as well as an identity not based on dominant stereotypes. It is difficult to identify as Nepali and come together as Nepalis when there is no clear definition of what it means to be Nepali.

However, in Pab's stories, prevailing definitions of who is South Asian/Nepali/Asian American, who belongs, and who can find support often work to negate the supposedly empowering acts of identifying and coming together as Nepali(s). For example, mainstream institutions such as colleges tell Pab that South Asians are not a "real" minority and, thus, are unable to be helped by affirmative action. Nepali American community members, including her mother, tell her or indirectly teach her that she is not a real or "normal" Nepali because she is not straight. Even her young Asian American peers tell Pab that she is not "actually Asian" because of her dress, her speech, her academic achievement, or her homelife, and in contrast tell her that she is "being White" because of her friends or her activism. So, while identifying as South Asian/Nepali/Asian American has its political and social purposes and benefits, competing definitions of who is authentically any of these identities work to normalize those identities, regulate those who can conform, and exclude those who cannot or do not.

My reading of Pab's stories helps me conclude that changing oppression involves saying more than "Asian Americans have to be less homophobic"; it also involves saying, "We have to change what it means to be authentically Nepali/South/Asian American." As it is for Pab, it is important for me to read Nepali culture in a way that affirms its differences but also troubles the very notion of *a single* Nepali culture. It is important to resist understanding Nepali culture only in its homophobic incarnation, and instead to seek multiple, perhaps contested, but certainly situated definitions of "Nepali." It is important, in other words, to engage in the labor of changing what "Nepali" cites. "Nepali culture" can include queer relations. These reading practices are not unlike what I argued in chapter 2 are paradoxical ways that educators can teach about cultures and about differences in general: students can simultaneously learn about differences while troubling that new knowledge and the ways we came to know it. For Pab, for me, and for teachers and students, reading about different cultures involves rereading and looking beyond the very ways those cultures and differences have come to be defined. And it involves reflecting on how different ways of reading cultures make possible different understandings, different identities, and different responses.

Second Route: Rereading Normalcy in Christopher's Stories

The notion that cultural and racial groups privilege certain identities is not new. As I turn to Christopher's stories, I am reminded that, for decades, black feminists (such as hooks, 1984 and 1994) have made similar arguments, even concerning activist movements. They have told us, for example, that "feminism" is often racialized as White, failing to address Black American women. Nellie McKay (1993) notes,

> For Black women, issues of gender are always connected to race.... Black women cannot choose between their commitment to feminism and the struggle with their men for racial justice. Many white feminists still do not recognize the structures that differentiate their experiences from those of Black women, structures that make the gender question, by itself, central to white women against patriarchy. (p. 276)

Conversely, Black or antiracist activism is often male-centered—that is, is often gendered as male. Thus, Kimberlé Crenshaw (1992) explains that

> the specific forms of domination to which black females are subject sometimes fall between the existing legal categories for recognizing injury. Underlying the legal parameters of racial discrimination are numerous narratives reflecting discrimination as it is experienced by black men, while the underlying imagery of gender discrimination incorporates the experiences of white women. (as cited in Williams, 1997, p. 277)

Black American women, in other words, do experience gender-based and race-based forms of oppression, but are often excluded by the White-centered and male-centered efforts to challenge them.

In addition, Black American women often experience unique forms of oppression based on the intersections of race and gender. For example,

Patricia Williams (1997) describes a "de-aesthetizing masculinization of Black women" in which they are "figured more as stand-ins for men, sort of reverse drag queens, women pretending to be women but more male than men" (p. 285). This gendered form of racism ascribes to Black American women a deviant femininity (and a hyper-masculinity) that denies them cultural acceptability as women (Higginbotham, 1992). As I argued earlier, oppression is not merely additive: in addition to racism in mainstream society and sexism in mainstream society, Black American women also experience Eurocentrism in feminist movements, male-centeredness in Black communities, a gendered racism in mainstream society, and presumably other forms of oppression as well. The experiences of Black American women are not merely the sum of Black (male) and female (White) experiences. Yet, activists often ignore ways in which *woman* is racialized and *Black* is gendered.

A similar situation exists for Black American queer men insofar as *queer* is often racialized and *Black* is often sexualized. Many queer Black American men have talked about the privileging of heterosexuality in their ethnic communities and the privileging of Whiteness in queer communities; many have felt excluded from their ethnic communities because they are queer, and from their queer communities because they are Black American; and many have experienced the exoticizing of deviant genders and sexualities attributed to Black American men, queer or otherwise, such as with the stereotype that they all have "big dicks" (Kumashiro, 1999a; Monteiro & Fuqua, 1995; Murray, 1996; Sears, 1995). Like Black American women, Black American queer men experience multiple forms of oppression simultaneously, and are caught between activist movements that, intentionally or not, exclude them from their efforts.

Such was the case with Christopher, who just turned thirty years old. Part African American and part Cherokee, Christopher identifies as a gay Black man. In our interviews, Christopher spent a significant amount of time talking about the relationship between racism and homophobia, as well as the unique forms of oppression facing queer Black men. He spoke not only of a racialized heterosexism in Black American communities, but also a unique form of racism in queer communities. His discussion of racism was eye-opening for me. With Williams (1997) in the back of my mind, I expected Christopher to argue that, similar to Black American women, Black American men are attributed a hyper- or deviant masculinity. Also in the back of my mind was a lecture I attended on pornography several years ago in which the speaker displayed cartoons of buffed, hairy, gorilla-like Black men with disproportionately large penises that had appeared in mainstream "soft porn" magazines like *Playboy* and *Hustler*. As I recall, the speaker argued that the cartoons dehumanized Black men as a way to boost the self-esteem of the predominantly straight, White male readership. Assuming this view of Black men to be prevalent in U.S. society, I expected Christopher to argue that the deviant masculinity attributed to Black men often takes the form of Black man as savage or as animal, and that this image would help to explain why Black men are often exoticized in queer communities. In particular, I expected Christopher's responses to suggest that many queer men see Black men as animal-like, bestial, or at best as noble savages.

This was not quite the case. My reading of Christopher's stories does suggest that many in U.S. society—queer and straight—hold dehumanizing views of Black men. But rather than a metaphor of savagery, Christopher's stories suggest to me something a bit different:

> Racism and homophobia.
> The relationship between them?
> I think that we don't want to be forgotten.
> If you start talking about homophobia inside ethnic communities
> then we start getting concerned because they're not looking at
> the race issues.
> If we start talking about race issues in the LGBT communities
> then we're concerned because they're not focusing on
> the fact that we're gay.
> You know, there's that going back and forth.
>
> That has to do with a lot of cultural,
> the way that we're brought up.
> Being part of the Black community
> I know that most Blacks don't think that Blacks are gay.
> "It's a White thing."
> [*laughter*]

You know it's,
"it's something that
you hang around too many White people and then you start
acting like them"
you know, it's that attitude
it's definitely seen as a choice
you know,
"White people do that."

That comes back to what I was talking about before with
not wanting anyone to stop focusing on them.
One of the big things that a lot of people in the
Black community holler about
is classifying gays and lesbians as a protected class.
Because they feel like it takes something away from them.
But you know, it still binds them.
One of my favorite quotes
and I haven't put it up on my wall yet but I need to do that
is from *Star Trek*.
Yeah I'm a big *Star Trek* fan
but you wouldn't know it from looking around.
It's from Captain Pickard,
"The first chain,"
no,
"The first chain forged,"
I can't remember the quote now,
"binds us all irrevocably."
And he went on to say that, when one of us
and our freedoms
and our rights are taken away,
we're all,
all of our rights are taken away.
And uh, and the majority of the Black community hasn't seen that yet.
It's still a focus on, you know,
"What have you done for me lately?"
you know,
"After you finish helping me

then we can talk about possibly doing for someone else
but that's after I'm empowered."

See
the biggest thing is they think their first priority is the color of their
skin.
And I don't know that that's untrue or true
but I think a lot of people think that.
The Black community doesn't think it can have homophobia.
They tend to ignore us
and then we say something
and then the way they perpetuate homophobia is by saying,
"It's not the same,
when they walk down the street
you don't know they're gay.
You know I'm Black."
Well, they're still gay.
You know, some people, you do know they're gay
when they walk down the street.
And they're discriminated against.
And of course some in the Black community will say,
"Well, they invited that."
Uh, you know, that's like saying that you invited it,
that, "You were Black when you walked down the street,
what you do that for?"
[*laughter*]
One of my favorite new phrases that I heard was
DWB
Driving While Black,
getting pulled over for DWB.

I've done two interviews with [a local news station].
One was about [an organization that claimed to "cure" homosexuality].
The second one was about nontraditional adoptions.
And then I've done several interviews as the spokesperson for
[the community LGBT organization].
The reason I was doing those was I,

I got tired of hearing Reggie White and Ron Greer be
the voice of Black Wisconsin.
And then people couldn't really respond to them because if they did
then they were interpreted as being racist.

I think,
not just the gay community but the community at large
is afraid to say anything bad about anyone in the Black community
because if they do they're automatically branded a racist.
But
there's a lot of racism still within the LGBT community
and we don't want to acknowledge it
in the same way that the Black community
doesn't want to acknowledge homophobia.

Society in general
and the Black community
and the gay community all have stereotypes that
all Black men are extremely well-hung.
I've only been sexually intimate with two
and they fit the stereotype
but I'm sure there are more out there who don't.
One of my favorite lines is from Arsenio Hall
before his show went off the air.
He was trying to tell viewers that,
"I know the secret to [the movie] *The Crying Game*."
This is before
you know, people were still talking about the secret.
And uh, he said, "the secret,
there's a brother with a liiiiiittle tiny weewee."
[*laughter*]
Physically,
another stereotype,
uh, big butt.
Yeah, that's another Arsenio line.
He had Patti LaBelle,
he kept trying to talk with her and she's trying to get ready to sing

and she finally told him,
"Just sit your little butt down."
He sat down on the ground and everyone started laughing and he said,
"She called my butt little."
A lot of people see Blacks as, you know,
wanting to have sex a lot,
which could be a similarity between that and gays,
what the community thinks,
"Well, they have sex a lot."
I think the difference is that in society
we don't think of Blacks as having sex with multiple partners a lot.

I think
a lot of the gay community thinks of getting involved with a Black man
or having sexual relationships with a Black man
as, uh, a treat?
As opposed to the real thing.
You know, this is something you do just so you can say,
"Ooh, I did it."
I think it ties into the stereotypes about Blacks in bed and about
the size thing.
It's kind of treating like property.
Yeah,
"I use this for, you know, a long time
and toss it out
like a Glade Plug-in."

I see at least one connection between Christopher's stories and Pab's stories: both discuss the regulatory nature of ethnic communities. Just as Asian
American communities narrowly define what it means to be Asian, Black
American communities narrowly define what it means to be Black, and this
definition leaves no room for queer sexuality ("It's a White thing"). But
while both stories focus on ways in which ethnic communities regulate their
own members—by defining what it means to be authentically Asian or Black,
and by limiting their activism to issues concerning race ("they think their
first priority is the color of their skin")—Christopher's stories also explore
ways in which ethnic communities regulate nonmembers. For example,

both queer communities and mainstream society refrain from criticizing Black American communities out of fear of being "automatically branded ... racist." It is this silence surrounding "anything bad" about Black American communities that allows heterosexism and homophobia to persist in these communities.

Of course, Black American communities are not the only problem since queer communities, too, are often oppressive spaces. Here, I am reminded once again of Michael's stories of being a queer Asian American man (Kumashiro, 1999b). According to Michael, many in mainstream society read the Asian American man as lacking in masculinity and, therefore, sexually undesirable, while many queers read that same "lack" as exotic and, therefore, hyperdesirable. Asian American men often confront a form of anti-Asian racism in queer communities that cites the long history of U.S. Orientalism in mainstream society. Similarly, Black American men often confront a form of anti-Black racism in queer communities that cites a form of racism in mainstream society, and my reading of Christopher's stories suggests that the racism cited is the history of slavery. As Christopher tells us, Black men are to be owned ("like property"), are to be used, are to serve the White man, and when they are no longer desired, they can be gotten rid of, tossed out "like a Glade Plug-in." They are not worthy of loving relationships; they are merely a "treat." After all, they are not real men. They are too masculine to be normal men, as symbolized by their too-large penis, the "size thing." Perhaps not surprisingly, both Michael and Christopher had been told on numerous occasions that they should be flattered that some men find Asian American men or Black American men especially desirable, but both sharply criticized such fetishes as being racist, and my reading of their stories reveals that such desires or fetishes do indeed have associations with racist views and practices.

I should note that, like Christopher, Michael pointed to racist stereotypes in queer communities that focus on penis size, noting that stereotypes of Asian American men as unmasculine often involve stereotypes that they have "small dicks." I do not find it insignificant that both Michael and Christopher talked about the size of the penis. I do not find it insignificant that the small Asian body and penis emasculate Asian American men while the large black body and penis hypermasculinize Black American men. And I do not find it insignificant that the deviant masculinities attributed to Asian and Black American men are a primary reason that they feel fetishized by other queer men. This is not to say that all Asian and Black American men are always stereotyped in this way. Sometimes, Asian American men experience a hypermasculinization through, for instance, stereotypes inspired by media images of martial arts experts like Bruce Lee or Jackie Chan (Tasker, 1997) or of gangsters (Gee, 1988). Sometimes Black American men experience emasculation through, for instance, associations with pop icon RuPaul or media images of the disempowered victim (hooks, 1995). Regardless, stereotypes that trouble the masculinity of Asian and Black American men do often involve an insistence that their penises are different in size than those of the White norm.

Clearly, talking about the penis involves talking about a lot more than, well, the penis. The penis is highly, though crudely, symbolic of masculinity and male privilege. It is the penis, after all, that helps visibly distinguish males from females, and that penetrates women and signifies the "top" (the aggressor) in both hetero- and homosexual relations. Not surprisingly, in a patriarchal society, physical attacks on marginalized men often focus on this symbol, the penis. For example, we can look back to the decades following the U.S. Civil War and see that public lynching of Black men often involved castration. As Robyn Wiegman (1993) explains, castration exemplified the fear felt by many White American men of extending to men of other races the privileges of patriarchy heretofore reserved for themselves. That which threatened gender sameness needed to be removed, both symbolically and physically. Modern-day gay bashing cites this history of castration, especially when it involves physical attack directed on the genitals. R. W. Connell (1995) describes how one such attack, which resulted in death, involved "stomping on the head, jumping on the genitals, and snapping the ribs by dropping on the torso with the full weight of the attacker's body" (p. 155). For the attacker, it was not enough to kill the man by destroying the head and heart. As with lynching/castration, the goal seems to have been to destroy the genitals in order to symbolically strip the man of that which had granted him power in a patriarchal society. With men of color, attacking the genitals symbolizes preventing them from receiving privilege (which they never *really* had); with queer men, attacking the genitals symbolizes retaliating against them for betraying the privilege that they may have *already* had (before coming out as queer).

There is a reason, then, that physical attacks often involve destroying or removing the genitals. There is a reason that stereotypes and verbal attacks often involve insisting that the genitals are abnormally small or abnormally large. As my reading of Christopher's stories suggests, people often do what it takes in order to allow them to continue reading the bodies and identities of others in commonsense ways. We desire reading the Other as "different from me." We desire maintaining some sense of our own normalcy.

When reading Christopher's stories, it is important that readers focus not only on understanding the experiences of queer Black American men, but also the forms of oppression that harm them while privileging others. After all, Christopher's stories are the stories of only one person, and cannot reflect the range of experiences that queer Black American men have with various forms of oppression. This is not to say that the development of such critical knowledges is not important; equally important, however, is that readers focus on how and why they often desire reading and understanding the queer Black American male body in these ways, and how and why they often desire reading oppression in ways that do not significantly trouble their own sense of selves. In other words, in addition to what they read, it is equally important that readers focus on how and why they read as they do—that is, how and why their desires shape the ways they read.

The desire to read the Black male body in queer ways often does reflect a desire to maintain the normalcy of the White male body. Since Whiteness is defined in opposition to Blackness (Morrison, 1992), the image of White American men as sources of security and goodness in society requires that the image of Black American men symbolize "all that is dangerous in the world" (Williams, 1995, p. 241). And since one symbol of White American male power is a penis of particular color and size, it is not surprising that disempowering stereotypes emerge such that "the Negro is eclipsed. He is turned into a penis. He *is* a penis" (Fanon, 1970, p. 120; emphasis in the original). The existence of a White norm requires the existence of an opposite (in this case, a Black queer), which means that the desire to maintain a sense of normalcy requires producing queered views of the other (Foucault, 1978). We often *desire* to read Otherness queerly.

In fact, the desire to read the Black male body in queer ways reflects a desire to maintain the normalcy of the reader's body, White male or otherwise. It is easy to talk about the queer Black male body without talking about my own body. It is easy to examine ways the queer Black male body is "different" without examining ways my own body feels normal (or also different, but perhaps in different ways). It is easy to discuss what I read on the queer Black male body without discussing how I conduct that reading in comparison to or in contrast with my own body. This ignoring of my own body is problematic. Just as feminists have critiqued the silences in research surrounding the researchers' emotions and personal experiences, so too have queer theorists critiqued the silences surrounding the researchers' bodies and sexualities in research (Honeychurch, 1998). They argue that such silences mask ways that the researchers' emotions, experiences, embodied desires, and sexualities always influence the ways they read and research, and consequently, mask ways that only some of their perspectives are privileged and considered objective. In other words, by ignoring the body and attempting to be objective, researchers actually maintain the privileging of only certain bodies and only certain ways of embodying desires, knowledges, identities, and so forth.

I cannot deny that the ways I view my own body and sexuality influence how I read Black male bodies and the stories of a Black gay man, and I tried to make that explicit by putting Christopher's stories next to Michael's (since Michael talks about the queer Asian American male body, which could be my own). Clearly, my desire to trouble prevailing stereotypes of Asian male bodies influenced how I read Black male bodies, such as with my emphasis on castration. However, even with this recognition, I need to keep asking, In what other ways do I desire normalcy, and how do those desires lead to both helpful and harmful readings of Christopher's stories? Did I, earlier on, fail to read slavery in the stereotype of Black male bodies because I desired not to confront my own socioeconomic class privileges? Am I now able to read slavery in Christopher's stories because, as a person of color, I desire to build alliances with other people of color? Does my insistence on thinking about the body in research feed on my desire that other researchers acknowledge how the body of Kevin Kumashiro does influence how they read my research, as when they think differently of my work *because* I am queer or of color? What am I still failing to read in Christopher's stories, and how do those failings relate to desires I have yet to articulate?

My focus in this discussion has been the bodies of queer Black American men. But the same applies to other differences and identities, such as the gender roles of straight Jewish girls, the learning styles of young Native American students, and the socialization of Latino/a urban teens. There are many ways to read stories, and it is important to reflect on how our desires lead us to read in only certain ways. In the case of Christopher's stories, it is important to examine how our own bodies and desires lead us to read in ways that normalize only certain bodies while Othering other bodies. It is important, in other words, to put our desire for normalcy at the forefront of our readings and ask, How does my desire for normalcy require me to read Others in queer ways? How we read can maintain the status quo, but it can also bring about change. This is not unlike what I argued in chapter 2. Antioppressive reading/learning/teaching practices are not neutral practices that merely aim for more knowledge. Rather, they are always and already shaped by our desires, our identities, and our prior knowledges. Consequently, learning about how we are already implicated in the knowledge we produce and reproduce involves reflecting on the reading/learning/teaching practices themselves. Antioppressive reading/learning/teaching practices do not aim merely to change the ways we read others. They also aim to change the ways we read ourselves. They aim to queer our very senses of self.

Third Route: Rereading Intersections in Matthew's Stories

As I turn to Matthew's stories, I am reminded that our desires are heavily influenced by the cultures that surround us. In the fall of 1999, at the time that I was first analyzing these stories, commercials began airing for the first televised concert of pop singer Ricky Martin. Only a few months earlier had I even heard of Ricky Martin, when Christopher joked of his attraction to him in his first interview with me. Since then, Martin had appeared frequently in the media, and as rumors began spreading that he was queer, people began offering multiple readings of his sexuality and of his ethnic background. On mainstream radio stations, I heard commercials that praised Martin for desiring to bring visibility and pride to Latino/a and Puerto Rican music, culture, and identity. In the queer press, I saw articles and letters debating the virtues of Martin's public image. Some complained that Martin should come out, if he is queer, because he can drastically change the perception that no Latino/as are queer. But some praised Martin for desiring to keep his private life private and for not discussing his sexuality, or at least, for discussing only his heterosexual relationships, since being out as queer could ruin a career built largely on sex appeal to a female audience. I had conversations with a friend who worked in Hollywood whose "connections" confirmed that Martin is queer. I had conversations with straight as well as queer friends who thought that such rumors were simply wishful thinking by queer men.

I then remembered Michael's discussion of stereotypes that queer identities are a White thing. I remembered Pab's discussion of forms of antiracist activism that require identifying with a homophobic culture and, therefore, make it difficult to affirm queer identities. I remembered Christopher's discussion of communities of color that do not often believe they are homophobic when they really are. And I started to realize that separating a Latino identity from queerness is not simply a choice that Martin makes on his own. In contemporary U.S. society, making visible and affirming both identities is often quite difficult. In fact, building Latino/a pride often requires that Martin not come out, that he not disrupt assumptions that he is heterosexual. This is because common understandings of "traditional" Latino/a culture and identity often cite homophobic discourses.

Rafael Campo's (1999) research is illustrative. He attributes the slow response of Latino/a communities to the rapid spread of AIDS among Latinos/as to "the vicious homophobia of a machista Latino culture that especially fears and hates gay people whom it believes 'deserve' AIDS" (p. 20). He notes that

> AIDS has long been considered a disease exclusively of homosexuals—
> especially in Spanish-speaking communities, where not only is HIV
> strongly associated with gayness, it is further stigmatized as having been
> imported from the decadent white world. Since we cannot speak calmly
> and rationally of homosexuality, we certainly cannot bring up AIDS, per-
> haps the only affliction that could be worse. (p. 22)

In other words, in Spanish-speaking communities, AIDS and queerness are associated with Whiteness and the "decadent White world." This is not unlike my earlier analyses in which queer sexualities are called a "White disease" or "a White thing." AIDS is characterized by a racialized heterosexism. But the AIDS epidemic is also linked to the centrality of Catholicism in Latino/a communities. As Campo notes,

> Hand in hand with both sexism and homophobia goes Catholicism.
> Latinos are overwhelmingly Catholic, and the Catholic hierarchy
> remains overwhelmingly not only anti-gay, but also opposed to the use of
> condoms as a means to prevent HIV transmission. . . . While on the one
> hand preaching about the sanctity of life, our religious leaders have
> abetted the deaths of countless Latinos by refusing to endorse the use of
> condoms as a means to prevent AIDS transmission. (p. 22)

The strong connection between being Latino/a and being Catholic gives many Latinos even more reason to distance themselves from AIDS-related issues. Not surprisingly, "Latinos are dying at an alarming rate from AIDS":

> In the U.S., Latinos accounted for one-fifth of all AIDS cases reported
> to the Centers for Disease Control last year, while making up only one-
> tenth of the U.S. population; AIDS has been the leading cause of death
> since 1991 for young Latino men in this country; in areas with especially
> high numbers of Latinos . . . AIDS deaths among Latina women were
> four times the national average since 1995. While the infection rate
> among whites continues to decline, today, and every day, 100 people
> of color are newly diagnosed with HIV infection. Behold our isolated
> and desperate substance users, the most marginalized of the marginal-
> ized, our forsaken impoverished, and our irreplaceable youth people.
> (p. 20)

Unfortunately, although faced with this crisis, "few Latinos dare even to mention the epidemic" since AIDS is not a "Latino/a issue" (p. 20).

Similar arguments are made in Matthew's stories. Matthew, who is in his early thirties, identifies as a gay Puerto Rican man; he concentrates his activist efforts on queer youth, community AIDS education, and homophobia within Latino/a (what he calls Hispanic) communities. Drawing on his own experiences growing up, he spent much time discussing how queerness is marginalized in Hispanic communities because of its associations with race, gender, and religion. I found his stories to be complex and troubling:

> My main focus is LGBT youth
> that's what I want to really concentrate on.
> Another concern is combating homophobia and

ignorance regarding HIV and AIDS in Hispanic communities
which is two areas that really need a lot of work.

Oh
Homophobia is much more intense
is so much greater in the Hispanic community
[than in mainstream society].
I think it's cultural
I think it's part of the Hispanic culture
and I think it's true in most minority communities.
And then with HIV/AIDS
for whatever reasons
HIV/AIDS disproportionately affects Hispanic community.
About 12 percent of the population is Hispanic but
approximately 19 percent of the cases of AIDS is Hispanic.

I think that, um,
there are cultural traditions
like toward the man being the head of the household
strong male head of the household
very sexist
very dominating
I mean all those images
you know the traditions of
the family
getting married
having children
you know that's very heterosexist
and very much entrenched in the Hispanic community.
Also the strong influence of Roman Catholicism in Hispanic community
has a lot to do with homophobia:
"It's against God
it's unnatural
it's abominable
it's perverse
it goes against nature
if you are, then you must be possessed,"

you know, "You're sick
you're confused
someone who's sexually promiscuous
someone who's not a moral person
someone that molests children."

There are many things about my culture that I really love,
like the sense of community
I think is one of the things that I really miss
living in American society.
I mean if it weren't for the fact that my culture is really homophobic
I'd go back to Puerto Rico in a second
because I really love that sense of community
that really getting to know your neighbor
your neighbor becomes like a family.
Everyone you know gets to know one another.
I mean here you can go your whole life and
not know who your neighbor is,
you know?
And that really hurts me,
it bothers me.
And yet
how can I partake of that sense of community,
how can I partake of that community when they reject me
when they repress me?

Now,
for me the more important work is the antihomophobic work
because that's what has cost me the most.
I haven't suffered so much in my life because of racism.
And I think that in part has to do with, you know,
the color of my skin.
Even though I'm Hispanic
I appear to be White.
And even though I never hide the fact that I'm Puerto Rican
even when that comes out
there are some people for which it's okay to be Puerto Rican

because I'm White
but if I were Puerto Rican and Black
or Puerto Rican and another shade between
then it would make a difference to them.
Unfortunately.
And even within minority communities
there is discrimination based on the shade of your skin.

I guess for me
I've suffered more because I'm a gay man than
because I'm Hispanic
because as a Hispanic man I had at least a community and support.
You know, I had my family
and that was critical,
both my immediate family and the rest of my family.
I had a cultural identity
I had people from whom I could learn what is it to be Hispanic
and yet as a gay man I didn't have anyone that could fill that role
until I came to [this town].

The degree of oppression I feel
depends on the extent of support or lack of it that I feel.
With racism
if you have the support of your family
and you have the support of your ethnic group,
I mean most people,
I'm a little bit uncharacteristic in that we moved around a lot
so we never really lived in a Hispanic community
at least not in the later years.
Without that community
you don't feel that sense of strength and support.
If you're growing up as an LGBT person
you don't live in an LGBT family
you don't, you don't live in an LGBT community,
that's not something that you enter until later in life.
So I think that's a big difference
that from a very early age

you can have the support of your family and community
if you experience [racism],
and that can help you overcome.
But from a very early age
if you recognize that you're in a minority
with respect to sexual orientation
you don't have any support there
and that's why it's so difficult.
The reason it's taken me so long to come out,
that's where my ethnic identity has such a big role to play
because of the discrimination I felt within my own family
my own community.
That's why I haven't come out so long, in part.

And so I want to work toward helping to
change that community
so that um, I can then rejoin it
and make it better.

Our multiple identities can lead to contradictory relationships with our own communities. Among Hispanics, it seems that Matthew's racial identity promotes feelings of belonging, while his sexual identity prompts experiences of exclusion. This exclusion results, in large part, from the heterosexism and homophobia of Roman Catholicism, which has become central to Hispanic culture ("the strong influence of Roman Catholicism . . . has a lot to do with homophobia"). In other words, "traditional" Hispanic culture and identity cite homophobic discourses by citing Roman Catholicism. Being an "authentic" Hispanic requires being Catholic, which requires being heterosexual. Of course, Roman Catholicism is not the only reason that heterosexism and homophobia exist in many Hispanic communities, but it does play a central role in Matthew's stories.

Matthew's stories are somewhat similar to Michael's stories. In both Asian American and Hispanic communities, heterosexism and homophobia result in part from the longing for a "traditional" culture that values (heterosexual) marriage, family, and procreation. However, their stories differ in the particular ways that queer sexualities are marginalized. While Asian American communities denigrate queer sexualities as a "White disease,"

Hispanic communities denigrate queer sexualities as religiously immoral. Heterosexism can take on many forms: racialized in one context, Catholicized in another.

This should not imply that the Catholicized heterosexism that Matthew has experienced in Hispanic communities is not also racialized. Catholicized heterosexism is racialized, but in a significantly differently way. In Asian American communities, different sexual identities are often associated with different racial identities, insofar as Asians are "supposed" to be straight and queers are "supposed" to be White. A similar racialization of sexual identities does not occur in Hispanic communities. Being queer is not exclusively or even predominantly a "White thing." In fact, when asked about how Hispanics generally talked about queers, Matthew said they usually referred to queers who were Hispanic, not White. Both Hispanics and Whites can be queer, and both can be straight.

What are racialized are not sexual identities, but sexualities, and in particular, different heterosexualities. According to Matthew, the institution of heterosexual marriage and even the ceremony of the heterosexual wedding valued by Hispanics derive from traditions of the Roman Catholic church in modern Europe (and not, say, from traditions specific to or originating in Puerto Rico). In contrast, as Matthew later told me, stereotypes of Hispanics held by the White American mainstream are of "promiscuous" heterosexual beings that procreate "like rabbits." It may be true, then, that heterosexuality is central to the Hispanic identity, but it is a *White* heterosexuality that is being privileged. Not all heterosexualities rank equally. Mainstream White heterosexuality is often considered the ideal, the standard against which, for instance, wedding ceremonies are imagined and practiced.

This racialization of heterosexualities is perhaps not surprising. When Hispanic communities privilege Roman Catholicism, they are simultaneously privileging a history, leadership, and set of doctrines and traditions that are Eurocentric. In fact, unlike Asian American communities that engage in Othering Whiteness (which is the opposite of what often happens in mainstream society), Hispanic communities are merely maintaining what is already privileged in mainstream society, namely, Whiteness and a White heterosexuality. Couched in the language of common sense, "Catholic tradition," and "traditional Hispanic culture," this racialization is insidious, difficult to challenge because it remains invisible.

In contrast are Hispanic heterosexualities that can only be *deviant* heterosexualities. This queering of Hispanic heterosexualities is not unlike the queering of early Chinese American heterosexualities. Jennifer Ting (1995) argues that the image that they all lived in "bachelor societies," common in written histories of early Chinese American communities, "insists on both the absence of Chinese women in the U.S. and the exclusive heterosexuality of Chinese immigrant men" (p. 277). According to this bachelor-society trope, Chinese immigrant men were heterosexual, but theirs was a "deviant heterosexuality," a heterosexuality characterized by a homosocial living arrangement and by sexual activity with female prostitutes. Only through assimilation—that is, only with the creation of Chinese American communities that resembled mainstream White America's family-centered communities—did Chinese American men come to be seen as having "overcome" deviant heterosexuality and achieve some normalcy. So, too, with Chinese-American women, since only with the immigration of wives did Chinese women in North America start to engage in "normal" (conjugal and procreative) sex instead of abnormal, prostitutional sex. Like Matthew's stories, Ting's research reveals that a White heterosexuality is often the norm that other heterosexualities are compared to, contrasted with, and/or modeled after.

The notion that Hispanic communities often privilege Whiteness is also reflected in Matthew's own experiences (or lack thereof) with discrimination. Early on, Matthew learned that mainstream society accepts him as Hispanic so long as he looks White: "the color of [his] skin" appears "to be White," and his ability to "pass" as a White American helps explain why he rarely experienced overt acts of racism while growing up in the United States. However, Matthew also came to learn that even Hispanics discriminate against people on the basis of skin color. Looking White has its advantages: "even within minority communities, there is discrimination based on the shade of your skin." Matthew's experiences suggest that what it means to look and be Hispanic does not directly trouble White privilege.

The same holds true of male privilege. According to Matthew, Hispanic communities often adopt from the Catholic Church and mainstream society sexist views of the roles of men and women in the household. He tells us that "there are cultural traditions, like toward the man being the . . . strong male head of the household," that are "very sexist, very dominating." Being Hispanic requires filling one's "proper" role in the family. Such notions of "family" and "proper" roles do not trouble patriarchy and gender oppression, and reveal how efforts to challenge oppression on the basis of, say, race cannot be separated from efforts to challenge oppression on the basis of gender and other social markers. Of course, Matthew's descriptions do not likely reflect all Hispanic, Latino/a, and Puerto Rican communities in the United States, but they do signal ways in which multiple identities and cultures can intersect in oppressive and insidious ways.

As I reflect on my reading of Matthew's stories, I realize that the notion of *citation* was indeed helpful in revealing some complexities that arise at the intersections of various identities, communities, and oppressions. I was able to see, for example, that "Hispanic" often cites "Catholicism," "White heterosexuality," and "patriarchal family," and that these restrictive associations are what Matthew's activism aims to change. I was also able to see that "Hispanic" often cites things that Matthew desires, such as a strong sense of community, and that these favorable associations are what motivate Matthew to work toward "helping" that community. Matthew seems to work to change oppressive citations within his Hispanic community so that he can then rejoin it. In a similar way, antioppressive educators can use the notion of *citation* to examine the intersections and interrelations of multiple forms of oppression and the situated nature of oppression, as well as to explore the changes made possible when laboring to alter oppressive citational processes. In chapter 4, I will discuss in more detail what this can look like. My point here is that poststructuralist frameworks for reading/teaching/learning do make possible insights and changes not commonly explored in educational research and practice.

Fourth Route: Reading beyond Beth's Stories

Common to my discussions of Pab's, Christopher's, and Matthew's stories is the notion that antioppressive routes of reading involve attending to what is read as well as how it is read. As I argued in chapter 2, *looking beyond* the stories we read involves reading paradoxically: learning from the stories, while troubling the very knowledge we produce and reproduce; affirming our differences, while troubling the very identities and cultures that offer affirmation; imagining new forms of activism, while troubling the ways that any practice is always and already partial. By putting our routes of reading themselves under analysis, we foreground the desires, resistances, and senses of self that otherwise could hinder our own abilities to identify, act, relate, and change in antioppressive ways. As I turn to Beth's stories, I explore in more detail a route of reading that aims less to understand difference, and more to change ourselves and our senses of normalcy. I try to look beyond her stories to see what antioppressive changes are made possible in me. In our interview, Beth asked that I not say much about her to start off. She wanted the reader to be introduced to her through her own words:

> My father's very old-fashioned.
> We were in Taiwan and he was watching this
> Chinese soap opera set in the dynasties,
> the kings, the knights and horses,
> where the father's the absolute ruler of the household,
> his wife cannot leave the house without his permission
> and he chooses who his children marry,
> you know?
> Anyway, I was like,
> "Gee, how can you watch that?"
> because the women were objectified and the children were objectified
> and it was just very patriarchal and monarchal.
> And you know what he said?
> Well, this was not very long before he said that I was mentally ill.
> He was like,
> "Well, this is the way things should be."
>
> I can't believe how naive I was.
> There were signs all through my life that something was wrong
> starting from first grade
> when I chose to play with the other girls on the playground because I
> preferred their style of interaction.
> I could see no point to the boys' needless and endless
> aggression and competition.
> After Chinese school, all the kids would go to the gym
> because there was nowhere else to go, nothing else to do.
> It was very male-oriented.
> Actually, the only thing you could do there was play basketball.

My sister and friends would just sit on the basketballs
and play house.
I usually played the role of mother
I didn't enjoy it so much when I had to play father.

My parents were always yelling at me about playing with girls
and talking on the phone so much.
They tried to get me to play rough-and-tumble sports with boys,
but fortunately they drew the line at football.
But it's so silly, really.
My mom kept asking,
"Why can't you learn to skateboard like our neighbor's boy?
Look at him!
He's so strong and he has wide shoulders."
Not only that
she wanted to buy me a brand new skateboard if only I would use it.
And of course
the neighbor's boy's mom was really surprised.
She was trying to get him to stop skateboarding
because it was so dangerous.

My father didn't let me play the piano when I was little because
he said it was a "girl's" instrument.
I had to wait until my younger sister was old enough to start
piano lessons
before he finally
let my mom even buy a piano.
RRRRRRRR!
That bastard wasted four years of my life when I could have
learned so much.
And even after I started he would never stop
trying to get me to quit.
He argued with my mom about what a waste of money my lessons were.
Of course the issue of my sister's lessons and money never came up.
And he would say things to me like,
"Well, you can either grow up to be a man
or you can grow up to be a woman

it's up to you"
in an effort to shame me into quitting
but for some strange reason it never bothered me
I just shrugged and kept playing.

I think it could have been different if I were a girl.
Could have?
Of course it would be different!
If I were a "real" girl
I would have been accepted by the girls with no problems
my parents and lunch monitors would not have asked why I never
played with the other boys
my classmates would not have called me "gay-wad."
Can you believe that?
Coming from elementary school students!
I'm glad I never knew what it really meant.

I suffered a lot of physical abuse from my father too.
He was upset because I hung out with girls
and I hung out with [White] Americans.
He started out spanking me
and when spanking didn't work
I mean, it didn't mold me into what he wanted me to be
then he started hitting me on the head with knuckles
and then that didn't work either
so after a while
he started shoving my head into ninety-degree corners of walls
and then several times he tried to push me down stairs.
He'd just get so mad
and I never understood why until one day he actually said something
other than just being angry
and what he said was,
"What's the matter with you, are you gay or something?"

[*sigh*]
You know, in first grade
I wanted to be a girl.

I was really ignorant.
I never even heard of the words transsexual or transvestite
let alone know what they mean.
Now that I'm older
I would never say that I want to be a woman.
There are certainly a lot of annoying things that women have to put up with:
not being taken seriously at the hardware store
being hit on
being fearful when walking alone at night
having to wear those horribly uncomfortable bras every day
and not being able to go topless when it's really hot.
I haven't experienced a lower salary yet but I'm sure I will soon.
But my sadness isn't so much that I have to be a woman
I just wish I didn't have to go through all this
I missed growing up as a girl and having a
best friend during my childhood.

When my sister came of age
she would go to the library and borrow some
really good books.
Some of them were about teenage girls and going through puberty
and others were just "regular" books.
Oh, I loved to read *Nancy Drew*!
I liked to read all the books she borrowed
it didn't bother me that I found her books interesting
it wasn't for sexual gratification or anything
I was just curious about what adolescent girls have to go through
and I wanted to see the world from their perspective
I didn't mind putting myself in their shoes.

My mom kept a lot of blouses in my closet along with my dress shirts.
I had a dream once that my sister and friends—
all girls, of course—
and I were standing around in my closet
and trying on clothes.
I remember that I was wearing women's underwear
and when I took a peek inside

I had a vulva!
But when I saw it
I didn't feel upset.
Instead I was delighted.
What a pleasant surprise!
I was happy to be a "real" girl!
Unfortunately
it was only a dream
and I woke up feeling sad, wistful . . .
I always wished that dream would come back
but it never did.

Sometimes
when I was home alone
I would secretly dress up in my mom's clothes and
fantasize about being a woman.
This was possible because the high schools got out
earlier than the middle schools
where my sister went.

My high school was fairly peaceful and safe
compared to other high schools
but of course there's always a few troublemakers.
Once, a couple juniors got suspended for setting off a pipe bomb
in the boys' bathroom.
Someone was actually in there when it went off.
They said he was damned lucky he wasn't
using a urinal at the time
or he would never be able to be a father.
There was porcelain and pipes all over the place
that took months to repair.
I remember thinking at the time that I
don't think I would mind if I could
never be a father for that reason.
In any case, I was a bit jealous of the guy who was in there when it went off.
He missed his chance,
I thought.

And then
for my philosophy class in college
I was browsing through the textbook
and I came across this story,
it was really talking about how the seat of consciousness
your sense of identity
is in your brain.
The main character's body got destroyed by some accident
but his brain was intact
and it got transplanted into a woman's body.
Of course, as a man he was very upset about this
but when I read it
I felt very sad and wistful.
I remember thinking that if it happened to me
I would be actually quite happy
and then I started wishing that it would really be possible.

But I can't believe how naive I was!
After all this time and everything that happened to me
I still did not know that I was transsexual.
And then I read somewhere that some percentage of children
wish they were of the
other gender
and by the time they're adults, it becomes less
but there's still a small number who never outgrow that.
When I saw that
I felt a lot better.
Oh
it was so relieving to know that I wasn't alone
that a lot of people are like that.
Before
I felt very isolated and guilty and ashamed for having
those feelings
but now it gave my problems some legitimacy.

Later that year
I was in a friend's dorm room

and all of a sudden
there was a short item on the radio
that talked about how expensive sex-change operations were.
At this point, I suddenly noticed that
everywhere I went
I just seemed to be bombarded with stuff about
transsexualism.
But, naive as I was
after all this time
and all this stuff
I still didn't realize that I was transsexual.

It wasn't until later that it all of a sudden occurred to me.
And surprisingly
the trigger had nothing to do with gender.
I was reflecting on something someone said about being a banana.
A banana is someone who is yellow on the outside and White on the
inside—
in other words,
an Asian person who acts culturally
American,
like me.
I remembered one of my childhood friends talked about being a
Twinkie,
same thing.
And then I realized that my problem was that I was a
man on the outside and a woman on the inside.
There.
It just came to me like that
totally out of the blue
and finally I knew what I was.
My father was always saying,
"Well, you're not American, you're Chinese
whether you want to be or not."
And you know, it's not something you can really answer.
It's like
why do I believe that I'm a woman when

"obviously, I am not."

Explaining it this way, I didn't feel ashamed about myself at all.

I was confident enough to ask my best friend if I could

borrow her clothes for Halloween.

And I borrowed a purse from another friend

and a headband from a third friend

and a pair of girly glasses from a fourth friend.

Part of it was to keep everyone in the dark

but I also didn't want to push anyone too far.

I was very nervous about going to classes and the cafeteria

dressed like that

but my nervousness lasted all of about thirty minutes.

After that, I just felt very natural.

Everyone told me that I was a very pretty girl, even without make-up

and people remarked that they've never seen me

so happy before.

A few people who weren't my friends said

I was having just a wee bit too much fun.

Oh-oh!

They knew then and there that I was doing it for more than just

Halloween.

Anyway, I enjoyed it so much that Halloween was technically

over for a couple hours

before I got out of my costume.

I was very sad that it was over.

I knew for sure

then and there

that I was more than just a cross-dresser.

It didn't feel like acting.

It was real.

I felt no sign of the fatigue that comes with

having to play a role for any extended period of time

even if you are a good acting person.

I felt like I would be

happy being a girl for the rest of my life.

I never wanted to go back to being my old male self
ever again.
I loved how nice the long flowing skirt felt against my legs
especially when blowing in a soft breeze.
I loved the freedom of movement
and even the feeling of wearing almost nothing.
I loved how soft the blouse felt on my shoulders
and I loved how pretty they were.
I felt a huge
sense of loss
when I finally had to return them to my friends
and go back to wearing my drab old male clothes.

That was Halloween 1995,
my birthday
as a woman.
I know being a woman is so much more than just
having the right body
or wearing the right clothes
but I was so comfortable with my new role
I knew I could live full-time without getting tired of it.
It was not a costume
and it was not an act that I had to maintain.
It was me.
The real me.
For once in my life
I felt that my identity crisis was over
just gone without even a wisp of smoke.
I was free,
free at last!
And I could never go back to that masquerade as a man
that prison.
All my life
I lived a lie
and now that I know the truth
no one can stop me from living my life
or just being alive.

If I were to try to "understand" Beth, I would argue that she destabilizes and critiques identities, and does so in several ways. She critiques the normative nature of racial identities, especially Asian identities that reflect the "old-fashioned" Chinese culture "where the father's the absolute ruler of the household." Asian identities, she tells us, are often "patriarchal and monarchal," but do not need to be. She also critiques the normative nature of gender identities, arguing elsewhere in the interview,

> There are these attitudes that must go.
> No more segregation of boys and girls.
> I'll tell you a story about what I saw on the bus.
> These two adults had about seven or eight kids with them
> from a nursery school
> and they were on a bus
> and they had all the girls sit on one side
> and all the boys sit on the other side.
> And that really made me mad
> because you see, right there
> even from a very early age
> they're saying you have to be either one or the other.
> No more emphasizing people's gender, like,
> "Oh, be a good girl."
> Why not, "Be a good kid"?
> And above all, no more of the attitude that "boys will be boys"
> because these days
> boys are committing really bad things like harassment and even rape.
> School officials have to be educated, too,
> to make sure they don't pathologize gay students or trans students.
> If girls want to wear their hair short
> they should be able to.
> If boys want to wear their hair long
> that shouldn't be a problem.
> If girls want to wear pants
> they should not be forced to wear skirts or dresses.
> If a boy wants to wear a dress to the prom
> they should let him.
> And they should have unisex bathrooms.

> I think that separate girls and boys bathrooms just serves to
> put people into
> two kinds of boxes.

According to Beth, traditional gender roles are transphobic, just as they are homophobic (as, for instance, when her father would "just get so mad" and physically abuse her, fearing that she was "gay or something"). Although she was told that "real" boys "act like boys" and are not gay, she argues that such does not have to be the case.

Trying to "understand" Beth could also lead me to argue that she stabilizes identities and treats them as less fluid. In terms of race, she differentiates Asians from White Americans, especially in her discussion of the "banana" and "Twinkie," where an individual can be "yellow [Asian] on the outside" and "White [American] on the inside." In terms of gender, she differentiates females from males, desiring the clothing (and "how nice the long flowing skirt felt against my legs") and body (as when she dreamt of seeing that she "had a vulva") typically associated with females, while disliking the clothing (the "drab old male clothes") and behavior ("the boys' needless and endless aggression and competition") typically associated with males. In terms of sexual orientation, she differentiates lesbians from gay men, and identifies as a "lesbian," a woman who loves women.

Because she both destabilizes and stabilizes identities, I could conclude that Beth operates in contradictory ways. She critiques the male-female gender binary, says boys do not have to act "like boys" (or girls "like girls"), and claims an identity (of "transgender") outside of the male-female binary; but she longs to be a "woman," and from her earliest memories, knew that she liked doing "girls' things" (like playing the piano and dressing in her mother's clothes). She critiques Asian cultures for being sexist and heterosexist, and knows that there are other ways to *be Asian* (since the traditional way is "old-fashioned"); but she adheres to traditional understandings of what it means to be Asian and White when discussing the possibility of being Asian on the outside and White on the inside. She identifies as transgender, thus problematizing the terms *heterosexual, homosexual, bisexual, gay,* and *lesbian,* all of which rely on the existence of only two genders; but she also identifies as lesbian *and* as one of the two genders she transgresses.

Perhaps none of this should have been surprising since, as I argued in chapter 2, antioppressive activism and education are always and already paradoxical. Beth's experiences illustrate how antioppressive practices are never fully realized, are always in the making, and can never be panaceas. They can involve helping marginalized groups to assert their differences from the mainstream while creating margins within those very groups. They can involve embracing identities in some ways and rejecting them in other ways. Enacted differently in different situations, antioppressive practices require being constantly worked through and worked over. Their partiality cannot help but lead to contradictory results.

We do not often desire contradictory results. In fact, common sense tells us that practices are antioppressive if their results are only antioppressive, not both antioppressive and oppressive. Common sense requires that the contradictions be resolved. This was how I initially read Beth's stories. Assuming that the contradictions in her stories were "problems" with either Beth (as if she were confused) or the stories (as if insufficient data were collected), I found myself wanting more information from Beth so that I could re-present her stories in "fully" antioppressive ways. I desired to silence her contradictions.

However, as I struggled to map Beth's stories onto my idealized image of *the* antioppressive story, I came to realize that something was deeply troubling with my reading of Beth. Why was I insisting that something was "wrong" with Beth or Beth's stories? Why was I insisting that only *certain* stories can be antioppressive? Why was I desiring to read Beth's stories in only certain ways? As I reminded myself of the antioppressive insights made possible by the various ways I read Pab's, Christopher's, and Matthew's stories, I began to realize that the contradictions I saw in Beth's stories are not themselves the problems. The problems are the desires, resistances, and identities that prompted me to read Beth in only particular, and regulating, and commonsense ways. What this means is, the contradictions do not prevent Beth's stories from being antioppressive; rather, they are exactly what can help Beth's stories be antioppressive, depending on how we read them. The contradictions in Beth's stories can be the tools I use to examine the problematic nature of my own routes of reading.

Drawing on what I suggested earlier to be a practice of looking beyond the stories themselves, I argue that the object of investigation when reading cannot be merely Beth's life, or Beth's ideas, or even Beth's stories. It is important that the object of investigation also be the route of reading itself—

how I make sense of Beth's stories, how I desire only certain interpretations, and how I resist others. My goal when reading can be not only to read Beth differently, but also to read *myself* differently, to change myself. And what helps to put myself at the center of my reading are the contradictions I initially find troubling. By asking why I find these contradictions troubling, I am making possible the analysis and change of my own routes of reading, my own desires, my own resistances, my own sense of self.

To do so, I need to ask a wider range of questions when reading. I cannot limit my questions to an understanding of transgender Asian Americans, as in, "What do these stories tell us about transgender Asian Americans? Who are they? What characterizes their cultural values and practices?" I cannot limit my questions to an understanding of the oppressions experienced by transgender Asian Americans, as in, "Which stereotypes of transgender Asian Americans do these stories confirm? Which ones do they disconfirm? What voices are silenced, and how do those silences perpetuate certain dominant discourses of who transgender Asian Americans are and should be?" And I cannot limit my questions to feelings of personal relevancy, as in, "How am I like transgender Asian Americans, and unlike them?"

While such questions are important, can help me learn about ways that mainstream society commonly reads and misreads transgender Asian Americans, and can even help me develop a sense of empathy, also important are questions on the very ways that I read, respond to, question, and feel about these stories. I might ask, "What did I desire to see repeated in these stories?" As I argued in chapter 2, we commonly desire to read things that confirm or repeat our own identities, knowledges, and values. Consequently, we conclude that stories or authors are problematic when they fail to repeat such things, such as our assumptions about transgender Asian Americans. It is important, then, for me to reflect on what I wanted to see repeated, and why. Was I pleased that Beth discussed the patriarchal nature of "traditional" Chinese cultures because I wanted her story to reinforce my discussion of the problems of "tradition"? Was I displeased that Beth did not discuss her own identities as more fluid (rather than as fixed "lesbian," "woman," and "banana" identities) because I wanted her story to validate my struggle to view my own identities as shifting, situated, and multiple?

I might also ask, "Did I resist reading the stories in ways that did not allow me to see myself in Beth?" As I argued in chapter 2, we are often comforted when we can see the other as like us, and discomforted when forced to see the Other as different but still equal. At a number of times when reading Beth's stories, I told myself that Beth was not much different than I am: like Beth, I disliked the aggressiveness of boys' play, I sometimes felt excited touching clothes traditionally reserved for women, I even viewed myself as less masculine than my male peers. But at times, I also found myself struggling to find similarities with Beth: I never dreamed of having a vulva, I don't recall wishing I was a girl, and I do not identify as lesbian. In my attempt to relate to Beth, I did find parallel experiences: she wanted a vulva, I wanted a bigger body; she felt a girl was trapped in her male body, I felt something queer trapped in my straight-acting body; she identifies as a queer woman, I identify as a queer man. However, such comparisons do not invite me to see myself any differently than I did before. Such a reading only invites me to see Beth's race, gender, and sexuality in ways that parallel how I have always viewed race, gender, and sexuality. How would I read Beth's stories differently if I did not insist on finding comparisons with myself? Does Beth's transgenderism take on different meanings if I no longer say that she is not much different than I am? Does Beth's transgenderism trouble my male privilege? Does Beth's transgenderism help me to think of my maleness in ways I have yet to imagine?

Another question I might ask when reflecting on my route of reading is, "Did I enter any crises when confronting the contradictions in Beth's stories, and if so, how am I working through those crises?" As I argued in chapter 2, we do not often expect to enter crisis when reading/learning, and yet, we cannot help doing so if we learn and unlearn things that trouble our identities, knowledges, and everyday practices. Antioppressive readings require that we change, and require that we work to do so. As readers, we cannot be passive, we cannot be voyeuristic, and we cannot do only what feels comforting. As I discussed in the preceding paragraphs, my readings of Beth's stories certainly troubled my identities as male, as queer, as Asian American, as an activist, and as an educator. While it was possible for me to maintain a sense of stability and normalcy in these areas by insisting on only certain routes of reading, it was also possible for me to explore different ways of *being* male/queer/Asian American/activist/educator by taking different routes of reading (as modeled by the questions in the preceding two paragraphs). My point, here, is that confronting my desires, working against my resistances, and working through the resulting discomforting spaces of uncertainty and instability can help me work against the repetition of commonsense that often hinders antioppressive change.

The Possibilities of Different Routes

Throughout this chapter I have tried to argue that different routes of reading suggest different understandings of oppression and different approaches to challenging oppression. If I had privileged a different theoretical framework (one other than poststructuralism), I imagine that I would have taken different routes of reading that shed light on other understandings and approaches. My readings do not reveal all there is to know from these stories about oppression and change, and future research should explore new possibilities and differences.

Nonetheless, I believe poststructuralism is able to contribute much to our understanding of what it means to challenge multiple forms of oppression. In the next chapter, I build on the insights from this chapter and juxtapose them with four more sets of stories from these activists as I aim more explicitly to explore implications for educational practice. What could it mean to teach in ways that put to use these more complex understandings of oppression? And what could it mean to read/teach/learn in ways that put to use the discomforting notions of desire, resistance, uncertainty, and crisis in education?

SAM: The work I do with the gay community, it really keeps me going. I mean, if I didn't have that, I feel like my life would be kind of boring. It's like risk taking: it's somewhat defying what you're expected to do. And you know, as with anyone [who's] a White, middle-class woman, you certainly have that pretty much laid out. And I think that that's really stimulating. It's also just like something in me, you know, that sort of says, Well, this isn't right, or, I'm frustrated with this. And how can you just sit there and say, Oh well, what a shame.

KEVIN: Why are you an activist when many other educators are not?

SAM: I think a lot of educators are not risk takers. On the other hand, I work with some fabulous teachers, you know, just incredible teachers and I'm just amazed at the things they do and they come up with. But I mean there's still a lot of fear about opening up things. That's one thing we talk about in our presentations [to other educators]. A lot of teachers don't want to talk about these because they're not sure that they'll be able to deal with the discussions and the conversations the kids will start in on, and they're not going to be able to pull them back into what they think they should be doing. I think people—you know, that aren't activists?—I think it's like, you're sheltered, and you don't know what to do with it. It's also being a risk taker. Because you can have the information, you can read about it in any newspaper, any books, but then take the next step and say, I'm gonna speak out. I'm gonna dare to go to a group.

KEVIN: What are you open to when you're a risk taker?

SAM: Well, you're open to not following the rules and being told that because you're not following the norm and the rules, that you're a bad person, or you don't belong there. Or getting fired. I mean in the teaching world, it's like, Well, if I say the wrong thing then I lose my job. And so I think that's part of it.

KEVIN: So you fear some sort of consequence, whether it's being fired, or just being seen as—

SAM: —not approved of. Yeah. Or that you're somehow not going to be accepted. You know, by me saying I'm a lesbian, well, there are gonna be people on my faculty that are not going to like me, or want to be around. And that was kind of scary when it first happened, but then I looked around and I thought, Who cares? You know?

KEVIN: Can you say more about how risk taking relates to unknowability in teaching?

SAM: Taking risks as a teacher?

KEVIN: Taking risks as a teacher, but also the need to take risks in becoming an activist as well.

SAM: *MM-HMM.* Let's see. I think so much of education is predictable to kids. Especially if they've gone through the entire system. Because I get them at the end, you know, and everything has been pretty much expected since kindergarten. And, kids are so bored because of that. And I think throwing kids off guard is really important. And just as much as you're saying we categorize students in our predicting where they will go or how they will learn and what we're giving them, students do that with teachers, too. They meet you and they're like, Ohhh yeah. And I think, God, it's just like, Why? All right, so you're a math teacher. Well, does that preclude the fact that you could also have a lot of other interests that you could weave into your curriculum? I mean that's one thing I like to do. I teach a lot of boys. The majority of my students are boys. And in the beginning of the year we do this thing where they do these minilectures, and so I model it. I think, Okay, they've got me stereo-typed, I'm an older woman and a mom, and what am I going to talk about in my minilecture? Well, I do the sumo wrestling. And I've got pictures, I've got stuff I've brought back from Japan, and they are like this [*drops jaw*]. Because they have so many stereotypes about sumo wrestlers. And I went to, actually went to a sumo stable and met the young guys who are becoming the wrestlers who are their age, I mean they were sixteen, seventeen, eighteen years old. They study poetry, they are very learned, they are good scholars. And they're like, "They're fat." And I showed them what they eat, the kind of, you know, tofu and vegetables. And they were just like, "Oh my god." But the main thing is, I'm throwing them off balance. I'm saying, "I'm interested in sumo wrestling. It's one of my hobbies and an interest." And then they're just like, Okay, I'd better start paying attention because this woman is going somewhere with this. But how do we get our teachers to be versatile and multifaceted and to share that and to put that into their curriculum?

You know, kids will often tell me, "Oh god, the teacher I remember most was the one who made us get up and do aerobics in class." She's an aerobics teacher as well as a classroom teacher, and she made them, you know, when they were doing math they had to get up and do aerobics. And kids ten years later are talking about [her]. Because it was like, "She kept us off balance, she did something different." And I think that's one way, it's like taking a risk, going somewhere with it, having them do a project that's going to go out of their norm, like who they hang out with or who they talk to. Getting students to talk to other teachers on a personal level or just finding out about them. And being able to break out of that expected role model that they have. Okay, now, what are we talking about? I'm getting lost.

KEVIN: The relationship between risk taking and unknowability in teaching.

SAM: Oh, okay, yeah. Oh, oh, and another thing. Because I don't have a curriculum, because I teach this nebulous thing, because what I'm really doing is doing speech language, but I'm cloaking it in a course so the kids will get credit because that makes them, you know, show up, basically. So I have to constantly be pulling from different areas and thinking of stuff. So when I'm off on a tangent or I'm in a hurry to plan a lesson, I always do this thing, I say, What is this going to do for this kid in life? Where is this going in life? And if I can hook it up with something, then I go ahead with it. You know, is it going to be good for on-the-job skills, is it good for interpersonal skills, is it going to help them read or be sure to vote? You know, instead of just doing something totally pointless. It's the whole thing about integration and cross-curriculum, and I love that. I really wish, you know, I think this whole thing about standards is pulling us away from that. I want to go back to that because it's so, it makes so much sense. It's also like bringing up stuff, if you know something about a student, bringing it out in the open. Like one of my students has a kid. Why should she go all day with nobody ever mentioning that she has a kid? I mean that seems so odd to me. You know, why do we think that certain things are taboo in the classroom, and then we act like those don't exist outside of school? I think that's risk taking, and knowing that it's okay. Oh, oh, I know another thing. Being able to bring up weaknesses in your students, and be open about it. You have to be careful because you can hurt kids. But if you allow kids to make fun of themselves, then the class can start doing it, kind of? And then it's like a caring laughing. It's like in a family, we know everybody's weaknesses. I think that the kid who can say, "No way, I can't spell, I absolutely can't spell," you know, if you're able to throw a word up and say, "Can you believe he—this is great—look at how he spelled this, look at how creative this was, isn't this a riot?" And then everyone's splitting their sides. And able to laugh at our insecurities, our disabilities, the ways that we are weak. And with men, oh my God, this is just huge. Girls bring it up themselves: "I'm so stupid, I'm so ugly, I'm so fat," blah blah blah. They're immediately throwing out all their insecurities and weaknesses. With boys, you've got to keep that close to your chest, you can't let everyone see that.

KEVIN: Why do you think it's helpful to be open about your weaknesses?

SAM: Because then I think it helps other people to meet you, to interact with you. If you always keep to yourself, who's going to want to be close to you and ultimately help you through your journey in life? And I found that so frequently, too, with going and giving talks about being a lesbian. You look at this audience and you're like, "shit, I can't come out to all these people." And then afterwards people are coming to you, they want to be close to you, they want to talk to you, they want to be with you on your journey. People you never ever imagine. And why can't we do that in school? I mean look at Littleton, Colorado. Wasn't a lot of it all about being isolated and not being able to see who people really were? I often think, Okay, is this kid ever going to be able to be in a relationship and be loved by someone? If they don't have that, what else are they going to have? So if I can teach him to be able to listen to that. So I think those are all risk taking, because in teaching you're basically told, you know, just don't do all these things.

KEVIN: Do you think risk taking has something to do with overcoming a resistance to something? Like we were talking earlier about resistance. What is it that they're overcoming a resistance to?

SAM: Being hurt. Being left out, being isolated, being rejected. It's got to be rejection. I mean, everybody wants people to look up to them, and have some kind of personal power, and if you show people your weaknesses, it's scary.

CHAPTER 4

Addressing Resistance through Queer Activism

Throughout the preceding chapters, I have described how students and teachers often resist changing their knowledges, identities, and everyday practices. In this chapter, I focus on ways to address these resistances and barriers to antioppressive change. I turn once again to the stories of four queer activists—Sue, Debbie, Matthew, and Pab—and ask what insights on resistance are made possible when I take different routes in reading their stories. I will argue that each of their experiences with queer activism suggests a different route of reading, and in particular, a different way to address resistance: doing "homework"; inverting and exceeding binaries; juxtaposing different texts; and catalyzing for action and change. As I describe these practices, I will also model them: I will use them to reread the activists' stories. As in chapter 3, I will focus my analysis on not only what I read, but also how I read. I am interested in exploring how different routes of reading can help readers/researchers/educators/students to address our resistances to antioppressive change.

First Route: Doing Homework
when Rereading Sue's Stories

Sue does not identify as sexually queer. Nonetheless, as the mother of a middle-aged White American gay man, she has been involved in fighting for civil rights for queers for many years. She has directed her local chapter of PFLAG (Parents, Families, and Friends of Lesbians and Gays), and recently earned a recognition award from the local queer community center. Although now retired from a long career as an academic advisor to university students, Sue continues to work in the field of education as a member of the local school district's board. She often links her activism with her work in education, such as by advocating for safer schools for queer youth. Sue's life is filled with activity and activism, which is perhaps not surprising given her decades of involvement in social justice movements within her Quaker religious community. According to Sue, Quakers have historically engaged in antioppressive activism, from supporting Japanese Americans during their internment in the 1940s to protesting U.S. involvement in the Vietnam War in the 1960s to creating inclusive policies and practices for queers within Quaker communities in recent years. Coincidentally, her involvement in Quaker movements is not unlike her involvement in anti-homophobia movements: both often result in being called a "queer" activist. As she will explain, Sue has long been used to being a "queer Quaker."

The notion that her Christian religion often takes a lead in social justice movements, including queer-rights movements, inspired me to learn more about ongoing debates on homophobia in the Judeo-Christian Bible. I was curious to see how differently people were reading the Bible, and how these different readings resulted in attitudes toward and interactions with queers. Soon after I interviewed Sue I perused a local bookstore and found a book by Daniel Helminiak (1994) titled, *What the Bible Really Says about Homosexuality*, that delineates two primary ways in which to interpret the Bible. One is through a "literal reading" of the Bible. This popular, commonsense approach is often used by Christian fundamentalists who argue that they are understanding the Bible exactly as it is written. They assume that the words in the Bible have always carried the meanings and assumptions and implications and values that they currently carry in U.S. society, and they interpret passages in the Bible accordingly. They conclude, for example, that the Bible condemns same-sex sexual relationships because certain biblical passages use words (in translation) like *abomination* to describe them.

In contrast is a second way to interpret the Bible, what Helminiak calls a "historical-critical reading." Drawing on works by such biblical scholars as John Boswell (1980), Louis Countryman (1988), and Robin Scroggs (1983), this reading acknowledges that the meanings, assumptions, implications, and values of words change over time and vary from one social situation to the next. Understanding the Bible requires researching what the words, phrases, metaphors, and so on likely meant to the people who wrote it (and, for that matter, to the people who prepared the translations), and then specifying implications for us here and now. In other words, "to say what a biblical text teaches us today, you first have to understand the text in its original situation and then apply the meaning to the present situation" (Helminiak, 1994, p. 26). Doing so requires researching not only how words and phrases are translated from one language into another, but also how social identities and physical acts are attributed different meanings in different contexts. For example, as Michel Foucault (1978) tells us, people who engaged in same-sex sexual relationships did not start self-identifying as "homosexual" until the twentieth century; and as I noted in chapter 3, people of the same gender might regard holding hands as an act of friendship in one context and an act of romance in another. Words and actions do not carry the same meanings and social significance at all times and in all places and with all groups of people.

Helminiak illustrates these two routes of reading with the story of Sodom (Genesis, chapter 19). In this story, a man named Lot urges two angels, who appear as men, to spend the night in his house. The (male) citizens of Sodom demand that Lot give them his visitors so that, presumably, they may use them for sex. Lot refuses. The angels then urge Lot to leave Sodom since God will soon destroy it. A literal reading would conclude that "God condemned and punished the citizens of Sodom, the Sodomites, for homogenital [same-sex sexual] activity" (Helminiak, 1994, p. 36). However, an historical-critical reading would recognize that "a cardinal rule of Lot's society was to offer hospitality to travelers" (p. 39), and would also recognize that Lot's society condemned male-on-male rape as a form of sexual abuse. Therefore, the sin of Sodom was not homosexuality but abuse, offense against strangers, and inhospitality to the needy. Indeed, all later references in the Bible to the sin of Sodom refer to *inhospitality*, not homosexuality.

Helminiak makes it clear that the Bible (and any text, for that matter) can be read in multiple ways, and that each reading privileges and marginalizes different social identities and relationships. What is oppressive is not the Bible itself, but dominant readings of it; and what promises antioppressive change is not the silencing of a Bible that some insist justifies homophobia, but an exploration of alternative readings and their implications for antioppressive change. Sue has long read the Bible in antioppressive ways. In fact, in contrast to many fundamentalists, she believes that the Bible calls on her to challenge homophobia. Sue's engagement in a nontraditional route of reading seems to facilitate her engagement in antioppressive activism. As I now turn to re-present her stories, and as I remind myself of Helminiak's insights, I anticipate that there are multiple ways of reading Sue's stories, and that reading them through a nontraditional route can facilitate my own engagement in antioppressive activism. At first, however, I was unsure as to what these multiple routes of reading might be.

Really
if you look at my background
my childhood upbringing
it couldn't have been more mainstream.
I was about as mainstream an American as you could have found.
My family were just as ordinary as you could be
they were lower-middle-class working people
who never discussed a controversial issue
except to have an opinion, like, "Roosevelt was terrible."
[*laughter*]

And then in [college] I discovered a wider world.
[My husband] and I went to a Quaker meeting in college
we both liked it
and we joined the Quakers right after college.
The Quakers are a peace church.
One of the basic tenets of those religions is they do not believe in war
and, you know, they sort of take this seriously,
"Thou shalt not kill,"
and an army doesn't make any difference
and there must be a better way to solve problems than killing people.

So it's kind of simplistic but uh
makes sense to me.
So at any rate, that's always been controversial
and then of course we lived through the Vietnam War,
we were very very active as Quakers and as peaceniks and
as antiwar people.
And the interesting thing is,
the word queer Quaker goes back for centuries.
A queer Quaker means
"These, these Quakers are queer because they're oddballs,"
you know.
[*laughter*]
And so, that queer word has been around Quaker for a long time.

[My husband] and I were both very big antiwar activists
and you know when fair housing came along
we were out campaigning for fair housing
and we've always been on the forefront of social change.
But you know, homosexuality:
"You know, I'm not prejudiced, mind you,
but it's somebody else's problem,
it's not my problem,
and I've got bigger problems like the war and other things."

And then
our son graduated from college
and came out to us.

I was giving him a haircut.
Actually, let me backtrack a little bit because
when he was in college,
you can see, [my son] is tall and handsome and uh,
women were always crazy about him, you know?
And he said,
"Mom, I think I'll tell this woman I'm gay and get her off my back."
And I looked at him with horror and said,
"Well, you don't have to go that far."

Can you imagine?

This liberal, stupid mother!

And then, I was giving him a haircut

and I don't know what we were talking about but,

maybe it was [the movie] *Seven Brides for Seven Brothers*,

and he said, "Well, mom, it's the brothers that turn me on."

And I said, "Are you trying to tell me you're gay?"

And he said, "I've been trying to tell you for some time."

And fortunately for me, and I tell you

my whole life has been absolutely

a series of wonderful coincidences.

Before [my son] came out to me

I was serving on the American Friends Service Committee board.

The American Friends Service Committee is

the social action arm of the Quakers.

And fortunately

at a board meeting

the panel speaking to the board

on spirituality and gay and lesbianism or something,

there were two males and two females, self-identified as gay or lesbian,

and they were you know,

I looked up there and,

Gee, I didn't know he was gay, I didn't know she was a lesbian.

[*laughter*]

You know, these were what we call weighty friends.

Very important people.

This was around two months before my son came out to me.

So we exchanged big hugs.

And I had to do some homework.

I read everything.

I, I wanted to read everything I could.

I was hungry for filling in the gaps in my education.

And there was so, there was not nearly as much written then

as there is now.

This notion of heterosexism was something new to me.

And, it was an assumption I made that I had to challenge in myself.

The difficult points were the realization that

he'd been raised in a homophobic home, unintentionally.

That was a crisis, an eye-opener.

I mean we didn't think of ourselves as homophobic

but the fact that there was no mention of it

the fact that there were jokes about limp-wristed people.

I mean we could think back over the,

my husband's prep school roommate was, uh,

he didn't know it in prep school

but he was a piano teacher and he would make a joke about

how he came in to play the piano like this [puts limp wrists in front],

you know.

And and you know we'd play charades

and somebody would act out Gaylord Nelson,

and what, what do you act out to get "gay," you know?

You just, you don't realize all the funny little

uh

and it really hit us hard when [my other son] was getting married

and [my gay son] was [abroad] and he wrote home and said,

"Well, he probably won't want me to be in the wedding anyway."

Aaagh!

How could he think that, you know?

So, these are the moments that you think,

What did I do wrong?

I've raised a homophobic kid

I mean he obviously had a lot of self-imposed homophobia.

So, my grandchildren have always been raised with,

that's why the wedding [between my gay son and his partner]

was so beautiful,

all my grandkids were there.

One of them spoke.

I've always been an activist and been

a part of a minority opinion for so long

so that controversial issues are something I've always dealt with.

And as a queer Quaker

this business of being a peacenik in times of war
very controversial
and yet you have a strong feeling that you're on the side of right.
And I think maybe that was where I was coming from
with the gay lesbian issue, too,
that while it's controversial
I felt truth was on my side.
But don't we all?
[*laughter*]
I've always been a leader.
You know, it's an interesting phenomenon,
people say, "People do certain things for glory."
No, you do it because it needs to be done and nobody else is doing it
you know?
And it always amuses me when,
when especially women are pointed to as power figures
when many of them are just picking up the pieces
and trying to get something done.
And this is the kind of thing I think I do.

And you know
that's why I ran for the school board
because the woman I was running against was very homophobic.
Although she claimed not to be homophobic
her actions spoke much louder than her words.
I ran as an active member of PFLAG,
Parents, Families, and Friends of Lesbians and Gays,
and the first newspaper headline was,
"Gay Rights Advocate Runs for School Board."
So the fact that I won that election I think was a statement
and made me feel quite good about the election in general
although I was careful not to make that a single issue.
I'm not going to stay there forever
but in my three years that I'm there
I have an elaborate agenda.
The so-called safe schools is very easy to sell
but it certainly doesn't answer the problem of eliminating homophobia.

Well, if we take one step at a time
I suppose you have to start somewhere
so I think you can't argue against safe space.
So it may be a starting point.
If it's a stopping point then it's bad.
But it's a foot in the door.
Of course that's what [opponents are] arguing about,
getting that foot in the door:
"It's just the beginning, they have an agenda."
Total tolerance,
that's probably our agenda.
Actually, not tolerance, even.
Mainstream equality is what is our agenda.
Beyond tolerance.
Civil rights.
My bumper sticker says
"Gay Rights Are Civil Rights."

Another rewarding activity is sitting at the table, the PFLAG table
during farmers market on Saturday morning
and you know a lot of people pass by and give you thumbs up
and just say, "Glad you're here."
You know, there's a lot of undercurrent of support that you feel that is
there
both with gays and straights as they pass by.

But
I've seen the resistance.
Well, they're desiring happiness for their kids.
Or
they're desiring,
now actually I had a mother call this week
and I must say I was almost disgusted with her
because we were in such different planes.
She was lamenting the fact that her daughter would never get married
she would never have children
she would never have the fun of having a shower for her daughter,

for having a wedding for her daughter,

and this all struck me as,

Ah, come on.

All the things that *she* wanted.

She was also very unhappy that her daughter hadn't come out to her.

She came out to her husband first.

And she had been closer to her daughter,

she had been um, the strength of the family, blah blah blah.

And in talking to this woman I could see in a moment why her daughter

would never come out to her

because she's obviously so homophobic.

I am sending this woman my PFLAG stuff,

she's really a case.

And it's kind of a throw back to some earlier,

it seems like we're not getting that kind of extreme parent

as much as we did five years ago in PFLAG

so maybe there is progress

but then this sort of person comes up and you realize that

they're still there.

And you're of course worried about their [kids'] physical welfare

and all the rest.

I know that when I speak out

and I'm asked to speak a lot,

some of the gay community says,

"Why don't they ask us to speak?

Why are you speaking for us?"

It's a real legitimate question, you know?

And the fact that straights find it easier for straights

to listen to other straights rather than gays

is really too bad.

It's not a good thing.

But

I guess I thrive on trying to do something that other people won't do.

And I'm very much at home with the GLBT issue, and I can,

you know nobody can out me,

I am as out as you can get,

and I'm a religious person

and I command a fair amount of respect in political circles
and so I've got nothing to lose,
you know?
And therefore I just feel like that kind of person has to speak out.
It's fascinating because
you know, you keep coming out
you keep coming out
trying to mainstream the issue.
Not, not thinking that it's a good thing to mention homosexuality,
but to mainstream it.
That's my hobbyhorse.

You know, it's an interesting thing.
Once I was on a committee
and I said, "Gee, it's nice to be on a committee that's noncontroversial."
And guess what?
I was taking controversial stands on the committee.
[*laughter*]
Why? I don't know!
I'd like to be in the mainstream.
I really would.
I'd like to win a war once in a while.
It was wonderful when Tammy [Baldwin] was elected [to Congress]
and I became mainstream!
[*laughter*]
Now I have a congressperson,
that's mainstream.
See, we've never been part of the mainstream, in many ways,
and so we're kind of used to be being different.
Even just being a Quaker is different.
But uh, when you get ordinary people
who are not used to being different at all,
who really are part of the mainstream,
then they've got a lot more to cope with.

I certainly feel about myself that I'm an ordinary person
who, for a variety of reasons, has had a life
of being an activist,

and you sort of stumbled into it because I
stumbled into these controversial things by
becoming a Quaker, becoming a peacenik in time of war,
and then having a gay son
and therefore defending at first that gay son
and then getting, sliding into activism.
One of the things I say about PFLAG parents is that they're
very ordinary people.
They come from all walks of life.
But they desire to
not be different
and do all the things that everybody's doing.

You know, activism is kind of a creative thing.
And I think promoting creativity is probably a
first cousin to being an activist.
Because the status quo,
isn't the status quo the opposite of activism?
And being part of the status quo is to be uncreative.
Seems to me, that's a truism.

How might I read Sue's stories in antioppressive ways? My training in how
to "do" educational research suggests to me that one way to read Sue's stories is to try to understand her experiences and ideas, and then explore their
implications for antioppressive activism and education. In what follows, I
will do just that, and as I noted at the beginning of this chapter, I will focus
my analysis on implications for addressing resistance to antioppressive
change. However, like Helminiak, I am interested in exploring the insights
made possible by multiple routes of reading the same text, and therefore,
am also interested in rereading Sue's stories. I believe these stories suggest
a second route of reading, one that, perhaps not surprisingly, parallels the
antioppressive readings in chapter 3 that aim less for understanding and
more for personal change. After my traditional reading of Sue's stories, I
will explore this second, reflexive route.

A Traditional Reading

Sue's stories reveal several paradoxes of being and becoming "mainstream." Her childhood upbringing "couldn't have been more main-

stream," and she feels that she is like many PFLAG parents insofar as she is "very ordinary." Yet, she is not part of the mainstream and has not been for a while since she is a Quaker, a "peacenik," a social activist, and an "out" mother of a gay son. She is queer, as a queer Quaker and as a queer activist. Yet, she does not identify as queer in terms of her sexuality, and she feels like an outsider when speaking for and about queer communities. She works to ensure that queers have civil rights; she works to mainstream queer sexualities and make them a part of the norm; she would "like to be in the mainstream" and "win a war once in a while." Yet, she believes that being different, not being part of the mainstream, and not doing "all the things that everybody's doing" are what make it easier for an individual to be creative, to disrupt the status quo, and to be open to antioppressive change.

Many in society do not share Sue's paradoxical experiences and desires. According to Sue, many "are not used to being different" and "really are part of the mainstream," and they are often the ones who desire to not be different and who resist Sue's efforts to challenge the status quo. This contrast suggests to me that it is Sue's earlier and ongoing departure or difference from the mainstream that helps her to work against her resistance to antioppressive change. She may still, like many in society, desire a sense of normalcy and of being mainstream, and she likely continues to feel discomfort when she experiences otherwise. However, rather than resist the differences and changes signaled by these crises, Sue often proceeds to work through these crises in antioppressive ways. Her many prior experiences doing what is queer has helped her develop queer desires to change the mainstream (by making homosexuality a part of it, by "mainstreaming homosexuality"), or at least, to be different from it (and be creative). Sue's experiences of being different are a significant part of the process of her being and becoming an antioppressive activist.

This reading of Sue's stories does have important implications for educators. In particular, it suggests that addressing students' resistance to antioppressive change requires that students have prior and ongoing opportunities to experience difference, to be out of the mainstream. Such opportunities need to be part of a K–12 curriculum. However, I am well aware that there is much more that Sue's stories could teach me. In particular, I am aware that this reading does not help me to look significantly beyond the theories of antioppressive education that I developed in earlier chapters. And perhaps that is not surprising. I wanted to interview Sue because I knew that she and I engage in similar kinds of antioppressive work.

In our earlier conversations, we agreed with each other about many aspects of political activism. During the interviews, I prioritized and worded and asked the questions that framed the conversation. Afterward, I pieced together the poem to make the points that I wanted to make about what Sue could teach us about antioppressive work: I selected the quotations, I organized the stanzas, I prefaced them with theory, and I followed them with my analysis. In these ways, my traditional reading could not help but be influenced by and reflect my theoretical framework. I could go on to argue that Sue's stories help us to think differently about theory when we look at how they illustrate theory in real life or how they disconfirm theory. Indeed, they do suggest that future research needs to explore further the notion of "experiencing difference," and what it means for curriculums to provide such opportunities, as ways to address resistance to antioppressive change. Nonetheless, this reading does not necessarily force me to look significantly beyond the ways I currently think about antioppressive activism and education.

A Reflexive Reading

As I reread Sue's stories, I am struck by her admission that she had much "homework" to do after her son came out to her. This homework entailed wanting "to read everything [she] could." She tells us that "there was not nearly as much written then as there is now" (this was about fifteen years ago). I presume that much of what was available was about queers, their histories, their identities, their communities, and their experiences with heterosexism and homophobia. However, in her stories, Sue did not discuss a desire to learn *about* queers. Nor did she talk much about what she actually read about them. Rather, she talked about how her readings caused her to turn inward, to critique the heterosexist "assumptions" that she had to "challenge in [her]self." She recalls reflecting on ways that she allowed homophobia to play out in her household and in interactions within her family, such as through silences, jokes, and charades. She recalls taking the initiative to change the dynamics in her household, such as by working to ensure that wedding ceremonies include queer people, and that her grand-children see themselves growing up in families that embrace sexual differences. And she recalls working to change her role in the community by becoming an activist for queer civil rights and by finding an alliance between her "queer Quaker" identity and LGBT queers. She admits that these processes were "difficult" and that she experienced crisis, such as with "the realization that [her son] had been raised in a homophobic home, unintentionally" and that he "had a lot of self-imposed homophobia." However, she took it upon herself to work through that crisis and address these problems. For Sue, doing homework (in the form of reading, and then self-reflecting, and then changing her identities and practices) and desiring to do this kind of homework exposed her to knowledges that gradually helped her change her relations with others (by "defending at first that gay son, and then . . . sliding into activism"). Doing homework was a way to work against her resistance to antioppressive change.

As I read Sue's stories, I find myself wondering whether I too should be doing homework, since my "traditional" reading does not require much homework. It is true that a traditional reading of Sue's stories can help me learn things I did not necessarily know about, say, members of PFLAG: they are "ordinary" people like Sue; they sit out every Saturday morning at the farmer's market and are told by passers-by that they are "glad you're there"; and they have been dealing with fewer rabidly homophobic and "extreme" parents over the past five years. However, such a reading does not necessarily address my desires and resistances. Are there ways to read her stories that get me to do the kinds of homework Sue had to do?

Sue's homework involved rereading herself by examining her *investment* in privilege, including her desire to be mainstream. My homework could similarly involve examining my own investments, including my investment in getting more people to engage in the forms of antioppressive activism and education discussed in this book. I might ask, How does this investment work against the very goals of this book? As I argued in earlier chapters, any knowledge, practice, and/or identity is defined in opposition to others: privileging one thing requires marginalizing others. Did I read Sue's stories in a way that privileged only certain models of *"ally," "activist,"* and so forth and refused to bring others out of the shadow? What forms of antioppressive activism are my forms defined in opposition to? Did my categorization and critique of various approaches in chapter 2, along with an emphasis on poststructuralism, function to dismiss certain approaches as ineffective or invalid? Are there other forms of antioppressive activism yet to be explored in educational research that needed to be silenced for mine to be validated? As I reread Sue's stories, my homework could involve looking beyond my own analysis to see what practices of and insights on activism in Sue's stories I am silencing. My homework could involve troubling my very notion of antioppression education.

Sue's homework also involved rereading herself by examining her often unintentional complicity with different forms of oppression, as was the case when playing charades. My homework could similarly involve examining my complicities, especially my complicities with oppressions that do not often target me, including sexism against women, anti-Semitism, child labor in Asia, and ethnic genocide in Europe. I might ask, How do my silences function to perpetuate the oppressions of already marginalized groups, or even create variations of oppressions within what I am calling "antioppressive" approaches to education? As I argued earlier, oppression is often multiple and intersected, and even activist attempts to address one form can comply with others. Did I read Sue's stories in ways that merely repeated the stereotypes I have in my head about parents, about straight people, about older White women, or about Quakers? Through its silences, did my readings of Sue's stories cite forms of oppression already existing in mainstream society, and perhaps give it new associations? How might I read Sue's stories in ways that foreground these complicities? As I reread Sue's stories, my homework could involve illuminating the margins I have unintentionally created in my theories of antioppressive education. I could work against ways that such margins are always being created.

Sue's homework also involved rereading herself by examining approaches to bringing about change that she had not previously known or used or desired to know or use, including changes in wedding celebrations and community activism. My homework could similarly involve examining new possibilities, especially forms of activism that Sue employs but that I do not or have not as of yet. I might ask, How does Sue's activism help me think differently about my own? Sue works in the community with everyday people. She is involved in local government, including a board that wields much control over local schools. She works with national religious groups. Although her poem does not reveal this, she works with organizations internationally. She even speaks to and through the local media. These are things I do not do, which is not to say that I should do exactly what Sue does, but these things do raise questions about my own work. For example, Sue's work with PFLAG targets families—especially parents—but in my own work, I have thought little about the role of the family in antioppressive education. Why is this the case? How might my theories and practices be different if I were a parent? Or a member of a Christian religious organization? Or a politician? What different insights, practices, relations, and changes are made possible and impossible?

By focusing on the notion of "homework," my reflexive reading of Sue's stories helps me to look beyond the ways that I currently think about, identify with, and practice antioppressive activism. As I extend this analysis to classroom practice, what becomes apparent to me is that school curricula and pedagogies need spaces for students and teachers to do this kind of self-reflexive homework. In other words, it is important that students and teachers have significant opportunities to reflect on their reading practices as they work to critique and transform their own investments and complicities and imagine new possibilities for bringing about antioppressive change. This applies to all grade levels and subject matters—learning new knowledge should not be separated from critically reflecting on the very ways we come to know. I imagine that many in schools and society will resist the centering of this type of "homework" since it requires that we exceed what we know, want, and do, and that we invite uncertainty, instability, and discomfort. Yet, as my reading of Sue's stories suggests, this type of homework can help us to look beyond the status quo, develop our creativity, and be more open to changing who we are and how things ought to be. Antioppressive education must involve doing this kind of homework.

Of course, different students, teachers, and contexts require different kinds of homework; there is no one best form. In each new situation, educators have their own work to do as they plan lessons that invite each student to do the kind of homework that will benefit that student in that moment. We all are constantly called on to do new kinds of homework.

I should note that "doing homework" is just one of many possible antioppressive readings of Sue's stories. I hope that I have shown the usefulness of this one route of reading, and I hope readers will feel invited to explore yet other routes and insights suggested by Sue.

Second Route: Inverting and Exceeding Binaries in Debbie's Stories

As I turn to the stories of Debbie, I again find it useful to do a reflexive reading. But what gets turned back onto itself is not the need to do homework. Debbie's stories suggest something quite different.

Debbie has been involved in activism for decades. Now in her forties and a parent of several grown children, Debbie identifies as a White American transsexual woman who is relatively new to making the transition from male to female. Over the past few years, she has assumed more and more leadership responsibilities in transgender activist movements. I was excited that Debbie agreed to be interviewed because of her insights on the complex intersections of gender- and sexuality-based oppression. The timing of the interview was significant for me because I had become fixated on such intersections, especially for boys. For months, I had seen the news media become inundated with analyses and remembrances of schoolyard shootings, such as those in Colorado, Kentucky, and Arkansas where young boys shot and killed students and teachers.

Three reports were especially troubling to me. One was a report on the television news program *20/20* that claimed that the number of schoolyard killings has actually declined in recent years while the number of news reports of such incidents has skyrocketed. I found myself wondering if this was because both the victims and the perpetrators of the newsworthy acts of violence were people who "counted" more in U.S. society—White, American middle-class suburban families.

Another report suggests that the answer is yes. This second report, from a queer news magazine, described and analyzed school-ground shootings and violence that had received less publicity than other shootings, or at least, had been publicized with little reference to the "faggot" factor:

> Barry Loukaitis, a sophomore at a Moses Lake, Wash., junior high school, gunned down fellow student Manuel Vela Jr. in retaliation for months of being called "faggot.". . . 15-year-old Michael Carneal killed three students and wounded five more at a West Paducah, Ky., high school after months of harassment following the publication of a student newspaper column in which it was rumored that Carneal was gay. . . . 15-year-old Matthew Santoni stabbed 16-year-old Jeffrey LaMothe to death in downtown Northampton, Mass., after months of being called "faggot."
>
> Why haven't you heard more about these incidents? Well, sadly, homophobic harassment in our schools is so commonplace that it is no longer news. And here's the real kicker: None of the boys who perpetrated these attacks identifies as gay. . . . We need to own up to the fact that our culture teaches boys that being "a man" is the most important

thing in life, even if you have to kill someone to prove it. Killing someone who calls you a faggot is not aberrant behavior but merely the most
extreme expression of a belief that is beaten (sometimes literally) into
boys at an early age in this country: Be a man—don't be a faggot.
(Jennings, 1998, p. 11)

I found myself wondering whether many in U.S. society resist engaging in
conversations about these events because they do not see as problematic the
use of homophobia to ensure that boys are "properly" masculine. And I
found myself wondering whether, when we do talk about these events, many
insist on understanding them only in terms of the victimization of queer
boys and of queerly gendered boys (and not in terms of the harmfulness of
maintaining gender privilege) because doing so allows heterosexual masculinity to remain untroubled, to remain the norm. Does the desire to
maintain a sense of privilege and normalcy by boys who bash queer people
parallel the desire to maintain a sense of privilege and normalcy by adults
who silence queer conversations?

The third report I found troubling suggests that the answer to these
questions is, once again, yes. This third report, from a queer activist
newsletter, argued that analyses of the shootings by Eric Harris and Dylan
Klebold at Columbine High School in Littleton, Colorado often failed to
account for ways in which "masculinity" regulates boys in society:

It's easier to crack down on nose rings than to confront a system that
assigns status in proportion to gender conformity, relegating boys who
can't meet the standard to the ranks of America's most despised minority, that legion of failed men known as "faggots." That's what the ruling
jocks called members of the Trench Coat Mafia. . . . The word *faggot* has
never merely meant homosexual. It has always carried the extrasexual
connotation of being unmanly. . . . Wielding the f-word is a way for some
guys to dominate others by convincing them that their masculinity can
be lost. . . . Harris and Klebold responded to their degradation in a typically compensatory way—they assembled their own cult of rogue masculinity. But the jocks who oppressed them didn't have to go in for Hitler
or Marilyn Manson. For these top men, homophobia was a socially sanc-
tioned way to rebel. . . . Athletic achievement was only the surface sign of
their status; bigotry was what made these jocks local gods. . . . So far, no

one has suggested that the administration at Columbine High is responsible for the homophobia that blew up in their faces. Better to blame the
killers' parents, exempting the rest of the community. (R. Goldstein,
1999, pp. 19–21)

This is not to say that homophobia alone caused the shootings. But it is to
say that examining different practices of and responses to homophobia can
help us complicate our understanding of why the shootings took place. The
"problem" was not just Harris and Klebold, but also a society that uses
homophobia to regulate masculinity; the "problem" was not just the way
certain boys were marginalized, but also the way other boys perhaps needed
to contribute to this marginalization in order to maintain some sense of
masculinity, normalcy, and privilege.

As I argued in earlier chapters, being privileged requires that a person
thinks, feels, acts, and relates to others in only particular ways; it requires
that a person be identified by others in only particular ways. For men, being
privileged as "masculine" requires being perceived as masculine; men can
never *be* fully masculine. Researchers have long argued that the dominant or
hegemonic masculinity in mainstream society is something that a person
can only constantly *become*, i.e., is something that must be constantly
"proven" (Connell, 1987). Masculinity is like a "relentless test"; it has a
"marketplace quality" insofar as a male needs to demonstrate to other males
aggressiveness, competitiveness, and excellence in a number of areas,
including athletic performance, physical fitness, sexual activity, and social
networking in order to be considered "masculine" (Kimmel, 1994). Unless
they constantly demonstrate masculinity, males risk being considered feminine (Arnot, 1984). In fact, to be masculine, males must constantly prove
that they are not feminine.

They often do this through acts of homophobia. Being "masculine"
requires distancing themselves from anything queer. After all, men deemed
queer generally fall at the bottom of the hierarchy of men. They are seen as
lacking in masculinity, more womanly than manly, despite the fact that
queer men do vary in the ways they perform different gender roles (queer
men can appear masculine, can appear effeminate, and can blur these lines
with ambiguity or androgyny). Perhaps this denigration of queers happens
because, as I argued in chapter 3 concerning castration, queerness defies
expectations of men in a heterosexist and patriarchal society, and betrays

and even threatens the privilege granted to men in such a society. Queer men disrupt our abilities to define as "normal" only certain gender identities and sexual relationships—namely, those around which commonsense notions of family, community, and society revolve. As Connell (1995) argues, "gayness, in patriarchal ideology, is the repository of whatever is symbolically expelled from hegemonic masculinity. . . . Hence . . . gayness is easily assimilated to femininity. And hence . . . the ferocity of homophobic attacks" (p. 78). Not surprisingly, most perpetrators of antigay violence are young men (Lipkin, 1995).

This link between queer sexuality and femininity helps to explain why boys (and girls) often use such terms as *girl, homo, fag,* and *sissy* interchangeably when insulting other boys. This link also helps to explain why gay bashing can be and is directed not only at boys who come out as gay or bisexual, but also at boys who fall into the broad category of queer, including boys who "look gay," or "look like a girl," or just look different. As Kevin Jennings (1998) has argued, not all targets of gay bashing self-identify as gay, lesbian, or bisexual, and of those who do, not all come out as such. A person's sexual orientation sometimes does not matter. Homophobia targets not only youth with queer sexual orientations, but also youth with queer genders, which often includes youth who are more visibly queer. Therefore, addressing homophobia requires addressing gender nonconformity, transgenderism, and transphobia.

Debbie makes a similar argument. Her understanding of the complexities and intersections of different forms of oppression has developed as her range of activisms has expanded. Here is how her queer activism began:

> I had started marching in the Pride Parade that we have every summer
> so it was like that activism stuff started waking up.
> Also at [the community radio station],
> I'd been volunteering there for quite a while,
> one day I saw a note on the bulletin board that said,
> "We're starting a new show
> and we're looking for lesbian, gay, bisexual,
> and transgendered people to host."
> And so at the organizational meeting I said,
> "Hey, did you really mean transgender?"

They said, "Yeah, why?"

"I'm your token transgender person."

[*laughter*]

So I became pretty heavily involved in [the new show],

met a lot of people in the LGBT community

and that kind of was a catalyst for becoming involved

in [the LGBT community center].

I had been talking to [the community center] a lot about transgender

because they wanted to serve the transgender community

but they really didn't have much of a way to do it.

I mean I was a peer counselor

but [as a peer counselor] I couldn't

meet somebody,

you know, for coffee to talk over their problem with them.

So we decided that I would start

[the transgender support group that meets at the community center].

It's a much different relationship.

The way I put it,

it is for cross-dressers,

transvestites,

transsexual,

pre-op,

post-op,

male-to-female,

female-to-male,

friends, family, and significant others.

Very inclusive.

I mean these are different "issues" to deal with

but

I think that all of those people are worthy of getting support.

Since then, I have become very activist.

I started going out on engagements for the speakers bureau

and also on my own I started speaking to

well, for example, I spoke to the various deans of students

about transgender issues
and the relationship to the college campus,
and I've given speeches to various classes
on [the nearby university] campus.
I've done some conferences.
I'm being asked more and more to speak,
I spoke at PFLAG this last weekend
I spoke at a high school this week
I'm going to be speaking to a group that's concerned with domestic abuse.
I will be going to Washington next month to participate in Gender Lobby Days.
I've approached a couple of city council members about
getting transgender people
or gender identity
or gender presentation
or words to that effect
put into the nondiscrimination ordinance
or I should say ordinances.
So you can see that it's all quite
you know, it's just mushroomed with me
I mean it's almost overwhelming
it's like something getting sucked into a vacuum.
There's nothing there right now.

To me
education is primary right now in transgender issues.
I think that there's a lot of misconceptions out there about
who transgender people are
and the only way to educate
is to be out, to be honest, to share a personal history,
and let people know, you know, that we all come from the same place.
I'm not out there to recruit.
I am out there, though, to be a role model if at all possible
because I remember how lonely it was being a kid.
I think, looking at the gay [and] lesbian movement over the last twenty years
it was really important to make people aware of all of the
wonderful things that was done by people who were gay and lesbian

and that to be such didn't mean that you were a freak.
And for transgender people,
there's so much that stigmatizes us
that I think it's important to get that message out
And the speaker's bureau was the way to do it.

I don't know,
you can talk about the history of people or whatever
but until you get to know others, people who are different,
it's pretty hard to make it resonate.
So, in my activist career, I think that's been the most powerful tool—
the sense of putting a real, a fleshing out of a person,
getting a sense that there are emotions
that there are feelings that go behind the ideas.
When we're talking about tolerance and such
I think that they have to get to know people.
I mean that's not to say that reading isn't good for certain things.
Books have been very helpful.
There's a book called *Gender Outlaw* by Kate Bornstein.
It was a very healing book for me.
She made it seem alright to be trans.
I mean that's just sort of a simplistic message but, not only that
she made the whole topic playful
it was something that wasn't to be feared
it was something to be experimented and understood
and that was one of the take-home messages I think was,
"There's no right and wrong gender
and you have to be able to be flexible."

The only contact that most people have with transgender
outside of a couple of sensational stories in the past
like Christine Jorgensen, Renee Richards, um,
is the TV talk shows
and we're paraded on the TV talk shows,
sensationalized on the TV talk shows.
Some of the shows have tried to deal with the education issue
and tried to demonstrate to people that,

you know, that we aren't freaks.

But often times, just by having,

I mean the underlying message about being on those talk shows is

that we're different

and so it's just the wrong environment for that kind of stuff

and I see the way people react

and what seems especially unjust to me is that there's this

silence in the press about it.

There have been seven trans murders in the past six months.

These are hate crimes too, and yet they're not covered as hate crimes.

It's hard to remain silent.

The traditional career path of a transsexual

is to come out of the closet,

because it's almost impossible to transition without somebody noticing

that there's something different about you,

and then once enough time has passed

and hormones have done their work

and you've acculturated yourself to that gender role

then you go back in the closet

and you don't want anyone to know about your past.

And if you pass well enough, you can just become that

traditional male or female person.

It's a closet with a swinging door.

They call it woodworking,

fading into the woodwork.

And that's why we aren't evident, that's why we're invisible

aside from the fact that our numbers are so few.

No, that's not me.

So for me it's been much different to come out

and I think I'll probably stay out for quite a while.

I've been fortunate, you know, to be out at work pretty much

and to have my job.

A lot of people aren't that lucky.

Going back to the [transgender support group]:

going around the room and listening to everyone's stories,
one person had lost their job, I mean more than one person,
I remember hearing this story about this person's struggle to
keep their job through their transition
and how everything was supposed to be in place and all right
but yet there was this undercurrent of discrimination that was happening
and some of it was rather overt.
And I say *discrimination* but I'm talking hatred.
And then hearing the story of the, um,
person who was a religious leader
who was afraid that they would be outed and lose everything.
Hearing about the myriads of people who lost their spouses
and were in the midst of what would have been two divorces
and thereby had lost their children.
This one person was trying to get the evidence and you know
get the cases together for a defense,
how much money they had spent for their lawyer
and all the nasty things about not allowing them to see their children
and this and that, you know
and going around the circle and hearing all these stories
it dawned on me that this stuff is very real
even though it was happening to me.
I had a very somber kind of a feeling
I could sort of feel myself becoming rather depressed.
My mood really did drop
but I kept listening, I stayed attentive, I didn't shut it out
and the more that I heard, I mean it sent my mind racing,
as opposed to other times when I would shut things out
and kind of go into a shut down mode.
It started to build into kind of an exhilaration that
there's a lot of work here that needs to be done
and I'm not sure exactly how to do it but I can see a few things right now.
And that was the moment that I thought that I had to be out
because I was sitting on the fence.
I didn't know what kind of a transperson I was going to be,
whether I was going to be a leader
or whether I was going to be a woodworker,

you know, at that point I just thought, "I can't not do these things.
I'm in a position to do it
I have the means
I have the abilities."

I want to challenge people
I want to pull a rug or two out from under people
and I want them, you know, not to take anything for granted.
Here's a kind of an educational tool that I use on myself
and unfortunately, it's a binary thing
but I often
if I learn a concept, I often try that concept
in reverse.
You know, if it's true one way, try it in reverse
and see, Will it be true also?
Because you'll be surprised how often they both can be true,
and then wonder, Well, what was the basis for the first one?
If A is better than B, you can always flip that around and say,
Well, does it make any more sense or less sense,
or are they both equally senseless?
[*laughter*]

Others were saying,
"You should try to change society
instead of changing your gender.
Change society to be more tolerant of you being a man
but having more of a range."
But I've only got, like, half a lifetime left
and I can't hope to change society by myself to do this.
I was going to live my life open, out, as a male-to-female transsexual
and
I was going to try to change the world
because then I could have it both ways.
And I know that I'm not going to hardly make a dent in the problem
but it's incumbent upon me to try
because it's the only way things will get done.
And I mean, it makes me feel good.

I used to have such a tremendous amount of guilt because
I felt sorry for myself.
And when I get active, that guilt subsides greatly
because I'm doing something
I'm taking an active role in the world.
Otherwise you're just letting it happen to you.

I think it's important for, at least in today's society,
to get the individual to a place where they can accept themselves
in order to deal with society as it is.
But also
I'd like to say,
change society,
tear down the male-female structure and allow for more fluid gender,
it's not as simple as black and white or A or B.
Letting them know, just the fact that
between one in a thousand or one in two thousand births is a
person with ambiguous genitalia
and that it's not always so clear-cut
there's a whole range of the way people are born
and this is not something to be afraid of.
I mean even the medical establishment causes this
there's this, you know, mad rush to surgically "correct" this
and it's done without regard for what the
internal gender of that child might be.
Most often the corrections go to female
because that's the easiest to construct.
So uh, just to get some of these issues on the table,
"Hey, what does it mean for . . . "
and see, this stuff spills over not just for transgender people but, uh,
"What does it mean to be a girl or a boy or a man or a woman?"
I mean right there you can see this touches on a lot.
The quote I've heard from so many people,
"I'm not a man born in a woman's body,
I'm a woman born in the wrong society."
So we're talking about medical politics,
we're talking about sociology, we're talking,

you know there's a myriad of ways that you can come to this
and lessons you can get out of it
that would be comforting for a person whose gender is
unexpected.

It's hard to understand transgender people
without being able to fight against the binaries
male and *female*.
I think it's important that educators allow themselves to think more
along a continuum.
And that I think is hard for people, awfully hard for most people.
That's what really I think offends people the most about transgender
because it just pulls the rug out from all of that stuff.
There is this sense of distress that one gets when you move
out of those boundaries
and it can be quite overwhelming.
People gotta steer back onto the path.
And it's only when somebody can allow themselves to take risks
that they're able to do that
and not have the reflexes kick in.
Sometimes it's good to mess around with the foundations, so that,
keep people a bit off balance.
I mean just think about it.
When you find yourself off balance
your adrenaline kicks in,
you're more aware of your surroundings,
you have that distressed kind of feeling
because you want to get back on solid ground.
I think that kind of a sense of things is sometimes a good way to
approach knowledge.

We all like to think that we have the world figured out
or at least have a pretty good sense of it
and when we learn something, I mean,
there can be this wonderful eureka-type sense of things
when you make a realization that
that the sun does not revolve around the earth,

but then after that thrill, after that initial thrill,

then we have to live with the consequences that can be

at times very painful.

I guarantee,

you start teaching a curriculum that challenged gender too much,

I mean

there's going against the gender stereotypes, in so far as,

"Look at all the things that girls can do now,

that women can do,

that we never could before,"

all that kind of stuff

that's one thing,

but when you start saying things like,

"Girls can be boys and boys can be girls,"

I think you're going to have the community jumping down your throat.

Here I am espousing all of this stuff about having more fluid gender.

It's easy to spout that kind of stuff

but why then don't I go around wearing a dress and sporting a beard?

You know, really challenging gender,

and what, I guess the vernacular is called, a "gender fuck"?

And, that's not me.

I tend to be more of the traditional female.

But I think both expressions need to have their own safe spaces.

I think we need both.

I think that people need to be able to be

comfortable in the body that they're in

and the place where their head is at.

But by the same token, people need sometimes to be challenged.

I wonder how I got here.

You know sometimes I just sort of like,

you know when you're falling asleep at night

and you're thinking about stuff that's happened,

How did I get here?

You know, a year ago, I wouldn't have done this [interview].

I have to say,

a fear of failure.

Not just that I'll make an ass of myself,

but just fear of failure.

I'll let too many people down.

As I read Debbie's stories, two things come to mind. One is Sue's stories and the importance of doing "homework." Debbie's stories remind me of stories I read several years ago, at a time when I felt perplexed by transgenderism. I did not understand why people who were critical of a gender binary would reinforce that binary by claiming the "other" gender. I wondered why they did not discard the binary altogether and claim a different, queer gender. There were people, after all, whose bodies were neither "properly" male nor "properly" female and who rejected the notion that there were only two "biological sexes," and they claimed an identity of "intersexual." But then I did some homework. I read several books suggested to me by friends and activists (Bornstein, 1995; Feinberg, 1993; Wilchins, 1997). And I realized that transgenderism is not as simplistic as I had assumed. Transgenderism involves contradictions. It involves paradoxical ways of troubling gender identities. In particular, rather than merely rejecting "male" and "female," it simultaneously embraces and looks beyond these identities. This paradoxical process refuses to stabilize gender identities, which is perhaps why I initially felt so troubled by transgenderism. It destabilizes my own gender identities.

This realization is not unlike my reading of Beth's stories from chapter 3, which is the second thing that comes to mind when I read Debbie's stories. In chapter 3, I argued that the contradictions in Beth's stories are exactly what make them useful for antioppressive change. There are many contradictions in Beth's stories, and perhaps not surprisingly, there are many contradictions in Debbie's stories. Debbie is normal and "like everyone else," but is queer in her refusal to conform to gender norms. She finds similarities and shared experiences between transgender people and gay/lesbian/bisexual people and embraces the joined acronym LGBT, but sees differences between sexual orientation and gender identity and sometimes desires separate spaces. She sometimes defines *transgender* as only male-to-female and female-to-male transsexuals, but sometimes broadens the definition to include people who do not perform their "proper" gender role. She identifies with the female gender, but also identifies as transgender (male-to-female). She sometimes presents herself as feminine, but sometimes does a "gender fuck" and presents herself in a mixed-gender fashion. She views gender as a continuum, but sees herself transitioning between two genders. She believes people can understand transgenderism through speakers and personal stories, but also believes that people cannot understand transgenderism because it exceeds binary knowledge. She works to change herself and fit the gender binary, but also works to change society so that she does not have to fit the gender binary. She is out as transgender, and "back in" as a transitioned, passable woman.

These contradictions of Debbie's sexual and gender identities are not accidental. As I reread her stories, I realize that these contradictions are central to her efforts to increase others' understandings of transgenderism and challenge transphobia. Her activism revolves around contradictions in two ways: she works to occupy both sides of binaries, often going back and forth between the two (as when using the "closet with a swinging door"); and she works to step outside of binaries and demonstrate other ways of being and acting in this world (as when doing "gender fuck"). In other words, she works to invert as well as exceed binaries. For example, she talks of being of one gender (male), and then of critiquing the entire binary gender regime, and then of being of a gender again (female). She talks of people being comfortable at first, and then of pulling "a rug or two out from under" them, and then getting them "back onto the path." And she talks about trying things "in reverse" as a way to work against her own complicities and change herself in such a way that she ends up *neither the same nor the opposite*. Such might have been the goal of an activity for youth that she observed at a religious convention:

> One year at this convention
> they have like the meetings for the adults
> but they also have like a whole weeklong retreat for the kids.
> I guess you would call it a retreat,
> it's kind of more like a camp or so.
> Now, you can take various activities at the camp
> and it's meant to be a learning experience.
> One of the activities that they did was for several days

they swapped genders
and were expected to live that way for
you know
twenty-four, seven.
And I thought, what a neat concept.

This activity is not unlike Debbie's practice of sometimes coming out as transgender and other times passing as a woman. Both can involve teaching about the socially constructed nature of identity, as when we teach that a man being a woman is no less artificial than a man being a man. Both can involve experiencing identity as a performance or an act of identification rather than an essential part of who we are, as when we learn that a man must constantly prove his masculinity but never fully is masculine. Both can involve seeing how different enactments of different identities are interpreted, valued, and responded to in different ways depending on the situation, as when we see that the "proper" roles for boys and girls and the rewards for being proper (and the punishments for not) vary by time and place and community.

My reading of Debbie's stories suggests that "being" identities that contradict one another, that invert social hierarchies, and that exceed binary logic can be exactly what helps to bring about antioppressive change. In the classroom, these processes of inverting and exceeding binaries can go in many directions. I can imagine a class where students work constantly to become the "other" gender at the same time that they work to become or ally with something outside of the gender binary, such as "gender fucked" or intersexed. I can imagine a class where students work constantly to imagine a society that is the "opposite" of their own (where, for instance, being deaf is the norm) as well as a society that is neither the same nor the opposite. I can imagine a class where students work constantly to learn criticisms of what they are being taught as well as tools to ask questions that have yet even to be asked. What is central in these paradoxical approaches to teaching is the *third party*, the thing that needs to be excluded from binaries in order for binaries themselves to have meaning and stability and structure (as with bisexuality and the hetero-homo binary, or intersexuality and the male-female binary). Debbie's activism centers not only on troubling the terms within binaries, but also on troubling the binaries themselves. Antioppressive activism and education involve both working within and looking beyond binaries. Contradictions can play a central role in such efforts toward antioppressive change.

Third Route: Juxtaposing Matthew's Stories to Other Cultural Texts

As I turn to the third route of reading, I return to Matthew, the gay Puerto Rican activist who appeared in chapter 3. His name (actually, his pseudonym) is what first suggested to me this third route. When juxtaposed with a central theme of his stories, namely, the theme of "dying," his name conjured in my mind associations with a Matthew whose death, at the time of our interview, had been preoccupying my thoughts. I asked Matthew if he had this other Matthew—Matthew Shepard—in mind when he chose the pseudonym Matthew. He explained that he had not, but the parallel was nonetheless striking.

Matthew Shepard directed national attention to antiqueer violence in the fall of 1998 when he was found brutally beaten and tied to a fence post in Laramie, Wyoming. He died soon after. Like many others, I was horrified at the senselessness and brutality of the crime. I was fearful that this attack on a shy, slightly built young man symbolized the violence directed at so many other queers, and that I myself was not immune to such attacks. I was angered that we live in a society that allows this kind of violence to take place, especially toward youth, and that sanctions it with homophobic laws and public policies. I was sad for Matthew Shepard and his loved ones. But it was not until several weeks after this tragedy was first reported that I became saddened to a point of paralysis. I remember that I had just come home that day and was flipping through a newsmagazine when I came across a short article about the attack. I do not remember the point of the article. Perhaps the article was saying something about how the police, at first, did not realize that Matthew Shepard had been beaten so badly because there was not much blood on his face. All I remember is that, according to the article, there was not much blood on his face because, while tied to the fence post, as if being crucified, Matthew Shepard's tears had washed away his blood.

For many minutes, I remember sitting with the article in my lap, stunned. I cried. I felt paralyzed. I later told a friend about this article, and getting tearful again, explained that I was not quite sure why that image upset me so. She suggested that the image suggests to us how alone Matthew Shepard must have been feeling at that moment. And how alone many queer youth feel every day of their lives. And how many queer youth actually *do* die alone every day.

Matthew, my participant, suggested that the isolation and loneliness of many queer youth help explain their disturbingly high rates of suicide. The website of the Gay, Lesbian and Straight Education Network (http://www.glsen.org) compiles statistics from a range of studies (citations are listed on their website). According to these studies,

+ Gay and lesbian youth are 3 or 4 times more likely to attempt suicide than other youth; and they represent 30% of all completed teen suicide. Nearly all gay and lesbian suicides occur between the ages of 16 and 21.
+ 30% of gay and bisexual adolescent males attempt suicide at least once. Young men with more "feminine gender role characteristics" and those who recognize their same-sex orientation at an early age and act on those sexual feelings face the highest risk of self-destructive behavior.
+ 53% of transexuals attempts suicide.
+ 36% of African American lesbians (compared to 21% of White lesbians) and 32% of African American gay males (compared to 27% of White gay males) attempt suicide before age 18.

This should not be surprising given that

+ 97% of students in public high schools report regularly hearing homophobic remarks from their peers.
+ 80% of gay and lesbian youth report severe social isolation.
+ 26% of adolescent gay males report having to leave home as a result of conflicts with their family over their sexual orientation.
+ 90% of gays and lesbians experience some form of victimization on account of their perceived or actual sexual orientation, and 1 in 5 gay males and 1 in 10 lesbians said that they have been "punched, hit, kicked, or beaten."

Perhaps one reason, then, that so many queer youth attempt and commit suicide is that long before the physical act of suicide, they are already dying, emotionally, spiritually, and socially.

Matthew's stories illustrate this point. A gay man now in his early thirties, Matthew had a very difficult childhood and young adult life. What made a difference, though, was a series of situated and paradoxical encounters with queer activism. He begins his stories in the fall of 1998 when he was about to begin another semester of graduate school, but decided instead to drop out of graduate school and begin activist work with almost half a dozen different queer, youth, and AIDS-related organizations:

> The really bizarre thing is
> last September
> maybe a week into the semester
> I just
> woke up one morning
> and said,
> I have to do this.
> There was no cataclysmic event.
> It's just, you know
> the balance shifted finally
> where it was no longer tolerable to be
> in the closet
> and it was no longer tolerable to just
> sit back and do nothing.
> The balance shifted.
> And it was a matter of
> feeling strong enough to take that step.
>
> It's important that you know
> I'm now thirty-three and I'm just
> now
> coming out full force and taking a more active role in the community.
> I know this sounds really bizarre.
> I mean I've been avoiding
> talking about this because it's hard
> but the reason I'm just now coming out
> is because, um,

the very home I grew up in was oppressive.
My father was a very abusive man, physically and emotionally.
In Hispanic culture
the firstborn, especially the firstborn male,
is held to a different standard
and that carries with it certain expectations
of carrying on the family name, and that sort of thing.
If he had a certain view of what it meant to be a man
he was gonna make sure that I met that image.
I don't know if he had any sense that
I was maybe more effeminate than the other boys
or I was weak and timid.
I was always very shy
I didn't like to do "boy" things
I didn't like sports.
So he was kind of forcing me to play baseball or play on the soccer team
you know, doing those kinds of things
and that just held me back.
You know, all this time it's held me back.

I think that's what it stems from.
I didn't come out for so long
because I feared for my own personal well-being
because I believed that if I did come out
I would be hurt.
It was purely a fear of being hurt.
It was an irrational fear.
You know not everyone is going to beat you up because you're gay.
But
I was abused when I was young—
young.
That's why I think the fear was blown out of proportion so much.
You carry that with you.
And it wasn't until I came here and
saw that it was possible to be out without being hurt
that I started unraveling that.

And that began,
I don't know if the kiss-in was the first time that I was confronted with
homosexuality in [the college town]
but it's one of the ones that sticks out in my mind.
I remember when I first came here
in '88
I was walking through [campus]
and some people were doing uh
I don't know what you call it
a kiss-in
a kiss-out
whatever
where gays and lesbians were just getting together and
just necking
as a form of
speaking out.
I mean they weren't saying, you know,
"Combat homophobia," blah blah blah,
but by their very act of being there and
pushing people's buttons
you know?
I think that was a significant moment
because that may have been the first time that I recognized that
gay people are open here.

At once, it pushed all my buttons because it
made me scared
because you know it made me see a part of me that I had suppressed
and I was really good at it too.
I had learned to live with the fact that I was
never going to be able to express my own sexuality.
It was very easy to pretend
to live in the heterosexual world.
There were no examples,
there were no successes.
I only had the stereotypes to—
I mean I didn't want to be like that,

I didn't want to be like what they were saying.
In fact, I was afraid of those people that they were talking about
I didn't want to be with those people
and seeing them made that all that come back to the surface
and that drove me even deeper in the closet
but it made me face it
and that was the beginning
of undoing all the damage that I had done to myself.

At first
I thought there wasn't any place where anybody could do that
without being assaulted.
And now seeing that,
well, gee, it's possible,
I thought that I would never be in a place where they were
I would never be so comfortable that I could do something so bold.
But here was a space.
And mind you, we're talking about a practically
ten-year-long process.
But
being put in crisis,
as you put it,
led to the slow unlearning of my fears
and led to the slow process of empowerment.
It wasn't until I faced other visions of homosexuality
that I started confronting my own stereotypes.
That was keeping me from being myself.
I can't begin to recount the number of times there was
something on the radio
or on the news
or in one of the school papers
or I would see an announcement about the LGBT dances
or I would hear about [the community center] for the first time.
Little by little all these bells would ring up
and I was thinking,
Oh my God, there's a whole world out there.
I didn't even know there was such a thing as an LGBT community.

I thought there were just all these LGBT folks hiding out in their homes
and leading secret lives.
And even though I didn't have any contact with it
even though I didn't know any activist
I was aware of their work
I saw what they did
I heard them speak
and ever so slow a manner over the last ten years
they have had an influence on me.
Now I'm going to be devoting my life
to serving the needs of the LGBT community.
And everything I do will be out.
There will be no question as to who I am.

Whatever the costs may be
there are some rewards to coming out
and I think chief among those are achieving
a sense of dignity and respect.
You know the cry,
"Silence equals death?"
Well, I think the same applies to not coming out.
When you don't come out
you're going through a sort of death
because whenever you do not speak out
you're in a sense affirming
what somebody else in the room may be saying.
Like if someone says something homophobic
and you say nothing
you're living a little death in that moment.
I viewed every waking moment as a
series of little crises
because every time I was with someone
I was in a sense stabbing myself in the back because
I was letting them believe that
I was like them
that I was one of them.
You know

every time I spoke to my parents on the phone
and they asked me,
"So, do you have a girlfriend?"
No.
That's true, but you know,
every time you affirm that which you are not—you know?—
you are living a little death
you're going further toward affirming those stereotypes.
And you're making it more difficult for yourself to live whole.

That repetition can go one of two ways.
It can bring you to a point of crisis
or it can serve to keep reaffirming the same old prejudices.
For example, if all throughout your schooling
all you ever heard is that Africans achieve nothing,
that can either make you so mad that you go out there
and try to find out the truth,
you know, can bring you to a point of crisis,
or if you hear it often enough
you're going to believe it.
It can simply immerse you even further in falsehood
until you take it to be true.
If you buy into the stereotype that all Hispanics are lazy
that might lead you to seek to achieve less
or it can bring you to the point of crisis where you say,
"I can't accept that I'm less than, you know, the White guy next door."

That gets to the heart of something that
I hope we have a chance to talk about, and that is
that activists have an important role to play in education.
Because that's what I think made a difference to me in my life.
That's what made a difference.
Because there was a point in my life where I thought,
I'm never going to be able to be like him or her
look at all the things that she's doing or he's doing
for the LGBT community,
gosh, you know, I wish I had that inner strength.

But it was seeing them that made me turn this way instead of that way.
It was seeing them that ever so slowly, over ten years,
I began to see,
Well, maybe I could, you know?
Maybe I could, because they did it
and I know that if I did take these steps
that there are people out there like me that are going to
help me through this
and I know that I can draw from their strength.
And that made all the difference in the world.
It was the lack of leadership where I used to live that kept me in the closet.

That would be my reason for that morning
deciding that I can't be in the closet anymore.
I was tired of dying.
Slowly the balance was tipping
and that morning I said,
I can't go through this anymore.
It hurts too much.
And I finally reached the point where that became unbearable.
The need to be
and to be whole
superceded the need for safety at that point.

I came out because the oppression that I felt
by not coming out
was greater than any pain or suffering I could suffer
because I was now out.
It became intolerable.
And I think you reach a second stage
at the point of activism
where not taking action becomes an
intolerable situation
because you feel that there are issues that need to be addressed
and so sitting back is
not even a choice.
I have to do something in which my identity is the center of what I do

and I have to do what I can to make sure that other young folks
don't waste fifteen years of their life because
they felt oppressed.
For the first time in my life
I'm putting my identity as a gay man in front
instead of in the background.
I don't want to live in a society where anyone
stands the risk of being killed
simply because they're LGBT.
I want to live in a setting where it's safe
for everyone to be whoever they want to be.

Matthew's stories suggest to me that an ongoing encounter with heterosexism and homophobia can be experienced as a series of "deaths," as when he was repeatedly lying to others, denying who he was, and "stabbing himself in the back." This is not to say that everyone experiences living in the closet as a form of dying, and that everyone therefore should come out, but for Matthew, each failure to challenge heterosexism and homophobia was a moment of crisis that, cumulatively, became a repetitive process that did indeed feel like dying. His insight is not unlike the poststructuralist insights described in chapter 2, which conceptualize oppression as the repetition of harmful citations and associations. What felt like dying was when Matthew was living through the heterosexist/homophobic associations between straight and normal, queer and sinful, that have traditionally permeated society. This is what he worked to change.

Such work was and is not easy. As I argued in chapter 2, changing repetition—especially when that repetition is the status quo—is often something people find uncomfortable and, therefore, resist. In Matthew's case, encounters with heterosexism and homophobia and a life in the closet were the norm, and trying to associate straightness and queerness with new things and stop the process of dying entailed confronting pretty discomforting knowledges. Most notably at the kiss-in, queer activists were trying to change traditional readings of *queer* by confronting viewers with transgressive performances of queer acts. They were giving traditionally chagrined acts (of same-gender kissing) new representations (of many people doing it at once), new contexts (in public during a political event), new social values (which insist that doing so is acceptable), new purposes (for activism, rather than for romance), and so forth. Not surprisingly, by changing what *queer* cites, and by insisting that it cites things that go against common sense, the activists led Matthew to feel a form of crisis, fear, and anxiety. As Matthew put it, "it pushed all my buttons because it made me scared."

Interestingly, the same type of queer activism that led Matthew into crisis was what helped him work through that crisis. In both experiences, Matthew was responding to queer activists who were insisting that *queer* mean something different. They were out, they were bold, and they were out and bold in various ways. They spoke through radio and newspaper announcements, planned social and support gatherings, advocated for changed policies and practices, and increased their visibility in the community. Their persistence helped Matthew to resist shying away from the discomforting image of queers kissing in public (which was his initial tendency) and from continuing to believe that being queer is bad, and instead helped him to confront his discomfort and gradually begin embracing things queer. It helped that their activism was multiple and paradoxical. They constantly insisted that he (and others) see them *being queer* at different venues, through different acts, in different performer-audience relations, and so forth, making it possible for him to experience queerness in various and sometimes contradictory ways. After all, Matthew's experiences of the performances could be voyeuristic (as when seeing someone be strangely queer), vicarious (as when wishing to be queer like them), reflexive (as when finding similarities with or implications for his own queerness), and so forth. They showed that *being queer* can be understood and experienced and reacted to in various ways. And perhaps that is what was so helpful to Matthew. The different experiences with queerness helped Matthew enter crisis in one moment, work through crisis in another, and presumably enter and work through and invite others into crisis at others. Queer activism was helpful because it could be read in different ways in different contexts. Like Debbie, Matthew suggests that differences and contradictions can help make queer activism useful for bringing about change. And like both Debbie and Sue, Matthew suggests that experiencing difference, experiencing what is queer, can help invite people to desire a process of bringing about change that is neither straightforward nor easy to do.

Furthermore, Matthew's stories suggest that changing oppressive repetitions in society is not something that is ever completed. Working against oppression requires constantly working; it requires ongoing activism. What

Matthew found "intolerable" was not just "dying" from heterosexism and homophobia, but also "not taking action" and living complacently with repetitions that continue to oppress himself and others in society. Matthew argues that repetition can go "one of two ways," and that it takes ongoing work to change harmful identities, practices, and social relations, or to prevent unharmful ones from acquiring harmful associations. Such an insight parallels Pab's insight from chapter 3 that cultures, identities, practices, and relations do acquire new meanings over time—sometimes more oppressive ones, but sometimes not—and we can and do help determine these changes. Without ongoing activism, it should not be surprising that oppressive repetitions will either continue to exist or eventually come into existence.

Thus far, my analysis has focused on insights suggested by the juxtaposition of Matthew's stories to cultural texts on Matthew Shepard. I am aware that this reading of Matthew's stories was inspired by my initial juxtaposition of the pseudonym "Matthew" and the theme of dying. This leads me to ask, What other readings of Matthew's stories are suggested by the juxtaposition of other aspects of his stories? I expect that the focus on other themes, such as "balance shifting," child abuse, and fear of safety could lead to very different insights on challenging oppression. Even within the focus on Matthew Shepard and dying, I expect that different insights can be made possible when Matthew's stories are juxtaposed with different cultural texts on Matthew Shepard. After all, even when they are all focused on the same topic, different cultural texts "say" different things.

For example, I might juxtapose Matthew's stories with the recent movie about Matthew Shepard (*Anatomy of a Hate Crime*) produced by and aired on MTV. Because the movie emphasized different aspects of and perspectives on the tragedy than did the news articles I read, I find myself thinking about different issues as I reread Matthew's stories. The movie showed the future killers commenting hatefully to each other when seeing flyers being posted about a queer-supportive event, which makes me wonder about the ways queer activism can ironically *increase* antiqueer sentiment. In contrast, the news articles tended to suggest that Matthew Shepard lived in areas where more queer activism was needed. The movie showed a straight person, who was working at a queer student center, help her boyfriend conceal his bashing of Matthew, which makes me wonder about the ways the same person can "do" both queer activism and queer bashing. In contrast, the news articles suggested that people were either open-minded and allies, or closed-minded and perpetrators. Juxtaposing the stories of my participant Matthew with the MTV movie urges me to ask different kinds of questions concerning queer activism, which in turn raises different questions about antioppressive education, such as, How do we address right-wing responses to antioppressive education, and how do we address those who may already be acting in contradictory ways and who perhaps always will?

This is not to say that there are "better" texts to juxtapose to Matthew's stories, or that they provide "better" readings. Rather, this is to say that reading Matthew's stories requires constantly reflecting on what different juxtapositions make possible and impossible. Juxtaposing Matthew's stories to different texts helps us to use his stories in paradoxical ways: learn from them, while looking beyond what we are learning. What makes juxtaposition helpful for antioppressive education are the multiple and contradictory insights, questions, and practices it can open up.

In a classroom, I can imagine juxtaposing my reading of Matthew's stories (and its theme of repetition and crisis) to the journals of my students in an attempt to critique my own teaching practices. I might ask, What do their journals suggest are harmful associations being repeated in my curriculums and pedagogies? How do my students desire and/or resist living through such repetitions? How do my classroom dynamics comply with and/or disrupt such repetitions and even create new ones? What do I bring and what can I bring to the classroom to help them experience and develop a desire for difference and change? What is inviting them into crisis and helping them work through it, and what else could make this happen? Were I to juxtapose different texts and ask different questions, I would learn different things about my teaching. And that is why antioppressive teaching can never be foretold. Many texts that can invite new antioppressive questions, insights, and practices are rarely if ever used in these ways, and many more have yet to be written, by our students, ourselves, and others whose voices have been silenced from these conversations. Many more insights await our readings.

Fourth Route: Reading Pab's Stories as Catalysts for Action and Change

As I turn to the fourth and final route of reading, I turn back to Pab, the high school student who appeared in chapter 3. I have little to say as I introduce

her second set of stories, except to urge the reader to read with this question
in mind: What are Pab's stories calling on you to do?

How do I want to be introduced?
I don't know.
This is kind of asking me who I am.
I think if I were to describe myself
I would describe myself as a very emotional person
that everybody kind of looks at and says,
"Wow, she's just got things figured out,"
but yet I really don't.
I do so much because I feel a lot,
like I have a lot of anger locked up inside of me
and instead of venting my anger as anger
I vent it through activism.

Being an activist is a very strong part of my identity.
I don't know,
everybody says I have a really strong identity.
I'd be told that I'm the [most] racist person they've ever met.
But I'm, like, "Why?"
And then we start talking about it
and after a while it's like,
"Wow, you're really not racist
you're just really connected into how you feel,"
and therefore because I'm able to joke about it and make blunt state-
ments
they kind of see it as being racist.
So I'm very blunt.
And I'm young.

I worked on this thing called Diversity Days.
I started it.
At my high school, I got all the groups together:
there were Latinos, Asians, uh,
Hmong Club, Asian Club,
African American,
gay-straight alliance,

and we all worked together
and we all became really close, you know?
And I was able to open up myself to these minorities as being
both gay and a minority
and it was a great experience.
We had speakers and performances, panels,
we had a potluck
and it was the most wonderful sight I've ever seen
because we had foods from all over the world, you know?
And it was homemade, it wasn't like this crap that you buy, you know?
And we charged very little for it, we gave a lot of food [away]—
there was all sorts of food.
The gay group didn't have anything to bring
so we brought cake and just sort of put it out.
And just, there's this time when there's five of us in there
trying to make rice.
And I started making rice the way we make it
where we wash rice and put it in the rice cooker.
And then one of my friends who's Latino came up to us and said,
"That's not how you make rice."
She started making rice her own way.
And then the Hmong friend came up and she's like,
"No, that's not how you make rice."
And then we had like,
one of my friends who's in the gay-straight alliance who's White
and she's like,
"We don't make rice but when we do we put it on the stove."
And like there's like five different styles of rice being cooked
and it was great.
And then we had an African American, they were like,
"No, this is how we cook rice."
And then just like having everybody serve the food.
Like you saw all these people dancing to Latino music that were
Asian, Latino, gay, Black, White, everything.
And it was probably the best thing I've, being like,
"Wow, this is something that I helped start;
it was my dream and it's here."

I have always dreamt of—
to have people come together.
Not only helping other people
showing the people that were buying the food that there's this diversity,
but having the people connect
and not just superficially just to work together
but having people talk about personal lives
having people be able to hug and hold hands and dance together
and two females dance together that weren't gay, you know,
in front of people.
And, we had a huge party at my house
I hang out with people still
it wasn't just this thing that dissolved
and that's why I find that a great success.

I got a lot of questions like,
"How the hell is this helping?"
You know?
And I didn't know how to answer except for,
"Well, do you see this mix of people,
and now you can see it all over because we're being forced to just mix,"
you know?
Teenagers, kids are growing up with all sorts of other
different types of kids
and being best friends with someone that's Asian or Black or whatever,
you know?
I think that is one way to grow and unify
is to have little kids grow up together.
But another way is to show that once they get into high school,
'cause they start separating again, and in middle school,
is to show that, "look, you can still unite."
I mean one of the largest questions is,
How can I set out to maintain my own culture but unify?
I think Diversity Days was a perfect way 'cause you got to
express your culture
but also unify with other cultures.
It's like we're all here together.

And I don't want any part of a culture to get lost.

I helped start a gay-straight alliance
and we became one of the largest clubs at [my high school].
We went to a lot of meetings
we did teacher orientations
and all sorts of things
anything we could do.
And at the beginning of the year
it was wonderful because one of our main goals was to
stop the use of the word *gay* as a bashing term.
At the beginning of the year you could hear everybody being like,
"That's so gay"
or, "He's such a fag."
And at the end of the year, you know, we were trying to keep count of it
and we couldn't hear it that often.
And we even heard people that we would have thought
would have been really discriminatory being like,
"You know what, I don't like the use of that language."
And just getting more people to say that all the time helped
and just spreading that knowledge.
We started that.
We just *told* people, you know?
We totally went out there
and we were going to stand strong
and I think a lot of the people at [my high school],
you know, I became close to a lot of people,
my friends became close to a lot of people,
through that we just got, you know, spread out.
It was almost like a little mission.
Um, we did it naturally, and it worked.

Another group I was involved in was [a multicultural drama group];
it was a class.
The drama teacher
she had thirteen kids of all different kinds go around
making up skits for the first quarter,

and second quarter we toured it to all the elementary schools.
We did it every morning.
And it was a great impact on the kids, they loved us,
you'd see them on the streets be like,
"you're from [the drama group]!"
We talked about racism, gender, sexuality.
It was great.
The best part was just going to little kids
and having them look at it
and we'd have a talk-back session
and having them talk about these issues
and seeing how they felt and everything.
Showing them that there were people that were gay out there
or showing people that were Asians, or Asian gays, or whatever.
And I learned that some kids are really really homophobic
and some kids are the most open people that I've ever met.
I was in this one class where they were like,
"No, that's so gay, they're gross, my mommy told me they're gross."
And we even had a one class where they were like,
"My mommy told me if you see a gay person or hear the word gay,
you whistle, really loud."
And just learning all these little things that
parents teach their kids was amazing.
In this one class there was this girl that was just like,
"Well, maybe your mommy's wrong."
And talk about racism, also!
They're more attuned to racism because they're taught that
you have to be PC,
you can't be racist.
But with homophobia, it's not there.

High schoolers are so PC.
And they're like,
"Of course I'm accepting"
or "Of course I'm this,"
and then you hear them say something, it's like,
"Whoa, shit, they're really not getting it."

But then, the high schoolers can do a lot more, too.

They can go out and be activists if they choose to open their eyes.

There were a lot of people in [the drama group] who

loved it while they were doing it but

something I never got was they never did it after that.

And I think that's something that showed me a lot about high schoolers

and a lot about when you get older, and about the teacher,

like the teacher that did [the drama group]—

she never brought her kids to any part of Diversity Days.

And I didn't understand that.

That was the most interesting thing to me.

It was like you have your own thing but after that you don't do it.

But not to be saying that they can't be activists.

I don't want to say anything that's generalizing

but maybe it's just that some people

just want to try to live a normal lifestyle

and being an activist is not leading a normal lifestyle.

And trying to be gay and trying to be accepted,

you know, go to work every day, come home, be with family,

I'm going to be gay but I'm not going to tell anybody,

I'm going to lead that normal lifestyle.

And a lot of gay youth also,

after they realize they can do something about it,

they just have too many personal problems

with growing up

and trying to learn who they are,

they don't have enough time to go out and try to help other people

when they have to help themselves.

That's with minority students, or other minorities

like Blacks, Asians, they don't have time to, you know?

They gotta work, make the money, to get out of wherever they are.

And I think that's why a lot of them aren't activists.

And it's very simple and it's very understandable.

A lot of the work I do has to do with who I am.

Everything is very personal, nothing is disconnected.

I wasn't ever, like, hardened, as in,

I've never been beaten up because I was like Asian or gay
but just seeing all these people use the word *gay*
or seeing all these people never accepting other people
and being one of those people that wasn't accepted.
Like in [other places I lived],
and being like, "Wow, this is not right."
And just seeing my family members in Nepal
always wanting to come to America
but if they come to America there's nothing here.
And trying to have people live their own life and be happy with it
but then you can't be happy when your country's overpolluted
and there's nothing there, you know.
That's probably what led me to want to help so much.
And just talking to my friends
and winning awards.
It didn't make me stop—
it's not that I want to win more awards—
it's that I think that I owe it to the community after I win an award to just,
like the first award I won I was like,
Wow, I should start doing a lot more for the community, you know?
And having my friends tell me that,
like, I'm an idol to them?
If I gain the knowledge in ways to—
not the knowledge, but parts of knowledges—
I can't do anything better with my time
or my life.

There are times when I don't know how I'm helping.
I'm doing something, but I don't know what that's doing.
And I feel like it's not doing anything
and people kind of question me
and I do not know how to answer that.
[My best friend's] like,
"you know what, Pab?
I see you as a type of person that has motivation
that has the courage
that has the energy

that has everything to go out and do something, and change the world."
And I just started crying
'cause I'm eighteen
and people tell me things like that all the time
and I don't know what to do.
I don't want to choose a fight but I don't know,
I feel like I have to choose something right now
and that rushing is probably the hardest part.

How can I help
it isn't just racism and gay rights
it's also oppression in other countries
and how to help my village in Nepal from becoming overpolluted
or help save my country
or help women around the world
or help anybody, you know?
It's just like, there's so much that you can do out there
and so much I could just be involved in
and that's a large part of my life right now
is like, How am I going to do this?
Like I could just dictate the world
and I wish I could do that
but I can't.
And I'm not saying I have all the right answers either.
I don't, at all,
I don't have any answers.
I just kind of have some knowledge
and I have a lot more to learn
and I'm not just going to learn that through school,
I'm learning that through traveling and being with different types of people.
That's where I've learned most of my stuff—
not from schools,
from people.

I see myself as someone who wants to learn all the time
I still have a long ways to learn.
I think just to be open and to acknowledge the fact that

you have the racism
the homophobia
whatever you're trying to fight,
you have it within you
and you have to deal with it yourself
before you try to deal with it in other people.
Or you deal with it at the same time.
I wish someone who's had the answers would be like,
"well, this is okay and this is not,"
like Yoda
or something like that,
but there isn't
so I have to talk to all sorts of people to figure out
what I'm doing right and what I'm doing wrong,
and if there's never a right and a wrong,
then that's something else that I have to figure out:
What part of it is right and what part of it is wrong,
how close is it?
Of course
I think that's just part of human nature
is that you always want to hear things that affirm your beliefs
and hear things that will help you say that
you're right or
you're good,
you're up there.
And I can't deny no human being ever has that, you know?
As an educator I can be more accepting that you have that
and sometimes that is a fault and sometimes that is not, you know?
Yeah, you will constantly want to be told that you're right, you're wrong,
but question yourself.
But not to question yourself where you never get an answer.
Question yourself once or twice.
Or just go ahead and do something without questioning yourself,
you know?
And be willing to take that responsibility if you're wrong.

One way that I confront people personally

and ways that I do activism,

people hate it sometimes,

is I'm very blunt.

I say things that will make people think,

that I know will anger them.

And I don't understand all of it myself

but like in front of [my girlfriend's] parents

sometimes I make comments about money

and make comments about being yuppy [*sic*]

and about having a yuppy puppy or having a yuppy cat or things,

you know?

Her mom is very uncomfortable around me

her mom is a very uncomfortable woman.

And she's a teacher.

She told my girlfriend that she's very uncomfortable around me at times.

And what I want is, I wish she would confront me

and talk to me about it.

That's what I like to do with people

I do a lot of things that I say bluntly to have people confront me

to talk to me.

And another thing was that her sister—

I love her sister—

she told her mom that I was one of the most racist people she's ever met.

And I heard that

and I was like, "wow."

And this is someone I admire, you know?

So we talked about it,

and I was like,

"I am racist

but I can't help it because it's just all this anger

locked up inside me that makes me have these comments"

but it's not racist to the point where I'm going to kill somebody

it's to the point where I want to talk about it

and talk about the fact that

I'm willing to acknowledge the fact that I have a lot of stereotypes on

White people—

especially White straight people—

but I'm also willing to talk about that.
And as long as they understand me,
or if I understand them,
they just have to accept it,
there has to be a two-way connection.

A lot of people get sick of the fact, like,
any time there's a chance,
I'll bring up gay, being gay.
We'll do a skit,
"why not have those two people be gay?"
They're like, "No, that's too confrontational;
you know, you can't just do that!"
I'm like, "Why the hell not?"
And people are so scared
and they constantly ask me why I have to be bringing up the topic.
They're like, "Why?
Why can't you just leave it alone once?"
And it makes no sense to me because I don't understand
how people plan to get anywhere unless they constantly think about it.
Or they work on it.
And it's not that I'm bringing it up *because* it's gay.
Like, people realize that the whole world is straight
is heterosexually run
but they're not bringing it up all the time.
If they're mentioning,
"Oh, he's with guys and girls,"
or they're not mentioning this and that with straight people,
but if I'm bringing up something that's gay,
I'm mentioning all the time,
my life is focused around that?
But *their* lives are not focused around *heterosexuality*?

People that shut down have never, never been confronted with it.
They've been very PC about it their whole life.
And it's not saying that they don't think
but it's saying that they do and that the way they deal with it,

and being so hard core,

front of your face, whatever, is not the way they do it.

[We need to] get people uncomfortable.

Get them thinking about things they've never thought about.

One thing I look for is, like, that pure state of mind

trying to clear my mind

because I feel like I'm so jumbled up

and I have been for the last four years.

I know there's an answer that I can find

but I don't know where it is.

And that's why I've been looking

but I haven't had time or energy or state of mind to go into that yet.

And part of going back to Nepal is to find that

and find just another way of living life

and maybe that would help me in finding more answers

to the questions that I want to know,

is how to help racism, homophobia, or homosexuality and all of that.

I am sometimes left speechless when thinking about Pab's stories. When I was a high school student, I, too, was involved in numerous organizations and activities, and was a leader in many of them. But unlike Pab, I did not identify as an activist. I did not explicitly work against multiple forms of oppression. I did not see my racial and ethnic identities as political ones. I did not come out of the closet, to myself or to others. I was quite different from Pab, and that difference makes it hard for me to imagine what her life must be like. It is hard for me to imagine how she finds the courage and the energy and the support, especially given the context of her activism. She is leading, she is taking risks, she is bringing about change; even though she does not have all the answers, she is constantly confronting hurdles, and has much to lose within her own family and among her peers. She is—or was at the time of this interview—still a teenager, in school, living at home, and in some ways, in the closet. But she is a *very active* activist. And she acts with a sophisticated understanding of oppression and a sophisticated critique of other activists in the back of her mind.

As I read Pab's stories, one main point stands out to me: she *acts*. And that inspires me to act. She reminds me that I can do no less. I see myself as an economically stable, socially supported adult with the resources and time and wherewithal to work substantially against oppression. How can I sit back when she is risking so much and doing so much? I share the feelings of admiration and motivation expressed by Sam, the antioppressive educator whose vignettes appear throughout this book: "I look at high school students [like Pab] and I think, 'Oh my God, how could I even spend one day being in the closet with these kids doing what they risk every day?'"

I could read Pab's stories for insights on activities that I could undertake with young students. I could read Pab's stories for insights on the barriers young activists today face in bringing about change in schools and with fellow students. I could read Pab's stories for insights on the relationship between identity and activism. I could read Pab's stories for insights on making people uncomfortable, on acknowledging that we will never have all the answers, on the importance of coalitions, and on the relationship between anger and the motivation to act antioppressively. Pab had much to say about such topics, and I expect all of these readings would prove worthwhile and meaningful. But sometimes, such as now, in that never-ending, always-troubling work of activism, I need to remind myself of my responsibilities and all that has yet to be done. I need to reconnect with others doing this kind of work, and rethink and readjust my life so that it does not feel isolated, depressing, and disconnected. I need the hope that can be borne only out of the promises of youth like Pab as I reenergize and remotivate myself. As she continues on her quest for "peace of mind," for "the answers," she never stops acting, never stops learning, and never stops troubling the practices that oppress us. I read her stories and cannot help but think I can do no less.

Her stories are no less contradictory than those of the other activists in this book, but they are nonetheless inspiring, eye-opening, and energizing. And that is why I end this chapter with Pab's stories. They can be catalysts to antioppressive activism and change. Or so they are for me. What are Pab's stories calling on *you* to do?

KEVIN: Why aren't you involved in working against other forms of oppression?

SAM: Why aren't I involved? Well, you know, I think in some areas I am, I have been involved. I think that fighting homophobia takes up so much time, and because I work full-time, and I'll often say, you know, someone says, "Well, do you want to do this, do you want to be involved in this?" I'm like, "Yes, yes, I do." But I keep saying, "Until we have equal rights, I have to keep focused on what I'm doing." And that's just how I choose to proceed. And, I mean I try to keep abreast of the issues and be well read and, raising my own children, I've really instilled, you know, all those things with them. I mean, we have amazing conversations. And so I think that is one way, I am an activist with my own family. But I would just say, and I've really learned this [in] dealing with GLSEN [Gay, Lesbian, and Straight Education Network], is that if you can't stay healthy, you're not going to be good to anybody. Because being an activist, it's everything. You're just constantly giving your entire soul, you know, not even to talk about your finances and your home!

KEVIN: Throughout your life what has been really helpful to you in addressing heterosexism and other forms of oppression?

SAM: Oh God, role models. Really important. Some days that's just what keeps me going. And there are other people in my life, I mean not especially famous people, but role models and just heroes who have done stuff and I, I just, I'm in awe of their strength and how they keep going. And then I say to myself, Well, hell, if they can do that, I can at least get my ass out the door and go to this meeting or make a phone call. Another thing is with young people. Seeing idealism and strength in youth really keeps me going.

KEVIN: Same here.

SAM: I'm just so overwhelmed by them. They're so incredibly brave. I know the kids in my school are just, I'm so amazed. The stuff they have to put up with and how they just keep going. I mean even my own kid, I mean she stands up against it every day in her classes and she shouldn't even have to be doing that, her teacher should be doing it.

KEVIN: Can you think of a time where you made that switch from being not so much an activist to being an activist?

SAM: Let's see. Oh, I know something else that's really encouraged me a lot. It's kind of hokey but, going to the huge marches, the big ones like the one in Washington, going to Stonewall 25, my partner and I were in the Gay Games, and that was just, to meet people from all over the world who are gay. And coming back from things like that. I mean, you're really encouraged to do more. And I think those are the very important times.

KEVIN: Why do you feel that was so encouraging?

SAM: Well, specifically, I'm thinking right now about Stonewall, and the Gay Games in New York. Because I saw people coming from these countries where there's so much oppression overall. And yet these people had somehow found a way to get to New York, and sacrificed so much to be there. And I realized, you know, in our country it's so much easier to be open, to be out, to write letters, to work with alderpeople and political candidates. I think, you know, when something happens like, well, when Matthew Shepard was killed, I was just like, every gay kid, I'm thinking mostly of the males, my heart was just crying for them. And that night when we did the candlelight vigil, and I looked at one of my friends, he's an undergrad here. He's just a waif. I mean, he just doesn't have any family. And I was just like, "My God, if this kid can risk so much, and here I have a nice house, you know, I have a job and everything. I think moments like that are really powerful. I think that's another thing which encourages people to do acts of, you know, activism, 'cause it's hard to sustain it forever. I know a lot of people in this community who are known as *the* activists. But they walk around in fogs half the time because they try to sustain it all the time and I just, I don't know that you can do that, when it's so personal.

KEVIN: Why are you an activist when other queer folks are not?

SAM: I don't know. I really don't. I don't get it. I would never want to be closeted. I mean I just find it so, it's so destructive, so oppressive. I mean, yeah, it's not fun to always be coming out to everybody, but I don't worry, like I hear people say, "Oh, I am just so worried someone's gonna throw a rock through my window or something." I don't know, how many people has that happened to? I think it's also that I'm in it with somebody else who's a total activist.

KEVIN: Being out is not a barrier to your students turning to you?

SAM: No, doesn't push them away. I mean it's scary, you're always a little concerned that it's gonna be a problem, it's gonna put up a barrier. And maybe sometimes it has, and I haven't even been aware of it. But the good thing is that in my teaching environment I also have three other out lesbians, or pretty out teachers, who also work with a lot of my students. English teachers. They do a lot of stuff with curriculum and reinforcement and through writing, videos, and they're also involved in the gay-straight alliance. So it's like these kids are getting it from other places. And I'll have some of their students who I would assume would be really, you know, stereotyping gay people or saying misleading information, and kids [who] are, you know, from lower-class families in [a nearby small town], and they're sitting in my class and they're saying stuff like, "Well, you know, gay people have the right to have full lives and they should be able to marry." And I'm just like, "Oh my God, they're getting it." Because they're hearing it from other people, too. And that to me is so thrilling. But I'm lucky. It's not that way at most high schools. There aren't other teachers who are willing to talk about it.

CHAPTER 5

Conclusions

In this book that refuses closure, I struggled to imagine an appropriate concluding chapter. At first, I thought of writing a somewhat conventional conclusion in which I summarize my main findings and arguments (on poststructuralist conceptualizations of oppression and queer activist approaches to addressing resistance to antioppressive change), reflect on my contributions to educational research and practice (through different routes of reading and what each makes possible and impossible), and suggest directions for future research (by looking beyond the current field of research, including the arguments in this book). While such a conclusion could certainly be helpful to people who have not read the entire book, I started wondering whether it could actually work against the book's goals. By ending with my summaries, my reflections, and my suggestions in this common and commonsense way, I felt that I would be not merely sharing my reading of my book, but doing so in a way that gave my reading authoritativeness. I did not want to engage in a traditional practice in educational research that does not necessarily invite readers to look beyond my book and my readings of it. I wanted an ending that would make it difficult for readers to read and to finish reading my book in traditional ways.

Helping readers to look beyond my own analyses and arguments was the purpose of interspersing Sam's vignettes throughout the book. So then I thought of writing a conclusion in which I reflect on some of the insights on antioppressive education made possible when juxtaposing Sam's vignettes with my chapters. I thought I might be able to model possible readings of that juxtaposition (looking for similarities, and differences, and complex and paradoxical relationships, and so forth), even while insisting that readers look beyond my models and find yet other ways to read Sam's and my contributions. I might focus, for example, on whether Sam's vignettes suggest yet another route of reading, and how that new route could help me reread my own book in antioppressive ways. However, while such a conclusion could certainly be helpful to people interested in hearing how I think Sam's ideas and practices trouble my own arguments, I again started wondering whether it would work against my goals. By ending with my reading of Sam's stories, I felt that I would be not only assigning some authoritative meaning to them, but also reducing their potential to invite readers to do their own work while reading, and while reflecting on what was just read. It seemed that modeling what I felt it means to use Sam's vignettes to look beyond my analysis disinvites readers to do their own work of *looking beyond* and instead makes it easier to feel satisfied that I have given out what readers should have gotten out of the book. Such a conclusion, in other words, makes it possible to continue to think of reading as a task of absorbing knowledge from a text rather than using the text in antioppressive ways (as when learning from it but also looking beyond it). I wanted an ending that would trouble my own authority, the authority of my own readings.

So then I thought of writing a conclusion in which I make some connection between routes of reading that refuse finality and approaches to teaching that refuse finality. I remembered that I had begun this book with anecdotes on the impossibility and problematic nature of traditional approaches to teaching and learning, and realized that such anecdotes could make for an interesting ending. I thought I might describe, for example, instances of my teaching that illustrated some of the issues in this book—such as paradox, uncertainty, and discomfort—and the ways they helped my students and me to address our desires and resistances and to challenge oppressions. I was excited by the idea of writing a conclusion that could help readers find feelings of hope and promise, which I admit were often lacking in my discussions of oppression and activist labors. However, I still wondered whether such a conclusion continues to invoke my authority as the expert on antioppressive education, because doing so implies not only that I know what it means to put these theories into practice, but also that I have already done so with encouraging results. I started to feel stuck in the process of concluding this book.

Perhaps this is not surprising. By trying to write in antioppressive ways, I am trying to teach through my writing. My writing is an instance of the type of antioppressive education that I am advocating. And this makes it likely that I will confront difficulties akin to those I have confronted as a teacher: a desire to control what cannot be controlled—namely, what students and readers learn, how they learn it, and how they change as a result.

Just as students enter our classrooms with a range of experiences, identities, desires, needs, and so forth, so too do readers engage with our texts while drawing on a range of such things. And just as each moment of teaching and learning is a highly situated moment that is never the same as the next because of these differences, so too is each moment of reading a highly situated moment in which readers read and respond differently than they do at other moments. By saying that I want my students to go from here to there, I am expecting to know that they are "here," I am expecting to know what they bring with them and how that influences how they will experience my lesson or text. In other words, by saying that I want them to learn or read *like this*, I am closing off the ways that *who they are* can take my lesson or text in directions appropriate and unique to *where they need to go*. This is not to say that I should not have my own goals, since I clearly do, and I strive to achieve them with conviction. However, this is to say that the ways I strive to achieve my goals of challenging oppression must constantly work against the ways that challenging oppression can paradoxically contribute to oppression.

Throughout this book, I have critiqued traditional approaches to teaching and learning for their tendencies to dictate who students are supposed to be and become, especially when that *who* is someone who fits into the oppressive status quo of society. In contrast, I have argued that antioppressive approaches to teaching and learning can trouble this tendency by creating new, activist possibilities for who students can be and become. I am not arguing that students must match only one particular image of "the antioppressive student," since such a prescriptive move is no different than that which I am critiquing. Rather, I am arguing that teachers and students must simultaneously enact different antioppressive forms of education while troubling those very forms; simultaneously be antioppressive in some ways while troubling those very ways of being. Antioppressive education needs to refuse to be a panacea, and those who propose antioppressive approaches need to refuse to speak as the authoritative voice.

One way I remind myself of the potential for attempts at antioppressive education to continue marginalizing students is by thinking back to my interview with Christopher, the gay Black activist described in chapter 3. A few years before our interview, Christopher had adopted a young child. As Christopher told it,

> In his preschool
> they have a hard time dealing with a child that's so
> difficult
> and so they had a hard time dealing with [my son] Lenny
> and they kept wanting to send him home,
> send him home.
> And then
> one teacher just wanted to say,
> "Look, he should just not be in preschool,"
> to have him out of preschool.
> And that's when I coined the phrase that I hope catches on eventually is
> disposable kids.
> Our society seems to believe in disposable kids:
> "If a kid gives you too many problems, get rid of it,
> we can't deal with their problem
> and when they're older
> they can go see a psychologist about it and deal with it then."
>
> And that's not to say that,
> you know,
> the situation that happened in Littleton recently,
> that those two boys should have been kicked out of the school system.
> But what did we do to try to avoid this happening?
> Or did we just figure it wouldn't?

We treated those two boys as disposable kids

and they have been disposed of.

They're not a problem that we have to deal with anymore.

That's how our society treats it.

And I have a problem with schools that have a philosophy of

disposable kids

and I absolutely refuse to allow them to treat my son as a disposable kid.

Christopher's notion that schools "dispose" of "difficult" students is certainly not a new one. I have heard students, parents, educators, and researchers alike argue that schools fail to address certain groups of students, especially those who do not conform to traditional images of "good students," and that doing so allows many of these students to fail out of and be Othered by the school system. However, the connection that Christopher draws between his son, a Black toddler from a working-class background, and the White middle-class teenagers from Littleton suggests to me that the disposal of kids he refers to might just be more widespread than traditionally assumed, and for that matter, that even well-intentioned educators might be disposing of some of the very students they are trying to address. Antioppressive educators have an ethical responsibility to reflect constantly on students they may be disposing of, and on how to rework their practices.

Therefore, my "conclusion" is really an insistence that this work never be concluded. My conclusion is really a call to continue the paradoxical work involved in antioppressive educational research and practice. I hope I have shown that educators have already made tremendous gains in theorizing and implementing approaches to teaching and learning that help to challenge multiple forms of oppression. And I hope I have provided some tools for educators to use as we build on their work while looking beyond and imagining new approaches to bringing about change.

Vignette 5

KEVIN: If someone were to say to me, Why did you interview a lesbian
teacher, what difference is she making to this field, what do you think
that answer might be? What are you saying that people need to hear?

SAM: Well, I think that, because I've been oppressed, as a woman and a lesbian. I just, I can't tolerate it. It sets me on fire and I want to make
changes. I can, like, get inside of people and I see it happening to them,
and it doesn't have to be just about gayness, or about being a woman. It
transcends to other areas, too. But, you know, that doesn't happen with
everyone, and why not? I try to think about that. We talked about the
bull dykes, you know, they play softball and they go to the bar. They
would never give money for a cause or go to a conference or walk in [a]
Gay Pride [parade]. They might come and watch, but they'd never think
of walking. So, what's the difference? I mean, I don't know, but I feel
there have just been things that have happened in my life that prevent
me from not doing this. So, the chapter in the book would be that I can't
watch intolerance. I want to educate, I want people to at least come to
common ground. I can't change how they will behave, but I want them
to know. And that's why I can't be closeted either. That's so unfair to
students for me to stay in the closet. It's just denying them the right to
an education—whoever they are.

References

Althusser, L. (1971). *Lenin and philosophy, and other essays*. London: New Left Books.

American Association of University Women. (1992). *How schools shortchange girls: A study of major findings on girls and education*. Washington, DC: AAUW Educational Foundation.

Anderson, G. L. (1989). Critical ethnography in education: Origins, current status, and new directions. *Review of Educational Research, 59*(3), 249–270.

Anyon, J. (1979). Ideology and United States history textbooks. *Harvard Educational Review, 49*(3), 361–386.

Anzaldúa, G. (1987). *Borderlands/La frontera: The new mestiza*. San Francisco: Spinsters/Aunt Lute.

Apple, M. W. (1993). The politics of official knowledge: Does a national curriculum make sense? *Teachers College Record, 95*(2), 222–241.

Apple, M. W. (1995). *Education and power* (2nd ed.). New York: Routledge.

Arnot, M. (1984). How shall we educate our sons? In R. Deem (Ed.), *Co-education reconsidered*. Milton Keynes, England: Open University Press.

Asante, M. K. (1991). The Afrocentric idea in education. *Journal of Negro Education, 60*(2), 170–180.

Askew, S., & Ross, C. (1988). *Boys don't cry: Boys and sexism in education*. Milton Keynes, England: Open University Press.

Athanases, S. Z. (1996). A gay-themed lesson in an ethnic literature curriculum: Tenth graders' responses to "Dear Anita." *Harvard Educational Review, 66*(2), 231–256.

Battersby, C. (1989). *Gender and genius: Towards a feminist aesthetics*. Bloomington: Indiana University Press.

Belenky, M., Clinchy, B., Goldberger, N., & Tarule, J. M. (1986). *Women's ways of knowing: The development of the self, voice, and mind*. New York: Basic Books.

Besner, H. F., & Spungin, C. I. (1995). *Gay and lesbian students: Understanding their needs*. Washington, DC: Taylor & Francis.

Bickel, W. E., & Hattrup, R. A. (1995). Teachers and researchers in collaboration: Reflections on the process. *American Educational Research Journal, 32*(1), 35–64.

Bishop, A. J. (1990). Western mathematics: The secret weapon of cultural imperialism. *Race & Class, 32*(2), 51–65.

Bishop, A. J. (1994). Cultural conflicts in mathematics education: Developing a research agenda. *For the Learning of Mathematics, 14*(2), 15–18.

Blackwood, E., & Wieringa, S. E. (1999). Sapphic shadows: Challenging the silence in the study of sexuality. In E. Blackwood & S. E. Wieringa (Eds.). *Female desires: Same-sex relations and transgender practices across cultures* (pp. 39–63). New York: Columbia University Press.

Bornstein, K. (1994). *Gender outlaw: On men, women, and the rest of us*. New York: Vintage Books.

Boswell, J. (1980). *Christianity, social tolerance and homosexuality: Gay people in western Europe from the beginning of the Christian era to the fourteenth century*. Chicago: University of Chicago Press.

Britzman, D. P. (1995). "The question of belief:" Writing poststructural ethnography. *Qualitative Studies in Education, 8*(3), 229–238.

Britzman, D. P. (1998a). *Lost subjects, contested objects: Toward a psychoanalytic inquiry of learning*. Albany: State University of New York Press.

Britzman, D. P. (1998b). On some psychical consequences of AIDS education. In W. F. Pinar (Ed.), *Queer theory in education* (pp. 321–335). Mahwah, NJ: Lawrence Erlbaum Associates.

Britzman, D., Santiago-Valles, K., Jimenez-Muñoz, G., & Lamash, L. (1993). Slips that show and tell: Fashioning multiculture as a problem of representation. In C. McCarthy & W. Crichlow (Eds.), *Race, identity, and representation in education* (pp. 188–200). New York: Routledge.

Burawoy, M. (1992). The extended case method. In M. Burawoy, J. Gamson, & A. Burton (Eds.), *Ethnography unbound: Power and resistance in the modern metropolis*. Berkeley: University of California Press.

Butler, J. (1990). *Gender trouble: Feminism and the subversion of identity*. New York: Routledge.

Butler, J. (1993). *Bodies that matter: On the discursive limits of "sex."* New York: Routledge.

Butler, J. (1997). *Excitable speech: A politics of the performative*. New York: Routledge.

Campo, R. (1999). Does silencio = muerte? Notes on translating the AIDS epidemic. *The Progressive, 63*(10), 20–23.

Capper, C. A. (1999). (Homo)sexualities, organizations, and administration: Possibilities for in(queer)y. *Educational Researcher, 28*(5), 4–11.

Casey, K. (1993). *I answer with my life: Life histories of women teachers working for social change*. New York: Routledge.

Chan, C. S. (1995). Issues of sexual identity in an ethnic minority: The case of Chinese American lesbians, gay men, and bisexual people. In A. D'Augelli & C. Patterson (Eds.), *Lesbian, gay, and bisexual identities over the lifespan* (pp. 87–101). New York: Oxford University.

Chan, S. (1995). On the ethnic studies requirement. In D. T. Nakanishi & T. Y. Nishida (Eds.), *The Asian American educational experience: A source book for teachers and students* (pp. 329–338). New York: Routledge.

Chase, C. (1998). Hermaphrodites with attitude: Mapping the emergence of inter-sex political activism. *GLQ: A Journal of Gay and Lesbian Studies, 4*(2), 189–211.

Cohen, C. J. (1996). Contested membership: Black gay identities and the politics of AIDS. In S. Seidman (Ed.), *Queer theory/sociology* (pp. 362–394). Cambridge, MA: Blackwell.

Committee on Gay, Lesbian, and Bisexual Issues. (1997). *Report to the faculty senate.* Madison: University of Wisconsin-Madison.

Conerly, G. (1996). The politics of Black lesbian, gay, and bisexual identity. In B. Beemyn & M. Eliason (Eds.), *Queer studies: A lesbian, gay, bisexual and trans-gender anthology* (pp. 133–145). New York: New York University Press.

Connell, R. W. (1987). *Gender and power: Society, the person, and sexual politics.* Cambridge: Polity Press.

Connell, R. W. (1995). *Masculinities.* Berkeley and Los Angeles: University of California Press.

Connell, R. W. (1997). Teaching the boys: New research on masculinity, and gender strategies for boys. *Teachers College Record, 98*(2), 206–235.

Countryman, L. W. (1988). *Dirt, greed and sex: Sexual ethics in the New Testament and their implications for today.* Philadelphia: Fortress Press.

Crenshaw, K. (1992). Whose story is it, anyway? Feminist and anti-racist appropri-ations of Anita Hill. In T. Morrison (Ed.), *Race-ing justice, en-gendering power* (pp. 402–436). New York: Pantheon.

Cronon, W. (1992). A place for stories: Nature, history, and narrative. *The Journal of American History, 78*, 1347–1379.

Crowley, S. (1989). *A teacher's introduction to deconstruction.* Urbana, IL: National Council of Teachers of English.

Crystal, D. (1989). Asian Americans and the myth of the model minority. *Social Casework: The Journal of Contemporary Social Work, 70*(7), 405–413.

D'Ambrosio, U. (1985). Ethnomathematics and its place in the history and pedagogy of mathematics. *For the Learning of Mathematics, 5*(1), 44–48.

Davies, B. (1989). *Frogs and snails and feminist tales: Preschool children and gender.* North Sydney, Australia: Allen & Unwin.

Delgado-Gaitan, C. (1993). Researching change and changing the research. *Harvard Educational Review, 63*(4), 389–411.

Delpit, L. D. (1986). Skills and other dilemmas of a progressive black educator. *Harvard Educational Review, 56*(4), 379–385.

Delpit, L. D. (1988). The silenced dialogue: Power and pedagogy in educating other people's children. *Harvard Educational Review, 58*(3), 280–298.

Doll, M. A. (1998). Queering the gaze. In W. F. Pinar (Ed.), *Queer theory in education* (pp. 287–298). Mahwah, NJ: Lawrence Erlbaum Associates.

Ellsworth, E. (1992). Why doesn't this feel empowering?: Working through the repressive myths of critical pedagogy. In C. Luke & J. Gore (Eds.), *Feminisms and critical pedagogies* (pp. 90–119). New York: Routledge.

Ellsworth, E. (1997). *Teaching positions: Difference, pedagogy, and the power of address.* New York: Teachers College Press.

Epstein, D. (1997). Boyz' own stories: Masculinities and sexualities in schools. *Gender and Education, 9*(1), 105–115.

Epstein, D., & Johnson, R. (1998). *Schooling sexualities.* Buckingham: Open University Press.

Fanon, F. (1970). *Black skin, white masks.* London: Paladin.

Feinberg, L. (1993). *Stone butch blues: A novel.* Ithaca, NY: Firebrand Books.

Felman, S. (1995). Education and crisis, or the vicissitudes of teaching. In C. Caruth (Ed.), *Trauma: Explorations in memory* (pp. 13–66). Baltimore, MD: The Johns Hopkins University Press.

Fine, M. (1991). *Framing dropouts: Notes on the politics of an urban public high school.* Albany: State University of New York Press.

Fine, M. (1994). Dis-stance and other stances: Negotiations of power inside feminist research. In A. Gitlin (Ed.), *Power and method: Political activism and educational research* (pp. 13–35). New York: Routledge.

Fleener, M. J. (1999). Towards a poststructural mathematics curriculum: Expanding discursive possibilities. *Journal of Curriculum Theorizing, 15*(2), 89–105.

Fordham, S. (1996). *Blacked out: Dilemmas of race, identity, and success at Capital High.* Chicago: University of Chicago Press.

Foster, M. (1994). The power to know one thing is never the power to know all things: Methodological notes on two studies of Black American teachers. In A. Gitlin (Ed.), *Power and method: Political activism and educational research* (pp. 129–146). New York: Routledge.

Foucault, M. (1978). *The history of sexuality, Volume I: An introduction.* New York: Vintage Books.

Frankenstein, M., & Powell, A. B. (1994). Toward liberatory mathematics: Paulo Freire's epistemology and ethnomathematics. In P. McLaren & C. Lankshear (Eds.), *The Politics of Liberation: Paths from Freire* (pp. 74–99). London: Routledge.

Friend, R. A. (1993). Choices, not closets: Heterosexism and homophobia in schools. In L. Weis & M. Fine (Eds.), *Beyond silenced voices: Class, race, and gender in United States schools* (pp. 209–235). Albany: State University of New York Press.

Freire, P. (1995). *Pedagogy of the oppressed*. (Translated by M. B. Ramos.) New York: Continuum.

Fuss, D. (1989). *Essentially speaking: Feminism, nature, and difference*. New York: Routledge.

Fuss, D. (1991). Inside/out. In D. Fuss (Ed.), *Inside/out: Lesbian theories, gay theories* (pp. 1–10). New York: Routledge.

Gee, D. (Director), & Asian Women United (Producer). (1988). *Slaying the dragon* [Videocassette]. (Available from National Asian American Telecommunications Association, 346 Ninth Street, Second Floor, San Francisco, CA, 94103.)

Gibson, M. A. (1988). *Accommodation without assimilation: Sikh immigrants in an American high school*. Ithaca, NY: Cornell University Press.

Gibson, P. (1989). Gay male and lesbian youth suicide. In M. R. Feinleib (Ed.), *Report of the secretary's task force on youth suicide. Volume 3: Prevention and interventions in youth suicide* (pp. 110–142). Washington, DC: U.S. Department of Health and Human Services.

Gilligan, C. (1982). *In a different voice: Psychological theory and women's development*. Cambridge: Harvard University Press.

Giroux, H. A. (1997). Rewriting the discourse of racial identity: Towards a pedagogy and politics of whiteness. *Harvard Educational Review, 67*(2), 285–320.

Giroux, H. A., & McLaren, P. L. (1989). Introduction: Schooling, cultural politics, and the struggle for democracy. In H. A. Giroux & P. McLaren (Eds.), *Critical pedagogy, the state, and cultural struggle* (pp. xi–xxxv). Albany: State University of New York Press.

Gluck, S. B. (1991). Advocacy oral history: Palestinian woman in resistance. In S. B. Gluck & D. Patai (Eds.), *Women's words: The feminist practice of oral history* (pp. 205–219). New York: Routledge.

Goldstein, B. L. (1988). In search of survival: The education and integration of Hmong refugee girls. *The Journal of Ethnic Studies, 16*(2), 1–27.

Goldstein, R. (1999, Autumn). The "faggot" factor: The chickens came home to roost at Columbine High. *Respect,* (2), 19–21.

Gopinath, G. (1997, April). *Nostalgia, desire, diaspora: South Asian sexualities in motion*. Paper presented at the meeting of the Association for Asian American Studies, Seattle, WA.

Governor's Commission on Gay and Lesbian Youth. (1993). *Making schools safe for gay and lesbian youth: Breaking the silence in schools and in families*. Boston: Massachusetts Department of Education.

Gramsci, A. (1971). *Selections from the prison notebooks*. (Edited and translated by Q. Hoare & G. N. Smith.) New York: International Publishers.

Greene, F. L. (1996). Introducing queer theory into the undergraduate classroom: Abstractions and practical applications. *English Education, 28*(4), 325–339.

Hall, S. (1990). Cultural identity and diaspora. In J. Rutherford (Ed.), *Identity: Community, Culture, Difference*. London: Lawrence & Wishart.

Haraway, D. (1988). Situated knowledges: The science question in feminism and the privilege of partial perspective. *Feminist Studies, 14*(3), 575–599.

Harding, S. (1994). Is science multicultural? Challenges, resources, opportunities, uncertainties. In D. T. Goldberg (Ed.), *Multiculturalism: A critical reader* (pp. 344–370). Oxford: Blackwell.

Helminiak, D. A. (1994). *What the Bible really says about homosexuality*. San Francisco: Alamo Square Press.

Higginbotham, E. B. (1992). African-American women's history and the metalanguage of race. *Signs: Journal of Women in Culture and Society, 17*(2), 251–274.

Holland, D. C., & Eisenhart, M. A. (1990). *Educated in romance: Women, achievement, and college culture*. Chicago: University of Chicago Press.

Hom, A. & Ma, M. (1993). Premature gestures: A speculative dialogue on Asian Pacific Islander lesbian and gay writing. *Journal of Homosexuality, 26*(2/3), 21–51.

Honeychurch, K. G. (1998). Carnal knowledge: Re-searching (through) the sexual body. In W. F. Pinar (Ed.), *Queer theory in education* (pp. 251–273). Mahwah, NJ: Lawrence Erlbaum Associates.

hooks, b. (1984). *Feminist theory: From margin to center*. Boston: South End Press.

hooks, b. (1994). *Teaching to transgress: Education as the practice of freedom*. New York: Routledge.

hooks, b. (1995). Doing it for daddy. In M. Berger, B. Wallis, & S. Watson (Eds.), *Constructing masculinity* (pp. 98–106). New York: Routledge.

Hune, S. (1995). Opening the American mind and body: The role of Asian American studies. In D. T. Nakanishi & T. Y. Nishida (Eds.), *The Asian American educational experience: A source book for teachers and students* (pp. 322–328). New York: Routledge.

Jackson, P. W. (1968). *Life in classrooms*. New York: Holt, Rhinehart, & Winston.

Jackson, P. W., Boostrom, R., & Hanson, D. (1993). *The moral life of schools*. San Francisco: Jossey-Bass.

Jacobs, S.-E., Thomas, W., & Lang, S. (1997). Introduction. In S.-E. Jacobs, W. Thomas, & S. Lang (Eds.), *Two-spirit people: Native American gender identity, sexuality, and spirituality* (pp. 1–18). Urbana: University of Illinois Press.

Jennings, K. (1998, September 29). My perspective: Be a man. *Advocate*, p. 11.

Johnson, J. A. (1997). Life after death: Critical pedagogy in an urban classroom. In I. Hall, C. H. Campbell, & E. J. Miech (Eds.), *Class acts: Teachers reflect on their own classroom practice* (pp. 107–126). Cambridge: Harvard Educational Review.

Kenway, J., & Willis, S. (1998). *Answering back: Girls, boys and feminism in schools*. New York: Routledge.

Kessler, S. J. (1998). *Lessons from the intersexed.* New Brunswick, NJ: Rutgers University Press.

Khayatt, D. (1997). Sex and the teacher: Should we come out in class? *Harvard Educational Review,* 67(1), 126–143.

Kimmel, M. (1994). Masculinity as homophobia: Fear, shame, and silence in the construction of gender identity. In H. Brod & M. Kaufman (Eds.), *Theorizing masculinities* (pp. 119–141) Thousand Oaks, CA: Sage.

Kozol, J. (1991). *Savage inequalities: Children in America's school.* New York: HarperPerennial.

Kumashiro, K. K. (1999a). "Barbie," "big dicks," and "faggots": Paradox, performativity, and anti-oppressive pedagogy. *JCT: Journal of Curriculum Theorizing,* 15(1), 27–42.

Kumashiro, K. K. (1999b). Supplementing normalcy and otherness: Queer Asian American men reflect on stereotypes, identity, and oppression. *Qualitative Studies in Education,* 12(5), 491–508.

Ladson-Billings, G. (1994). *The dreamkeepers: Successful teachers of African American children.* San Francisco, CA: Jossey-Bass.

Ladson-Billings, G. (1995a). Making mathematics meanings in multicultural contexts. In W. G. Secada, E. Fennema, & L. B. Adajian (Eds.), *New directions for equity in mathematics education* (pp. 126–145). Cambridge, England: Cambridge University Press.

Ladson-Billings, G. (1995b). Toward a theory of culturally relevant pedagogy. *American Educational Research Journal,* 32(3), 465–491.

Ladwig, J. G. (1991). Is collaborative research exploitative? *Educational Theory, 41,* 111–120.

Lather, P. (1991). *Getting smart: Feminist research and pedagogy with/in the postmodern.* New York: Routledge.

Lather, P. (1998). Critical pedagogy and its complicities: A praxis of stuck places. *Educational Theory,* 48(4), 487–497.

Leck, G. M. (1994). Queer relations with educational research. In A. Gitlin (Ed.), *Power and method: Political activism and educational research* (pp. 77–96). New York: Routledge.

LeCompte, M. D. (1995). Some notes on power, agenda, and voice: A researcher's personal evolution toward critical collaborative research. In P. L. McLaren & J. M. Giarelli (Eds.), *Critical theory and educational research* (pp. 91–112). Albany: State University of New York Press.

Lee, J. (1996). Why Suzie Wong is not a lesbian: Asian and Asian American lesbian and bisexual women and femme/butch/gender identities. In B. Beemyn & M. Eliason (Eds.), *Queer studies: A lesbian, gay, bisexual, and transgender anthology* (pp. 115–132). New York: New York University Press.

Lee, S. J. (1996). *Unraveling the "model minority" stereotype: Listening to Asian American youth.* New York: Teachers College Press.

Lee, S. J. (1997). The road to college: Hmong American women's pursuit of higher education. *Harvard Educational Review, 67*(4), 803–827.

Letts, W. J. (1999). How to make "boys" and "girls" in the classroom: The heteronormative nature of elementary-school science. In W. J. Letts & J. T. Sears (Eds.), *Queering elementary education: Advancing the dialogue about sexualities and schooling* (pp. 97–110). Lanham, MD: Rowman & Littlefield Publishers.

Lipkin, A. (1995). The case for a gay and lesbian curriculum. In G. Unks (Ed.), *The gay teen: Educational practice and theory for lesbian, gay, and bisexual adolescents* (pp. 31–52). New York: Routledge.

Loutzenheiser, L. A. (1997). How schools play "smear the queer." *Feminist Teacher, 10*(2), 59–64.

Luke, C., & Gore, J. (1992). Women in the academy: Strategy, struggle, survival. In C. Luke & J. Gore (Eds.), *Feminisms and critical pedagogy* (pp. 192–210). New York: Routledge.

Luhmann, S. (1998). Queering/querying pedagogy? Or, pedagogy is a pretty queer thing. In W. F. Pinar (Ed.), *Queer theory in education* (pp. 141–155). Mahwah, NJ: Lawrence Erlbaum Associates.

Mac an Ghaill, M. (1994). *The making of men: Masculinities, sexualities and schooling.* Buckingham, England: Open University Press.

Macedo, D. (1991). English only: The tongue-tying of America. *Journal of Education, 173*(2), 9–20.

Maher, F. A., & Tetreault, M. K. (1994). *The feminist classroom: An inside look at how professors and students are transforming higher education for a diverse society.* New York: Basic Books.

Maher, F. A., & Tetreault, M. K. (1997). Learning in the dark: How assumptions of whiteness shape classroom knowledge. *Harvard Educational Review, 67*(2), 321–349.

Malinowitz, H. (1995). *Textual orientations: Lesbian and gay students and the making of discourse communities.* Portsmouth, NH: Heinemann.

Marshall, B. K. (1992). *Teaching the postmodern: Fiction and theory.* New York: Routledge.

McCarthy, C. (1993). After the canon: Knowledge and ideological representation in the multicultural discourse on curriculum reform. In C. McCarthy & W. Crichlow (Eds.), *Race, identity, and representation in education* (pp. 289–305). New York: Routledge.

McKay, N. Y. (1993). Acknowledging differences: Can women find unity through diversity? In S. J. Jaimes & A. P. A. Busia (Eds.), *Theorizing black feminisms: The visionary pragmatism of black women* (pp. 267–282). London: Routledge.

McKay, S. L., & Wong, S. C. (1996). Multiple discourses, multiple identities: Investment and agency in second-language learning among Chinese adolescent immigrant students. *Harvard Educational Review, 66*(3), 577–608.

McLaren, P. (1994). White terror and oppositional agency: Towards a critical multi-culturalism. In D. T. Goldberg (Ed.), *Multiculturalism: A critical reader* (pp. 45–74). Oxford: Blackwell.

McRobbie, A. (1978). Working class girls and the culture of femininity. In Centre for Contemporary Cultural Studies (Eds.), *Women take issue: Aspects of women's subordination* (pp. 96–108). London: Hutchinson.

Metz, M. H. (1992). *Different by design: The context and character of three magnet schools.* New York: Routledge.

Middleton, S. (1993). *Educating feminists: Life histories and pedagogy.* New York: Teachers College Press.

Middleton, S. (1997). *Disciplining sexuality: Foucault, life histories, and education.* New York: Teachers College Press.

Miller, J. L. (1998). Autobiography as queer curriculum practice. In W. F. Pinar (Ed.), *Queer theory in education* (pp. 365–373). Mahwah, NJ: Lawrence Erlbaum Associates.

Miller, L. S. (1995). *An American imperative: Accelerating minority educational achievement.* New Haven: Yale University Press.

Minnich, E. K. (1990). *Transforming knowledge.* Philadelphia, PA: Temple University Press.

Monteiro, K. P., & Fuqua, V. (1995). African-American gay youth: One form of man-hood. In G. Unks (Ed.), *The gay teen: Educational practice and theory for lesbian, gay, and bisexual adolescents* (pp. 159–187). New York: Routledge.

Morris, M. (1998). Unresting the curriculum: Queer projects, queer imaginings. In W. F. Pinar (Ed.), *Queer theory in education* (pp. 275–286). Mahwah, NJ: Lawrence Erlbaum Associates.

Morrison, T. (1992). *Playing in the dark: Whiteness and the literary imagination.* New York: Vintage Books.

Murray, S. O. (1996). *American gay.* Chicago: University of Chicago Press.

Nelson-Barber, S., & Estrin, E. T. (1995). Bringing Native American perspectives to mathematics and science teaching. *Theory into Practice, 34*(3), 174–185.

Noddings, N. (1984). *Caring: A feminine approach to ethics and moral education.* Berkeley and Los Angeles: University of California Press.

O'Neill, M. (1993). Teaching literature as cultural criticism. *English Quarterly, 25*(1), 19–25.

Oakley, A. (1981). Interviewing women: A contradiction in terms. In H. Roberts (Ed.), *Doing feminist research* (pp. 30–61). New York: Routledge.

Okihiro, G. Y. (1994). *Margins and mainstreams: Asians in American history and culture*. Seattle: University of Washington Press.

Orenstein, P. (1994). *Schoolgirls: Young women, self-esteem, and the confidence gap.* New York: Anchor Books.

Osajima, K. (1988). Asian Americans as the model minority: An analysis of the popular press image in the 1960s and 1980s. In G. Y. Okihiro, S. Hune, A. A. Hansen, & J. M. Liu (Eds.), *Reflections on shattered windows: Promises and prospects for Asian American studies* (pp. 165–174). Pullman: Washington State University Press.

Osajima, K. (1993). The hidden injuries of race. In L. A. Revilla, G. M. Nomura, S. Wong, & S. Hune (Eds.), *Bearing dreams, shaping visions: Asian Pacific American perspectives* (pp. 81–91). Pullman: Washington State University Press.

Palumbo-Liu, D. (1995). Introduction. In D. Palumbo-Liu (Ed.), *The ethnic canon: Histories, institutions, and interventions* (pp. 1–27). Minneapolis: University of Minnesota Press.

Paxton, R. J. (1999). A deafening silence: History textbooks and the students who read them. *Review of Educational Research, 69*(3), 315–339.

Philips, S. U. (1983). *The invisible culture: Communication in classroom and community on the Warm Springs Indian reservation.* New York: Longman.

Pinar, W. F. (1998). Introduction. In W. F. Pinar (Ed.), *Queer theory in education* (pp. 1–47). Mahwah, NJ: Lawrence Erlbaum Associates.

Pitt, A. J. (1998). Fantasizing women in the women's studies classroom: Toward a symptomatic reading of negation. In W. F. Pinar (Ed.), *Queer theory in education* (pp. 299–319). Mahwah, NJ: Lawrence Erlbaum Associates.

Powell, A. B., & Frankenstein, M. (Eds.) (1997). *Ethnomathematics: Challenging eurocentrism in mathematics education.* Albany: State University of New York Press.

Powell, T. B. (1999). Introduction: Re-thinking cultural identity. In T. B. Powell (Ed.), *Rethinking the binary: Reconstructing cultural identity in a multicultural context* (pp. 1–13). New Brunswick, NJ: Rutgers University Press.

Reynolds, A. L., & Koski, M. J. (1995). Lesbian, gay, and bisexual teens and the school counselor. In G. Unks (Ed.), *The gay teen: Educational practice and theory for lesbian, gay, and bisexual adolescents* (pp. 85–93). New York: Routledge.

Rhoads, R. A. (1994). *Coming out in college: The struggle for a queer identity.* Westport, CT: Bergin & Garvey.

Richardson, L. (1997). *Fields of play: Constructing an academic life.* New Brunswick, NJ: Rutgers University Press.

Russo, V. (1989). *The celluloid closet: Homosexuality in the movies.* New York: Perennial Library.

Sadker, M., & Sadker, D. (1994). *Failing at fairness: How our schools cheat girls.* New York: Touchstone.

Salomone, R. (1997, October 8). Sometimes 'equal' means 'different': New York city schools should go the legal distance in defending single-sex public education. *Education Week*, 31–32.

Sanday, P. R. (1990). *Fraternity gang rape: Sex, brotherhood, and privilege on campus.* New York: New York University Press.

Scheurich, J. J. (1995). A postmodernist critique of research interviewing. *Qualitative Studies in Education, 8*(3), 239–252.

Schmitz, B., Rosenfelt, D., Butler, J. E., & Guy-Sheftall, B. (1995). Women's studies and curriculum transformation. In J. Banks & C. A. M. Banks (Eds.), *Handbook of research on multicultural education* (pp. 708–728). New York: Simon and Schuster Macmillan.

Scott, J. W. (1993). The evidence of experience. In H. Abelove, M. A. Barale, & D. M. Halperin (Eds.), *The lesbian and gay studies reader* (pp. 397–415). New York: Routledge.

Scroggs, R. (1983). *The New Testament and homosexuality: Contextual background for contemporary debate.* Philadelphia: Fortress Press.

Sears, J. T. (1987). Peering into the well of loneliness: The responsibility of educators to gay and lesbian youth. In A. Molner (Ed.), *Social issues and education: challenge and responsibility* (pp. 79–100). Alexandria, VA: Association for Supervision and Curriculum Development.

Sears, J. T. (1995). Black-gay or gay-black? Choosing identities and identifying choices. In G. Unks (Ed.), *The gay teen: Educational practice and theory for lesbian, gay, and bisexual adolescents* (pp. 135–157). New York: Routledge.

Secada, W. G. (1995). Social and critical dimensions for equity in mathematics education. In W. G. Secada, E. Fennema, & L. B. Adajian (Eds.), *New directions for equity in mathematics education* (pp. 146–164). Cambridge, England: Cambridge University Press.

Sedgwick, E. K. (1991). *Epistemology of the closet.* Hemel Hempstead, England: Harvester-Wheatsheaf.

Shah, N. (1993). Sexuality, identity, and the uses of history. In R. Ratti (Ed.), *A lotus of another color: An unfolding of the South Asian gay and lesbian experience* (pp. 113–132). Boston: Alyson.

Sheets, R. H. (1995). From remedial to gifted: Effects of culturally centered pedagogy. *Theory into Practice, 34*(3), 186–193.

Shulman, B. (1994). Implications of feminist critiques of science for the teaching of mathematics and science. *Journal of Women and Minorities in Science and Engineering, 1*, 1–15.

Shulman, B. (1996). What if we change our axioms?: A feminist inquiry into the foundations of mathematics. *Configurations, 3,* 427–451.

Simon, R. L., & Dippo, D. (1986). On critical ethnographic work. *Anthropology and Education Quarterly, 17*(4), 195–202.

Sleeter, C. E., & Grant, C. A. (1987). An analysis of multicultural education in the United States. *Harvard Educational Review, 57*(4), 421–444.

Smith-Hefner, N. J. (1993). Education, gender, and generational conflict among Khmer refugees. *Anthropology and Education Quarterly, 24*(2), 135–158.

Spivak, G. C. (1990). Poststructuralism, marginality, postcoloniality and value. In P. Collier & H. Geyler-Ryan (Eds.), *Literary theory today* (pp. 219–244). Ithaca, NY: Cornell University Press.

Stacey, J. (1988). Can there be a feminist ethnography? *Women's Studies International Forum, 11*(1), 21–27.

Stambach, A. (1999). Gender-bending anthropological studies of education. *Anthropology and Education Quarterly, 30*(4), 441–445.

Street, B. V. (2000, April 20). *School and Community Literacies and Numeracies.* Lecture presented at Swarthmore College, Swarthmore, PA.

Sumara, D. (1993). Gay and lesbian voices in literature: Making room on the shelf. *English Quarterly, 25*(1), 30–34.

Sumara, D., & Davis, B. (1998). Telling tales of surprise. In W. F. Pinar (Ed.), *Queer theory in education* (pp. 197–219). Mahwah, NJ: Lawrence Erlbaum Associates.

Sung, B. (1985). Bicultural conflicts in Chinese immigrant children. *Journal of Comparative Family Studies, 16*(2), 255–269.

Sylvester, P. S. (1997). Elementary school curricula and urban transformation. In I. Hall, C. H. Campbell, & E. J. Miech (Eds.), *Class acts: Teachers reflect on their own classroom practice* (pp. 179–202). Cambridge: Harvard Educational Review.

Talburt, S. (2000). *Subject to identity: Knowledge, sexuality, and academic practices in higher education.* Albany: State University of New York Press.

Tasker, Y. (1997). Fists of fury: Discourses of race and masculinity in the martial arts cinema. In H. Stecopoulos & M. Uebel (Eds.), *Race and the subject of masculinities* (pp. 315–336). Durham: Duke University Press.

Tedlock, D. (1983). *The spoken word and the work of interpretation.* Philadelphia: University of Pennsylvania Press.

Tierney, W. G. (1994). On method and hope. In A. Gitlin (Ed.), *Power and method: Political activism and educational research* (pp. 97–115). New York: Routledge.

Tierney, W. G. (1997). Lost in translation: Time and voice in qualitative research. In W. G. Tierney & Y. S. Lincoln (Eds.), *Representation and the text: Re-framing the narrative voice* (pp. 23–26). Albany: State University of New York Press.

Tierney, W. G., & Dilley, P. (1998). Constructing knowledge: Educational research and gay and lesbian studies. In W. F. Pinar (Ed.), *Queer theory in education* (pp. 49–71). Mahwah, NJ: Lawrence Erlbaum Associates.

Ting, J. (1995). Bachelor society: Deviant heterosexuality and Asian American historiography. In G. Y. Okihiro, M. Alquizola, D. F. Rony, & K. S. Wong (Eds.), *Privileging positions: The sites of Asian American studies* (pp. 271–279) Pullman: Washington State University Press.

Treichler, P. A. (1988). AIDS, homophobia, and biomedical discourse: An epidemic of signification. In D. Crimp (Ed.), *AIDS: Cultural analysis/cultural activism* (pp. 31–70). Cambridge, MA: MIT Press.

Ulichny, P., & Schoener, W. (1996). Teacher-researcher collaboration from two perspectives. *Harvard Educational Review, 66*(3), 496–524.

Unks, G. (1995a). Thinking about the gay teen. In G. Unks (Ed.), *The gay teen: Educational practice and theory for lesbian, gay, and bisexual adolescents* (pp. 3–12). New York: Routledge.

Unks, G. (Ed.). (1995b). *The gay teen: Educational practice and theory for lesbian, gay, and bisexual adolescents*. New York: Routledge.

Uribe, V., & Harbeck, K. M. (1992). Addressing the needs of lesbian, gay, and bisexual youth: The origins of PROJECT 10 and school-based intervention. In K. M. Harbeck (Ed.), *Coming out of the classroom closet: Gay and lesbian students, teachers, and curricula* (pp. 9–28). New York: Harrington Press.

U.S. Commission on Civil Rights. (1992). *Civil rights issues facing Asian Americans in the 1990s.* Washington, DC: Author.

Vogt, L. A., Jordan, C., & Tharp, R. G. (1993). Explaining school failure, producing school success: Two cases. In E. Jacob & C. Jordan (Eds.), *Minority education: Anthropological perspectives* (pp. 53–65). Norwood, NJ: Ablex.

Walkerdine, V. (1990). *Schoolgirl fictions.* London: Verso.

Wat, E. C. (1996). Preserving the paradox: Stories from a *gay-loh.* In R. Leong (Ed.), *Asian American sexualities: Dimensions of the gay and lesbian experience* (pp. 71–80). New York: Routledge.

Watney, S. (1991). School's out. In D. Fuss (Ed.), *Inside/out: Lesbian theories, gay theories* (pp. 387–401). New York: Routledge.

Weiler, K. (1991). Freire and a feminist pedagogy of difference. *Harvard Educational Review, 61*(4), 449–474.

Weis, L. (1990). *Working class without work: High school students in a de-industrializing economy.* New York: Routledge.

Whatley, M. H. (1992). Images of gays and lesbians in sexuality and health textbooks. In K. Harbeck (Ed.), *Coming out of the classroom closet: Gay and lesbian students, teachers, and curricula* (pp. 197–211). New York: Harwood Press.

Wiegman, R. (1993). The anatomy of lynching. In J. C. Fout & M. S. Tantillo (Eds.), *American sexual politics: Sex, gender, and race since the civil war* (pp. 223–245). Chicago: University of Chicago Press.

Wilchins, R. A. (1997). *Read my lips: Sexual subversion and the end of gender*. Ithaca, NY: Firebrand Books.

Williams, P. J. (1995). Meditations on masculinity. In M. Berger, B. Wallis, & S. Watson (Eds.), *Constructing masculinity* (pp. 238–249). New York: Routledge.

Williams, P. J. (1997). American Kabuki. In T. Morrison & C. B. Lacour (Eds.), *Birth of a nation'hood* (pp. 273–292). New York: Pantheon.

Willis, P. (1977). *Learning to labor: How working class kids get working class jobs*. New York: Columbia University Press.

Wilson, A. (1996). How we find ourselves: Identity development and two-spirit people. *Harvard Educational Review, 66*(2), 303–317.

Woog, D. (1995). *School's out: The impact of gay and lesbian issues on America's schools*. Boston, MA: Alyson Publications.

Wright, H. K. (2000). Nailing Jell-O to the wall: Pinpointing aspects of state-of-the-art curriculum theorizing. *Educational Researcher, 29*(5), 4–13.

Yanagisako, S. J. (1985). *Transforming the past: Tradition and kinship among Japanese Americans*. Stanford: Stanford University Press.

Zenger, A. (1999). Moving words: On teaching citation in a college composition course. *Journal of Curriculum Theorizing, 15*(4), 173–183.

About the Author

Kevin K. Kumashiro is assistant professor of education at Bates College, Lewiston, Maine. He is the editor of *Troubling Intersections of Race and Sexuality: Queer Students of Color and Anti-Oppressive Education* and has just finished editing a collection of autobiographies of queer Asian/Pacific American activists (forthcoming). His current research focuses on antioppressive teacher education.

Index